C000232557

Intermediate Student's Book

ASPIRE

Discover
Learn
Engage

John Hughes and Robert Crossley

NATIONAL GEOGRAPHIC LEARNING | CENGAGE Learning

Australia • Brazil • Japan • Korea • Mexico • Singapore • Spain • United Kingdom • United States

Contents

	Grammar	Vocabulary	Reading and Listening	Speaking and Writing	Culture
1 Exploring the world page 5	the present simple, the present continuous, the present perfect; reflexive and reciprocal pronouns	adjectives to describe people; exploration	**Reading:** Explorers making a difference; Exploring cultures **Listening:** The music explorer; Describing people	**Speaking:** Describing people **Writing:** Informal writing	Exploring cultures; Bronisław Malinowski
Unit 1 Review page 29	**Everyday English:** At the campsite				
2 What the world consumes page 17	quantifiers; the past simple vs the present perfect simple; the present perfect simple vs the present perfect continuous	food; alternative sources of energy; the environment	**Reading:** Solar cooking **Listening:** People's eating habits; Presenting information	**Speaking:** Presenting information **Writing:** An opinion essay	Our thirsty world
Unit 2 Review page 30	**Case Study:** The good earth				**Video:** One village makes a difference
3 Global opinion page 31	narrative tenses; *used to* and *would*	politics / global issues; countries, nationalities and people	**Reading:** Cultural diversity **Listening:** The EU's history; For and against	**Speaking:** Getting the message across; For and against **Writing:** A for and against essay (1)	The spoken word
Unit 3 Review page 55	**Everyday English:** Giving your opinion				
4 Culture and civilisations page 43	modals for speculating in the present and past; modals of obligation and ability in the past; order of adjectives	festivals and celebrations; adjectives for expressing emotions	**Reading:** Festivals and celebrations; The Mayans **Listening:** A photographer at a festival; Ancient civilisations	**Speaking:** Describing an event **Writing:** Describing an event	The great treasures of culture
Unit 4 Review page 56	**Case Study:** The Bering land bridge				**Video:** The lost temples of the Maya
5 A new home page 57	*will*; *be going to*; the present continuous; modals for speculating about the future	homes and furnishings; phrasal verbs	**Reading:** Unusual homes; Living in space; A house in the future **Listening:** An unusual home; Asking for information	**Speaking:** Asking for information **Writing:** Describing a place	Cultural tips for visiting someone's home
Unit 5 Review page 81	**Everyday English:** Find a flatmate				

	Grammar	Vocabulary	Reading and Listening	Speaking and Writing	Culture
6 Sports and competitions page 69	articles; language for comparison	sports and competitions	**Reading:** Choosing an Olympic city; A real winner **Listening:** the Paralympics; Karolina Wisniewska; Comparing and contrasting	**Speaking:** Choosing an Olympic city **Writing:** A for and against essay (2)	Unusual competitions
Unit 6 Review page 82	**Case Study:** Is our future in the stars?				
7 Careers and education page 83	relative pronouns; relative clauses	careers; education	**Reading:** A television correspondent; Home schools; Butler school **Listening:** Interviewing	**Speaking:** Interviewing **Writing:** A letter of application	Charles Dickens' *Nicholas Nickleby*
Unit 7 Review page 107	**Everyday English:** Talking to parents				**Video:** Dangerous dining
8 What's on your mind? page 95	verb patterns; passive voice; phrasal verbs	senses; learning styles; languages	**Reading:** Saving the world's languages; What's on your pet's mind? **Listening:** How people remember; Learning styles; Preferences and interests	**Speaking:** Preferences and interests **Writing:** A report	Where are you from?
Unit 8 Review page 108	**Case Study:** The Welsh language				**Video:** The memory man
9 News and Media page 109	indirect questions; reported speech	news; media; types of programmes on TV	**Reading:** Icelandic volcano; Freelance journalism **Listening:** An interview with a journalist; Reporting what you've heard	**Speaking:** Talking about news; Sounding surprised **Writing:** A film review	Media moments in history
Unit 9 Review page 133	**Everyday English:** On the television				**Video:** Living with a volcano
10 Technology changing our world page 121	verb patterns; conditionals: zero, first, second, third	technology; bionics	**Reading:** Fame on the Internet **Listening:** Documentary about a bionic arm	**Speaking:** Problems with technology **Writing:** A short story	Mary Shelley's *Frankenstein*
Unit 10 Review page 134	**Case Study:** Connecting the world				

Irregular verbs page 135

Grammar reference pages 144–158

Video worksheets pages 136–140

Pronunciation guide page 159

Communication activities pages 141–143

Aspire Intermediate Student's Book
John Hughes and Robert Crossley

Publisher: Jason Mann

Commissioning Editor: Alistair Baxter

Editorial Project Manager: Karen White

Development Editors: Kathryn Eyers and
Rachel Lovering

Editorial Technology: Debie Mirtle and
Melissa Skepko

Senior Marketing Manager: Ruth McAleavey

Project Editor: Amy Smith

Production Controller: Tom Relf

National Geographic Liaison: Leila Hishmeh

Art Director: Natasa Arsenidou

Cover Designer: Sofia Ioannidou

Text Designer: Natasa Arsenidou

Compositor: eMC Design Ltd.

Audio: the Soundhouse Ltd.

© 2013 National Geographic Learning, as part of Cengage Learning

ALL RIGHTS RESERVED. No part of this work covered by the copyright herein may be reproduced, transmitted, stored, or used in any form or by any means graphic, electronic, or mechanical, including but not limited to photocopying, recording, scanning, digitizing, taping, Web distribution, information networks, or information storage and retrieval systems, except as permitted under Section 107 or 108 of the 1976 United States Copyright Act, without the prior written permission of the publisher.

For permission to use material from this text or product, submit all requests online at **www.cengage.com/permissions**.
Further permissions questions can be emailed to
permissionrequest@cengage.com.

ISBN: 978-1-133-56447-8

National Geographic Learning
Cheriton House, North Way, Andover, Hampshire, SP10 5BE
United Kingdom

Cengage Learning is a leading provider of customized learning solutions with office locations around the globe, including Singapore, the United Kingdom, Australia, Mexico, Brazil and Japan. Locate your local office at: **international.cengage.com/region**

Cengage Learning products are represented in Canada by Nelson Education Ltd.

Visit National Geographic Learning online at **ngl.cengage.com**

Visit our corporate website at **www.cengage.com**

Printed in China by RR Donnelley
2 3 4 5 6 7 8 9 10 – 16 15 14 13

Exploring the world

Let's get started

1 Discuss as a class. Look at the person in this picture.

1 Why is this person doing this?

2 What kind of person becomes an explorer?

3 Describe a time when you, or someone you know, explored somewhere.

Vocabulary

2 Read the comments and match with an adjective in the box.

Example:

1 = *independent*

> helpful   positive   decisive   independent
> determined   ambitious   patient

1 'I don't need anyone else's help.'

2 'We're going to get there and nothing is going to stop us.'

3 'Let me help you with that.'

4 'Don't worry. I can wait for you.'

5 'There are two choices but I think this is the best one …'

6 'I feel great this morning. I feel certain today is the day we will reach the top.'

7 'I want to be the very best at what I do.'

3 Discuss in pairs. Which personal qualities in Exercise 2 are necessary for these occupations? Can you think of any other personal qualities that are important for them?

> teacher   manager   artist   doctor
> athlete   astronaut

4 Discuss as a class. Which personal qualities do you need to learn a language?

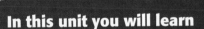

In this unit you will learn

- **Communication**: describing people, at a campsite
- **Vocabulary**: adjectives to describe people, exploration
- **Reading and Listening**: explorers making a difference, music explorer, exploring different cultures
- **Writing**: informal writing
- **Grammar**: the present simple, the present continuous, the present perfect, reflexive and reciprocal pronouns

1A Young explorers

Speaking

1 Discuss as a class. At what age are you allowed to …?

- drive a car on the road
- leave school
- leave home
- get married

2 Now discuss if you think the rules for these should change. Should the age be lowered or raised?

Reading

3 Read the article below about a young explorer. Decide if these statements are true or false.

		True	False
1	Jessica sailed round the world on her own.		
2	She wanted to sail round the world to visit different countries.		
3	She used the Internet to write about her journey.		
4	Her parents were angry with her for going on the journey.		
5	Some people thought her parents were wrong to let her go on the journey.		
6	Jessica thinks some people don't know what a 16-year-old can do.		

4 Discuss these questions as a class.

1 Do you think Jessica was too young for this journey? Why? Why not?

2 Which adjectives from page 5 describe Jessica's personal qualities?

3 Do people like Jessica inspire you? Would you like to try something similar?

5 Match the underlined words in the text to definitions 1–7.

1 to succeed in finishing something after lots of effort

2 to be satisfied and pleased with something you did well

3 to test skill or ability

4 to have the ability or skill to do something

5 to try to do something which is very hard

6 to have an opinion only based on how someone looks

7 to make other people want to achieve something

One way Jessica kept herself busy during the lonely voyage was by writing a blog in which she described monstrous storms, beautiful sunrises, seeing a blue whale for the first time and watching shooting stars at night.

As her journey finally ended at Sydney Harbour, the first people on board were her parents. The reunited family hugged each other and then Jessica stepped off the boat to thousands of cheering spectators. Her parents had received a lot of criticism for allowing someone so 'immature and inexperienced' to <u>attempt</u> something so dangerous. But Watson responded to those critics by telling the huge crowd that, 'People don't think you're <u>capable of</u> these things – they don't realise what young people, what 16-year-olds and girls, are capable of.'

16-year-old conquers the world

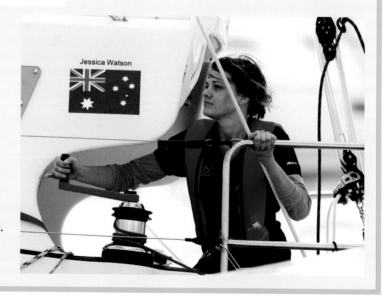

Jessica Watson

Jessica Watson became the youngest explorer to sail solo around the world. While many of her classmates at school were entertaining themselves with pop music and make-up, the 16-year-old Australian completed the 210 day voyage across 23,000 nautical miles (about 38,000 kilometres) on her own. She told the *Los Angeles Times* that: 'I wanted to <u>challenge</u> myself and <u>achieve</u> something to be <u>proud of</u>. And yes, I wanted to <u>inspire</u> people. I hate being <u>judged by my appearance</u> and other people's expectations.'

6 Work in pairs. Ask and answer these questions.

1 What has been your biggest challenge?

2 Which life achievement are you most proud of?

3 Have you ever attempted something but failed?

4 How much do you think people judge each other by appearances? Do you think this is good or bad?

5 Which person has most inspired you? Why?

7 Complete this text using the correct word (A, B, C or D).

1 A achievements B qualifications
   C ambitions   D grades

2 A competition   B activity
   C place   D challenge

3 A expectation   B ambition
   C attempt   D appearance

4 A afraid   B successful
   C capable   D critical

5 A judged   B interested
   C inspired   D determined

6 A determination B appearance
   C experience   D disorganisation

Aged 20, Geordie Stewart's (**1**) _____ already include climbing the highest mountains in North and South America, Africa and Europe. Now he faces his biggest (**2**) _____ by attempting to climb Mount Everest for the second time. He tried in 2010 but was unsuccessful. But if this second (**3**) _____ is successful, he will also become the youngest Briton to conquer the highest peaks on every continent. It's something he feels fully (**4**) _____ of achieving. Geordie remembers climbing Scotland's highest peak – Ben Nevis – when he was only 11. 'It was very exciting to reach the summit of Ben Nevis at that age, and I have no doubt it (**5**)_____ me. I've loved climbing ever since.' The legendary explorer Sir Ranulph Fiennes gave support to Geordie by describing him as 'an ambitious young man with genuine (**6**)_____'.

Listening

8 1.02 Listen to five speakers talking about Jessica Watson. How do they feel about her? Match the speaker to answers A–F. There is one extra answer.

Speaker 1	
Speaker 2	
Speaker 3	
Speaker 4	
Speaker 5	

A The speaker is inspired by Jessica.

B The speaker is critical of Jessica's parents.

C The speaker congratulates Jessica.

D The speaker describes the event.

E The speaker comments on how Jessica looks.

F The speaker knows Jessica personally.

Grammar: reflexive and reciprocal pronouns

9 Read sentences a–d and answer the questions about the pronouns in bold.

a *Most girls of her age entertain **themselves** with pop music.*

b *I wanted to challenge **myself**.*

c *Jessica kept **herself** busy by writing a blog.*

d *Her family hugged **each other**.*

1 What type of word does the pronoun follow?

2 Are the subject and object the same person?

3 Does sentence **d** mean Jessica hugged her parents and her parents hugged her?

4 Read the grammar summary below and complete the table.

Reflexive pronouns	Reciprocal pronouns
Use reflexive pronouns to show that both the subject and the object of the verb are the same person or thing.	Use *each other* or *one another* to say that each person or thing does the same to the other person/people or thing/things:

I	
you	yourself
he	himself
she	
it	itself
we	ourselves
you	yourselves
they	

They hugged each other = They hugged one another.

See Grammar Reference, page 144

Reading

1 Work in groups. Read about an explorer and then discuss these questions.

   1 What kind of an explorer is Ponte?

   2 Why is his work important?

Joshua Ponte works as a music producer and documentary film-maker. He's explored many parts of the world in search of music but has a special love for the Central African country of Gabon. Since 2001, he's been involved in a number of conservation projects in the country, including the recording of traditional Gabonese folk music. Previous archaeologists and explorers have found evidence of humans dating back 400,000 years in this region of Africa, so the music Ponte is recording must be some of the oldest on the planet.

Listening

2 1.03 Listen to a radio interview with Joshua Ponte. Decide if statements 1–5 are true or false.

		True	False
1	The explorer has lived in London.		
2	He's speaking from the city of Libreville.		
3	He's working alone.		
4	He thinks local children are leaving the villages because of modern technology.		
5	Local people and musicians are often suspicious of him.		

Grammar: the present simple, the present continuous and the present perfect

3 Study sentences 1–7. Which tense is the verb in?

   a the present simple

   b the present continuous

   c the present perfect

   1 Traditional forms of music are dying out.

   2 He's explored many parts of the world in search of music.

   3 He's recording traditional music in Gabon.

   4 Archaeologists have found evidence of humans dating back 400,000 years.

   5 Joshua travels ten hours every day.

   6 He's recorded hundreds of hours of music which you can listen to.

   7 He has a special love for the Central African country of Gabon.

4 Now match these uses (1–7) to the tenses (a–c) in Exercise 3. Use the sentences above to help you decide.

   1 a regular event or activity *a*

   2 a permanent state or situation

   3 events or activities now or around the time of speaking

   4 a current trend or development

   5 a past event with a result in the present

   6 an event in the past but we don't know when it happened (and it isn't important)

   7 an event/activity which started at a specific point in the past and continues to the present

Stative verbs

We often use certain verbs to describe permanent states. These include *be, believe, have, know, like, think, understand*. We don't normally use these *stative verbs* in continuous tenses:

He's an explorer. → *He's being an explorer.*

They love Gabonese music. → *They are loving Gabonese music.*

See Grammar Reference, page 145

5 Read parts of the interview with Ponte. Underline the correct verb form.

Interviewer	Where are you exactly?
Josh Ponte	I (1) *speak / 'm speaking* to you from a small town about 50 miles from the capital, Libreville.
Interviewer	Great. And (2) *are you / have you been* in Gabon a long time?
Josh Ponte	On and off since 2001.
Interviewer	So what (3) *are you doing / have you done* there at the moment?
Josh Ponte	Currently, I (4) *collaborate / 'm collaborating* with a team of musicians and film-makers to make audio and video recordings of traditional Gabonese music and dance from villages in the countryside. So far, we (5) *'re visiting / 've visited* about ten different villages.
Interviewer	Why is this work important?
Josh Ponte	Well, lots of the old traditional culture (6) *slowly disappears / is slowly disappearing* from Gabonese culture. For example, some of the languages and songs.
Interviewer	Do you mean it (7) *'s become / 's becoming* extinct?
Josh Ponte	That's right. The children (8) *don't stay / aren't staying* in the villages because of better-paid jobs in the cities. We (9) *hope / 've hoped* to save this culture using modern technology.
Interviewer	So, how (10) *does the project go / is the project going*?
Josh Ponte	It's hard work. We (11) *usually drive / are usually driving* about ten hours a day from one village to the next. The roads are really bad but then we (12) *always seem / 've always seemed* to get a great welcome from the local people. They (13) *love / are loving* to sing their music. We (14) *already make / 've already made* about 100 hours of recordings.

6 🔊 1.03 Listen again and check your answers.

Pronunciation: final sounds in verbs

7 🔊 1.04 Listen to these sounds and repeat them: /d/, /t/, /s/, /z/, /k/, /ŋ/

8 🔊 1.05 Listen to these sentences. Tick the final sound you hear at the end of the word in bold.

1 The number has **decreased**.
/t/ ✓ /d/ ___

2 What are you **doing** there?
/k/ ___ /ŋ/ ___

3 He's **worked** there since 2001.
/t/ ___ /d/ ___

4 She **loves** to sing.
/s/ ___ /z/ ___

5 It **takes** over from smaller languages.
/s/ ___ /z/ ___

6 He's **recorded** over 100 hours.
/t/ ___ /d/ ___

7 Local people **sing** traditional folk songs.
/k/ ___ /ŋ/ ___

9 🔊 1.05 Listen again and repeat the sentences.

Speaking

10 Work in pairs. You will each ask and answer questions about two different explorers and conservationists. Student A see below. Student B go to page 143.

1 Read about this explorer and answer Student B's questions.

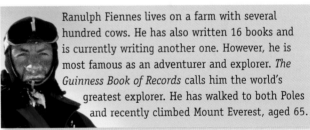

Ranulph Fiennes lives on a farm with several hundred cows. He has also written 16 books and is currently writing another one. However, he is most famous as an adventurer and explorer. *The Guinness Book of Records* calls him the world's greatest explorer. He has walked to both Poles and recently climbed Mount Everest, aged 65.

2 Now look at the missing information in this article about these explorers. Ask Student B questions and write in the missing words.

Example:

Where have his family explored?

The explorer Louis Leakey began searching for human fossils in the 1930s. Since then, three generations of his family have explored (1) _____ (**where**?). Meave and Louise Leakey work as (2) _____ (**what**?) in this region. They are currently running (3) _____ (**what**?) at (4) _____ (**where**?), where there are many ancient remains. Their discoveries have included a (5) _____ (**what**?).

1C Making a difference

A   B
C   D

Reading

1 Look at pictures of four modern explorers and answer the questions.

1 Match each picture to paragraph 1, 2, 3 or 4 in the article on page 11.

2 Prepare one sentence to describe how each explorer is trying to make a difference to the world (four sentences in total). Afterwards, compare your sentences with the rest of the class.

2 Now read the article again and match the sentences to the explorer. There are two possible answers for sentences 5 and 7.

1 This explorer is continuing a family tradition. ___
2 This explorer is worried about water on the planet. ___
3 This person explores the past. ___
4 This explorer wants to discover medical cures. ___
5 These explorers also need to spend time in their laboratories studying their findings. ___ ___
6 This explorer wants to find out about animals which are no longer living. ___
7 The work of these explorers includes educating people. ___ ___
8 This explorer saves animals. ___

Vocabulary

3 Study these pairs of words that have similar meanings but with slight differences. Match the words to definition a or b.

1 dead / extinct
   a something is no longer living
   b a species of animal is no longer living

2 ocean / sea
   a area of salty water partly surrounded by land
   b huge area of salty water

3 poison / venom
   a liquid that will kill you
   b liquid that comes from a snake that kills you

4 jungle / forest
   a a large area of trees and plants
   b area of trees and plants in very hot countries

5 education / awareness
   a to know something happens
   b to learn about something

6 poachers / thieves
   a people who steal things
   b people who kill or steal animals for money

7 raise / rise
   a increase
   b develop or improve of something (e.g. understanding/knowledge)

8 species / race
   a a set of animals with the same appearance (e.g. elephants)
   b a group of people with similar appearance

9 bones / fossils
   a the rock forms of ancient animals which are now extinct
   b white hard part inside the body

10 prey / predators
   a animals that another animal hunts and eats
   b animals which hunt and eat other animals

Explorers making a difference

In the past, explorers were people who travelled the world and discovered new places. Nowadays, there aren't many new places to discover. Instead, twenty-first century exploration is all about making the world a better place. Here are four explorers who are trying to make a difference.

Explorer 1

Most explorers expect to meet some dangers, but Zoltan Takacs goes looking for danger! He follows snakes, their prey and predators through the world's most remote jungles, deserts and oceans. He collects snake venom and, back at his laboratory, he analyses the venom. The reason is that snake venom can provide medication, including drugs for high blood pressure, heart attacks, diabetes and cancer. Takacs usually travels on his own with just a backpack and a camera. Sometimes he pilots a plane or rides a camel to reach remote places. His adventures include diving for sea snakes in the Philippines, running from stampeding elephants in the jungles of Congo, a helicopter rescue from civil war in Laos and surviving seven snake bites. 'Most of this is fun,' he says.

Explorer 2

Alexandra Cousteau had a famous grandfather and father – Jacques and Philippe Cousteau. As a girl she went with these men and explored the world's oceans. Nowadays, as a woman, she is exploring new ways to save the oceans. She believes water will cause the biggest problem this century because of the shortage of clean water for people to drink. Cousteau is involved in many projects to increase people's awareness of the future problems. She is currently writing a book and developing video games about water and climate. She is also planning a series of expeditions around the world to show how water is a global issue.

Explorer 3

On a beach in Nicaragua, Jose Urteaga is trying to protect the sea turtles. Nicaragua is home to five of the world's seven sea turtle species. It also has one of the world's few beaches where sea turtles produce 600,000 eggs. However, Nicaragua is quite poor. People live on $1 a day and they can sell the eggs and adult turtles for a lot of money. Urteaga understands this: 'I don't just work with turtles, I work with people. We can't only look at this from the turtle's point of view,' he explains. He tries to persuade the poachers to stop taking the turtles. He has started educational programmes with school children. He even helped set up concerts with Nicaraguan rock and folk music stars to raise awareness of the situation.

Explorer 4

Beth Shapiro is an explorer who travels back through time. She studies mammoths, dodos and other extinct animals. She looks at the last ice age and arrival of humans in North America. Her journey is made possible by ancient DNA samples. She uses genetic information from fossilised animals and plants to discover how evolution happens over time. To get the DNA, Beth also has to travel around the world. She has been to Alaska, Kenya, Siberia and Canada to collect small samples from bones, teeth, skulls and tusks. Back in her laboratory she can take out the DNA and study what happened to species of animals over 130,000 years ago.

Speaking

4 Work in groups and discuss answers for these questions.

1 Which species of animals in the text above are extinct? Can you think of one more?

2 Are there forests or jungles in your country? Have you visited them? When?

3 Does your country have a sea or an ocean?

4 Think of one animal. Is it prey or a predator?

5 Have you ever found a fossil? Where is a good place in your country to find fossils?

5 Discuss as a class. Which explorer do you think is making the biggest difference to our world? Why?

1D Describing people

Vocabulary

1 Categorise these words and expressions in the table. Some words can fit more than one category.

> medium-height teens late-twenties slim bald fair middle-aged well-dressed pale well-built short muscular smart streaky spiky elderly tanned dark shaved curly fashionable scruffy wrinkly

Age	Height and build	Hair	Skin / complexion	Dress and general appearance

Listening: describing people

2 1.06 Sandy Thoren is an explorer and professional photographer. Listen to her describe five of her favourite pictures. What part of the person's appearance does she mention? Match each description to categories a–e.

a age

b height and build

c hair

d skin / complexion

e dress and general appearance

3 We use certain verbs to talk about appearance. Write these verbs in the language summary below.

> looks like   have got   are   look
> are wearing

Verbs for describing appearance

Age / Build: *He's quite elderly. / They*
(1) _____ *huge.*

Clothes: *These people* (2) _____ *fancy clothes to the wedding.*

Hair, eyes and physical features: *The twins*
(3) _____ *long dark hair and brown eyes.*

Use *look* before an adjective: *The married couple*
(4) _____ *happy.*

Use *look like* before a noun: *This worker*
(5) _____ *she's been in the sun a long time.*

Speaking

4 Work in pairs. Talk about the appearance of the people in each picture on the left. Comment on their age, hair, build, complexion and dress.

Writing: informal writing

5 Read the email below. Are these statements true or false?

1 Giulia and Sally are both going to university this autumn.   True / False

2 Sally is saving money for her air ticket.   True / False

3 Sally's sister is going to study in Rome.   True / False

4 She has recently changed her appearance.   True / False

5 Sally and her sister are similar in appearance.   True / False

---

From: sally@geemail.com

To: giulia@geemail.com

Subject: Hi!

Hi Giulia!

Great to hear from you again! It must be two years since you were here. I'm so glad that your plans for university are working out. What subjects are you going to study? Hope you are going to have time to relax this summer before the term begins in October.

I'm also finishing school this year but my big news is that I've decided to take a gap year before starting university. I'm doing some part-time work at a shop at the weekends to try and save money for it. I've bought my ticket but I need some spending money. My flight goes to LA and then on to Australia. I can't wait!!

Anyway, thanks so much for agreeing to meet my sister in Rome and letting her stay for a few days. She's very excited about her course and I've told her all about you and your family. I've attached a photo of her. Unfortunately it's about six-months old and only shows her face. Since then she's dyed her hair, so it's brown with red streaks and she's wearing a lot of dark make-up these days, so she looks a bit unusual. Not sure if she'll still look like that when she arrives! Anyway, she's medium-height and most people say we look alike. She's got a photo of you as well, so I'm sure you'll find each other.

Her plane arrives on Tuesday 10th at midday and she's got your home number in case of any delays.

OK, I need to go now. I start work at the shop in an hour and I have to look smart!

Best wishes

Sally

6 How does Sally organise each part of the email? Number each part (1–6) in the order you read them:

___ talks about the main reason for writing

___ gives the reason for ending

___ refers to the previous letter

___ confirms the final arrangement

___ comments on friend's news

___ tells friend her news

USEFUL EXPRESSIONS informal writing

Starting

Dear … / Hi! / Hello

Refer to a previous letter / email

Thanks for your … / Great to hear from you again.

Introducing news

The big news is … / Did I tell you that …? / I can't wait! / Guess what?

Linkers

Anyway / But / Apparently / Maybe / By the way / Unfortunately

Enclose (with a letter) / Attach (with an email)

I've attached / enclosed a …

Ending

I need to go now …

Bye for now / Best wishes / Write soon

Tip

Notice how the writer uses a new paragraph for each new part of the letter.

7 Reply to a letter from a friend in England.

- tell him/her your news
- thank him/her for offering to look after your best friend
- describe in detail your best friend's appearance
- explain when and where the friend is arriving

Exploring cultures

Reading

1 Why do you think people travel and go on holiday to other countries?

2 Here are some reasons people travel. Which would be your main reason? Put them in order from 1–7 (1 = your main reason).

- ☐ to buy things they can't buy in their own country
- ☐ to lie on a sunny beach
- ☐ to have new experiences
- ☐ to be able to tell all their friends at home
- ☐ to go sightseeing
- ☐ to meet new people and make new friends
- ☐ to understand other cultures

3 Read paragraph 1 of the article on page 15 about the Polish-British anthropologist, Bronisław Malinowski. What was his main reason for travel?

4 Now read the whole article and match these headings A–F to paragraphs 1–5. There is one extra heading.

A Explorer, traveller and anthropologist

B Academic success

C Changing the way we view other cultures

D Remembering the importance of Malinowski

E The Kula Ring

F Becoming English

5 Read the text again and choose an answer for questions 1–5. Circle A, B, C or D.

1 Malinowski's biggest influence was on …

   A Polish culture.

   B writing.

   C other cultures.

   D how we study other cultures.

2 He first moved to Britain to …

   A study British culture.

   B escape the First World War.

   C study and lecture.

   D learn English.

3 The Kula Ring was …

   A a piece of jewellery.

   B an island.

   C a ritual.

   D the King of the Trobriand islands.

4 Malinowski's new approach to anthropology was to …

   A read about societies.

   B find out about their history.

   C interview the leaders.

   D become part of their society.

5 What is the author's purpose in this article?

   A to criticise

   B to praise

   C to agree

   D to inform

6 Discuss in groups. Imagine that a modern anthropologist wants to study society in your country. What do you think they would say about your …?

- food
- clothes
- architecture
- daily lives and routines

What else would they be interested in observing?

1 ___

'Imagine yourself … alone on a tropical beach …'
With those words, an explorer, traveller and famous
anthropologist begins one of his books. Bronisław
Malinowski was always happiest when he was
travelling and he wrote many diaries and travelogues.
But, more importantly, he changed the way we study
and talk about people from other cultures.

2 ___

Malinowski was born in Kraków on April 7, 1884 to
Lucjan and Józefa. He grew up in an educated upper-
class family and as a student he received his PhD
in Philosophy, Physics and Mathematics from the
Jagiellonian University in Kraków in 1908. In 1913,
he lectured at the London School of Economics,
where he earned his PhD in Science in 1916. It
was in England that he first became interested in
anthropology: the exploration of different human
cultures.

3 ___

One of his first and most famous anthropological
studies was with the Trobriand Islanders of New
Guinea in the southwest Pacific from 1915 to 1918.
He studied their day-to-day life and learnt their
language. He was particularly interested in their
beliefs and one of their rituals called 'the Kula Ring'.
The people on the different Trobriand islands gave
and took two types of objects from each other:
a necklace or a bracelet. The islanders would sail long
distances to exchange these gifts with people on other
islands. Necklaces travelled clockwise and the arm
bracelets travelled anti-clockwise. There were many
rules to the Kula Ring and Malinowski concluded that
the ritual helped keep friendly relationships between
the islanders and in particular show respect to the
different kings, who exchanged the special gifts.

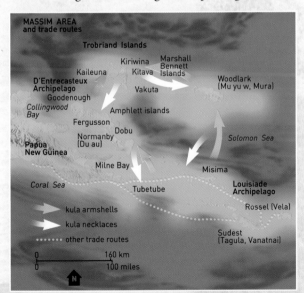

Bronisław Malinowski

4 ___

In 1920, Malinowski published his book about the
expedition called *Argonauts of the Western Pacific*.
The book was particularly important because, unlike
other explorers of the time, Malinowski was the
first anthropologist to use 'participant observation'.
In other words, he lived among the people he was
studying. It may seem obvious to us nowadays, but
Malinowski's approach was very new in those days.
He ate with the people, followed their daily routines
and attended their ceremonies. He stressed that
anthropology should be about understanding 'the
native's point of view, his relation to life, to realise his
vision of his world.'

> **'Malinowski changed the way we
> study and talk about people from
> other cultures.'**

5 ___

After this period, Malinowski mainly lived and
worked in England. He changed his citizenship to
British in 1931 and continued to travel widely. In
1934, he studied African tribes and he visited Indian
tribes in Mexico from 1941 to 1942. In later life he
lived in the USA and died on May 14, 1942 in New
Haven, Connecticut. Since his death, Malinowski's
research and books have continued to influence
anthropologists in their work. There is even the
annual Malinowski Award. It can be awarded to any
anthropologist who tries to understand and help
societies in the world.

At the campsite

Listening and speaking

1 Look at the two pictures and answer the questions.

1 Why do people go camping?

2 Compare the two types of camping in the pictures.

3 Which type of camping do you prefer? Why?

2 1.07 Two people have arrived at a campsite. Listen to the conversation at the reception. There are five mistakes in the advert and booking form. Correct the mistakes.

Camp Europe

With over 200 registered campgrounds across Europe, Camp Europe is one of the biggest networks for caravans, campers and traditional tents.

Discounts for students!

There is a 20% discount for all students holding a valid ISIC card.

Facilities

All our campsites are fully equipped with washrooms, outdoor swimming pool and a shop with all the basics.

Bike hire

Why not explore the countryside by bike during your stay? Bike hire is available at all sites for 50 euros a day.

Booking Form

Number of nights:	3
Site number:	E21

3 Look at these phrases from the listening. Who says them? Write *C* (camper) or *R* (receptionist).

We'd like to camp here for two nights. C

Do you have a reservation? R

We're fully booked. ___

There are a few spaces left. ___

Can you fill in this form? ___

I need to see your passport. ___

There's a discount. ___

It's 15 euros a day. ___

Can we hire two for tomorrow? ___

Anything else? ___

Have a nice stay. ___

4 1.07 Now listen again and check your answers.

5 Work in pairs. One of you is the camper and the other person is the campsite receptionist. Practise the conversation in the listening. Use the phrases in Exercise 3 and the information in the advert. Afterwards, swap roles and repeat the dialogue.

What the world consumes

In this unit you will learn

- **Communication**: presenting information
- **Vocabulary**: food, alternative sources of energy, the environment
- **Reading and Listening**: people's eating habits, solar cooking, the good earth
- **Writing**: an opinion essay
- **Grammar**: quantifiers, the past simple vs the present perfect simple, the present perfect simple vs the present perfect continuous

Let's get started

1 Describe the picture and answer the questions.

 1 How healthy is the food in the picture?

 2 Which of the food items do you often eat?

 3 Describe the best meal you or your family have ever had.

Vocabulary

2 Work in pairs. How many items of food and drink can you identify in the picture? Make a list.

3 Compare your list with the rest of the class. Which pair had the highest number of words?

4 Which of these categories describe the food in the picture?

- packaged
- fresh
- processed
- from the supermarket
- home grown or local
- healthy
- organic
- fast food

5 Think of examples of food for each of the other categories.

6 Which of the categories in Exercise 4 describe what you or your family eats?

Vocabulary

1 How healthy do you think your diet is? Tell your partner.

2 The food pyramid tells us what we should eat and how much per day. Match the five food groups to sections 1–5.

> dairy and proteins   grains   sugars and fats
> fruits   vegetables

3 Can you name all the food in each food group? Which are countable nouns? Which are uncountable?

Grammar: quantifiers

4 Read the comments by people discussing the food pyramid. Write the words in bold in the language summary table.

> I eat **a lot of** dairy products every day.
> My family probably eats / doesn't eat **enough** grains or bread.
> I like **a little** sugar on my cereal for breakfast but not **too much**.

> The pyramid tells me I eat **too few** fruits and vegetables.
> My sister's a vegetarian, so she doesn't eat **any** meat but she gets **enough** protein by eating things like beans and nuts.

Quantifiers

Both *plural countable nouns* and *uncountable nouns* follow these quantifiers except with *small amounts* and the *wrong amount* (see below).

Large amounts

lots of / _____ …

Small amounts

not much / _____ (+ *uncountable nouns only*)

not many / a few (+ *plural countable nouns only*)

No amount

_____ …

The right amount

_____ …

The wrong amount

_____ …

_____ / too little (+ *uncountable nouns only*)

too many / _____ (+ *plural countable nouns only*)

See Grammar Reference, page 145

5 Work in pairs. Do you and your family have a balanced diet? Make sentences using this table.

I eat / don't eat …	
My family eats / doesn't eat …	
lots of	grains
a lot of	dairy
much	vegetables
many	fruit
a few	proteins
a little	sugars
any	fatty foods
enough	bread
too much / many	meat
too few / little	other?

6 Peter Menzel is a photographer. He had dinner with 30 different families in 24 countries and took pictures of each family alongside the food they typically eat in a week. Here is one of the pictures. Discuss in groups:

1 Which part of the world do you think the family comes from?

2 How balanced is their diet? Do they eat the right amount of everything?

Listening

7 1.08 Listen to part of a documentary about Peter Menzel.

1 Why did he take the pictures?

2 Which places and countries are mentioned by the presenter?

8 1.08 Listen again and choose the best ending to sentences 1–4.

1 The family in Okinawa had the greatest impact on Peter Menzel because …

A they all lived to be over 100 years old.

B they all ate healthy things like fish.

C they all knew how to eat the correct amount of food.

2 In China, he took pictures of an urban and a rural family to show …

A how rural families are more healthy.

B how food says a lot about where and how we live.

C how urban families can afford food from supermarkets.

3 Peter often found that families …

A lied about what they ate.

B told the truth about what they ate.

C didn't know what they ate.

4 The family in the USA were exercising and so …

A they were losing weight.

B they didn't have time to cook food.

C they stopped eating fast food.

Speaking

9 Discuss as a class. Do you think people in your country have healthier diets nowadays? Are they eating more or less processed, packaged and fast foods? Is this a problem?

2B Animal power!

Grammar

1 What do you think the connection might be between these three pictures?

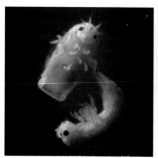  

2 Read this article. See if your predictions about the pictures were correct.

Animal power

Before the inventor Karl Benz created the first gasoline-powered engine in 1896, most transport with wheels needed a horse to pull it. Since his invention, cars and planes have taken over the roads and the skies, with horse power becoming a thing of the past. But now, as the world is turning away from its reliance on fossil fuels, some scientists have turned to animals once again to solve our transport problems.

Cow power

Milk isn't the only useful thing to come out of a dairy cow, according to farmer Darryl Vander Haak. His 1,000 cows also produce a lot of manure which produces the gas 'methane'. Haak has already built his own 'methane digester' which turns manure into methane and powers a small electrical power plant on his farm. The next step is to use the methane to drive his farm vehicles.

Gribble power

Have you ever seen a gribble? Probably not. They are very small (one to four millimetres) sea creatures and only ship builders have known about them because the species is a pest which eats through the wood of ships. But recently scientists have been studying the small pink creatures because after they eat the wood, they produce a substance which can be turned into bio fuel to drive engines.

Fat power

Maybe you've stopped eating fast food because everyone has been telling you how unhealthy it is for you. Well, now you can eat burgers and fries without the guilt because the billions of litres of animal fat that pours out of our food every year could be converted into engine fuel, according to creators of a fat-burning car engine. One group of people who could also benefit are the restaurant owners. They've been paying for the disposal of the fat from their kitchens for years. Now there's a way for them to make money out of it.

3 Read these statements. According to the text, are they true or false?

1 The author says we will use horses more than cars and planes in the future.
2 Some scientists think animals are important for alternative forms of energy.
3 Darryl Vander Haak only has cows for the methane they produce.
4 Haak already uses the methane for his transport.
5 Scientists put the gribbles inside car engines.
6 The writer suggests restaurant owners could sell the fat as engine fuel.

Grammar (1): the past simple vs the present perfect simple

4 Compare sentences a and b from the reading and answer questions 1 and 2. Then compare c and d and answer questions 3 to 5.

a *Karl Benz created the first gasoline-powered engine in 1896.*

b *Since his invention, cars and planes have taken over the roads and the skies.*

   1 Which sentence talks about the time when something started in the past and continues to the present?
   2 Which sentence talks about a finished action at an exact time?

c *Darryl Vander Haak has built his own 'methane digester'.*

d *Have you ever seen a gribble?*

   3 Which sentence talks about past experiences?
   4 Which sentence talks about a recent event connected to the present?
   5 In both sentences, do we know when the action began?

Past simple or present perfect simple?

The past simple talks about …

- the exact time when the finished action event happened: *He bought the car yesterday / last week / last year / in 2010.*

The present perfect simple (*have/has + past participle*) talks about …

- recent events which are connected to the present: *We've just launched a new kind of car.*
- past experiences: *Have you ever driven a car?*
- when the situation started and how long it has continued to the present: *I've studied English for two years/since 2010.*

See Grammar Reference, page 145

5 A journalist is interviewing the inventor of a car which is powered by water. Write the verbs in brackets in the past simple or present perfect simple tense.

A A company in Japan (1) _____ (just / launch) a new kind of car that runs on water. We (2) _____ (speak) to the inventor of the car last week in Tokyo …

… When (3) _____ (you / begin) work on the car?

B I suppose we (4) _____ (work) on this model for about two years.

A (5) _____ (you / ever / see) anything similar?

B Well actually other people (6) _____ (already / build) engines using water. For example, Isaac de Rivaz (7) _____ (make) the first water-powered engine in 1805.

A What is different about yours?

B We (8) _____ (create) an engine which only needs a small amount of water …

6 Work in pairs. Ask each other questions about things you have created or done. Start the conversation with *Have you ever …?*

- write a story or poem
- build something
- help animals
- invent something

Example:

A *Have you ever composed a song?*

B *Yes, I have.*

A *When did you write it? / How did it go? / Have you ever recorded it?*

Grammar (2): the present perfect simple vs the present perfect continuous

7 Read the grammar summary below. Then underline two examples of the present perfect continuous in the final paragraph of the text on page 20.

Present perfect continuous

You form the present perfect continuous with *have / has + been + verb + ing: Scientists have been studying the small pink creatures.*

The present perfect simple or the present perfect continuous?

You use the present perfect continuous to talk about recent continuous or repeated actions. In many sentences its meaning is similar to the present perfect simple. You can use either tense with verbs such as *work, live, teach, study*:

*Scientists **have studied** the small pink creatures. ✓*

*Scientists **have been studying** the small pink creatures. ✓*

We use the present perfect continuous to talk about temporary events and to say for how long:

Scientists have been studying the creatures all week.

But we use the present perfect simple with stative verbs and to say *how many*:

Ship builders have known about gribbles for years.

Ship builders ~~have been knowing~~ about gribbles for years.

Haak has used methane in three ways.

See Grammar Reference, page 146

8 Choose the present perfect simple or the present perfect continuous to complete the sentences.

1 I've *eaten / been eating* everything on my plate. Can I have some more?

2 Have you ever *tried / been trying* milk fresh from a cow? It's delicious!

3 People have *lived / been living* in my village for hundreds of years.

4 I've *driven / been driving* this car hundreds of times and it's never broken down before.

5 We've *been / been being* vegetarians ever since we watched a TV programme about meat.

9 Work in pairs. Turn to page 141 and read about five situations. Discuss what you think has happened or has been happening.

Example:

My mother has been cooking cakes all day.

2C Solar cooking

Reading

1 Look at the picture with the article.

  1 How do you think the cooker works? Describe the process.

  2 What do you think some of the advantages might be of cooking in this way?

  3 Tell the class about a meal you cooked.

Eating from the Sun

On a cool sunny day in Borrego Springs, California, Eleanor Shimeall walks from her kitchen and goes outside to a strange-looking piece of equipment. She opens a glass door and puts some bread inside. Then she opens another flap of a box made of glass and wood and pulls out a pot of chicken and rice. 'Ah, it's doing nicely,' she says. Shimeall's meal looks delicious but the remarkable thing is that she isn't using wood or **fossil fuels** such as gas or coal to cook her food. Instead, Shimeall is using the sun to make her meal, and she's done it almost every day for more than 20 years. Using her **solar** cooker, she can cook meat, fish, grains and vegetables – just about anything that you can cook on a normal cooker.

This method of cooking is becoming popular among people who are concerned about the environment and **global warming**. However, they aren't the only people interested in this unusual invention. In developing countries around the world, solar cookers have the potential to save lives. According to one expert, people around the world may soon not have enough traditional fuels. He explains in his own words, 'With sunshine you have an alternative to fire. And that's important for two and a half billion people to learn about because they're **running out** of **non-renewable** fuels.'

Eleanor Shimeall and her husband, Dr Bob Metcalf, founded a company to promote solar cooking around the world 15 years ago. They came up with the idea for Solar Cookers International (SCI) for two reasons: they wanted to help stop the terrible **deforestation** which is occurring in some countries, and they also wanted to make women's lives easier. The problem of deforestation is often due to the demand for trees and wood to use as fuel. The women who collect the wood often have to walk two to three miles. It's also their job to look after the fire and the smoke can burn their eyes and choke their lungs. According to the World Health Organisation this problem can be linked to the death of two million women and children each year.

SCI has already trained more than 22,000 families to cook their traditional food with a solar cooker. When the women first receive their solar cooker, it looks like pieces of cardboard and shiny metal. Someone from the organisation comes along to show them how to use it and the women are always surprised that it cooks a wide range of dishes such as soups, rice, potatoes, and bread. As well as being a safe way to cook without traditional fuels, SCI says it can make water safe to drink by heating it to the correct temperature. Even more importantly each cooker only costs about five dollars.

SCI has been making the lives of African women easier with their solar cookers and now similar projects are also starting in countries such as Nepal and Nicaragua. Their goal is to increase the use of solar cookers everywhere. Dr Metcalf adds, 'Science is supposed to help and benefit all of mankind and we've got something that is good science that could help half a billion people in the world.' With the need for **renewable** fuels at a global level, perhaps solar cookers could also have a place in richer countries as well as the developing world.

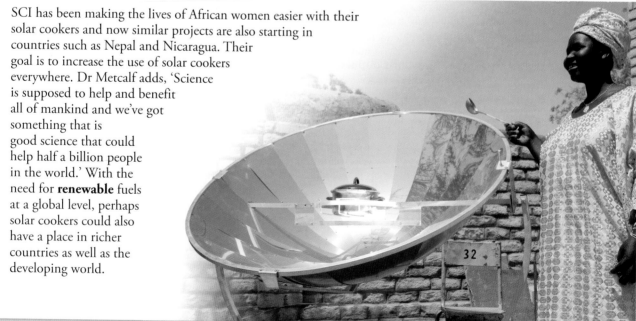

2 Read the article again and find the correct answers. Circle A, B, C or D.

1 The situation in the first paragraph takes place …

    A before the meal.   **B** during the meal.

    C during the night.   **D** after the meal.

2 The solar cookers appeal to …

    A people who are concerned about global warming.

    B countries with little wood left for cooking.

    C women and children whose health is affected by burning.

    D Answers A, B and C.

3 When the cookers are delivered to developing countries, someone from the organisation goes in order to …

    A collect the money for it.

    B plug it in.

    C teach people how to use it.

    D check that it works.

4 Currently, the cookers are used …

    A only in Africa.

    B in many parts of the world.

    C only in rich countries.

    D in all parts of the world.

Vocabulary

3 Match the definitions 1–7 to the words in bold in the text.

1 substances to produce heat such as coal, oil or natural gas _____

2 cutting down of trees in a large area _____

3 the problem of the world's rising temperature _____

4 cannot replace itself _____

5 coming from the sun _____

6 can replace itself _____

7 having no more of something _____

Pronunciation: word stress

4 ◎ 1.09 Listen to these words. Underline the stressed syllable and write the number of syllables. Which word has only one syllable?

deforestation (*5*)   energy ( )

environment ( )   fuel ( )

electricity ( )   renewable ( )

temperature ( )   nuclear ( )

alternative ( )

5 Which of these types of energy does the article on page 22 mention?

A

B

C

D

E

F

G

Speaking

6 Work in groups and answer the questions.

1 Which of these types of energy are most common in your country? Which do you use?

2 Which are renewable? Which are non-renewable? Which are running out?

3 Think of one advantage and one disadvantage of each type of energy. Compare your list with the rest of the class.

2D Environmental awareness

Reading: presenting information

1 Work in pairs.
Read about an
environmentally
friendly tent.

1 What is one of the
main problems
facing festival
organisers?

2 What do you think
the advantages of
a cardboard tent
might be?

Every summer, thousands of people
go to outdoor music festivals –
there are over 100 in Britain. They
listen to bands perform and have
a giant party. They also leave
a lot of mess. One of the biggest
problems for the organisers is
the number of tents that people
leave behind. Now James Dunlop,
a young design student, has
created 'myhab'. It's a tent made of
cardboard which can be recycled ...

Listening: presenting information

2 ⦿1.10 Listen to a short presentation about myhab
tents. Decide if these statements are true or false.

		True	False
1	You buy your tent from a shop.		
2	You set the tent up where you want it.		
3	Parts of the tent are reused.		
4	The cardboard on the tent is recycled.		
5	After using the tent, you have to take it down and return it.		
6	The speaker thinks myhab tents are good for the environment.		

3 ⦿1.10 Listen again and tick the expressions you
hear in the list below.

USEFUL EXPRESSIONS presentations

Start your presentation
☐ Hello.
☐ Thanks for coming.
☐ Today, I'd like to talk about ...
☐ Today, I'd like to present ...

The main part
☐ Firstly,
☐ The first thing you
   need to do is ...
☐ Secondly,
☐ You'll also need to
☐ Then
☐ Finally,

Ending the presentation
☐ So, to sum up
☐ In conclusion
☐ Do you have any
   questions?

Pronunciation: pauses

4 ⦿1.11 When you present or explain information,
it's helpful to pause between phrases. Listen again
to the first part of the presentation and notice
how the speaker pauses.

Hello. / Today, / I'd like to talk about myhab. / It's so
simple / compared to your traditional tent. / So, / the
first thing you need to do / is go online / and book
the tent you want from / myhab dot com. / You'll also
need to tell us / where you want the tent / and then
we set it up. /

5 Work in pairs. Try reading the text in Exercise 4
with the pauses.

Tip Notice how we pause where there's a full stop
or a comma. We also use pauses to emphasise
certain words. Pauses also make a long sentence
easier to say.

Speaking: presenting information

6 Now prepare your own presentation. You are
going to explain how to do something. Choose
from this list or think of your own idea:

• how to set up an ordinary tent for camping
  holidays

• your favourite cooking recipe

• how to change the wheel on a bicycle.

Practise your presentation and remember to
include pauses!

7 Work in groups of three or four. Take turns to give
your presentations.

Writing: an opinion essay

8 Students are writing paragraphs about the following statement.

> *'In the future the world will need an alternative to fossil fuels. Which alternative types of energy do you think the world should or shouldn't use?' Give your opinion.*

Read this paragraph and put the sentences in the correct order (1–7). Is this student's opinion positive or negative?

_1_ In my opinion solar energy will be one of the main alternatives to non-renewable energy sources such as oil and coal in the future.

___ One of its biggest advantages is that it's clean and there's an unlimited supply of it.

___ Firstly, it's used to heat water in some houses as well as run the cooling and heating systems in buildings.

___ This means that we could supply power to whole cities in the future using the sun.

___ Secondly, developing countries use solar energy for cooking food and this same approach could work anywhere.

___ It's also worth noting that the world already uses solar energy in a number of ways.

___ Thirdly, solar panels can convert the rays of the sun into electricity.

9 Complete this essay with the missing expressions. Is this student's opinion positive or negative?

> finally   it's also worth noting
> in my opinion   firstly   I strongly disagree
> in addition to that

Some people believe that we should use more nuclear power to replace fossil fuels in the future. However, **(1)** _____, this would be a bad idea.
(2) _____, there is the problem of safety at nuclear power stations. If there is an accident at a power station, radiation can leak into the atmosphere. Many people could be killed by such a disaster.
(3) _____ children born after the accidents will still suffer from radiation for years to come. **(4)** _____ that nuclear power produces waste materials which are very expensive to destroy safely. **(5)** _____, countries can also produce nuclear weapons using materials from nuclear power stations, so **(6)** _____ with this kind of energy.

10 Now it's your turn. Write a paragraph giving a positive opinion of using wind power as an alternative energy.

To help you, here are some reasons why wind power is a good idea:
- *Wind power is clean energy and not dangerous.*
- *There's lots of wind – it's an unlimited natural resource!*
- *Building wind farms provides jobs for people and helps the local economy.*

11 Write another paragraph. Choose ONE of these statements and write your opinion.
- 'The world's supply of water is running out. We must find ways to make these resources last longer.' What is your opinion?
- 'In some parts of the world people have more than enough food and in other parts they are starving, so those who have plenty of food should share it for free with those who don't have it.' What is your opinion?

USEFUL EXPRESSIONS an opinion essay

Expressing your opinion
In my opinion …
I think that …
I strongly believe that …
People should …
Structuring your arguments and opinions
Firstly, / Secondly, / Finally,
One of the biggest advantages is …
One disadvantage is …
Connecting your opinions
It's (also) worth noting …
Another reason is …
In addition to that …
This means that …
Even more importantly …

Our thirsty world

Speaking

1 Take this quiz. Check your answers on page 141.

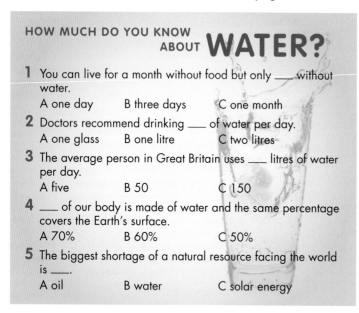

HOW MUCH DO YOU KNOW ABOUT WATER?

1 You can live for a month without food but only ___ without water.
   A one day   B three days   C one month

2 Doctors recommend drinking ___ of water per day.
   A one glass   B one litre   C two litres

3 The average person in Great Britain uses ___ litres of water per day.
   A five   B 50   C 150

4 ___ of our body is made of water and the same percentage covers the Earth's surface.
   A 70%   B 60%   C 50%

5 The biggest shortage of a natural resource facing the world is ___.
   A oil   B water   C solar energy

2 Analyse the information below. Then discuss these questions in pairs.

   1 What do the figures tell us? What's the problem?

   2 How do you think we could reduce the amount of virtual water we use?

   3 Do you ever have water shortages in your country? How do people try to conserve their water?

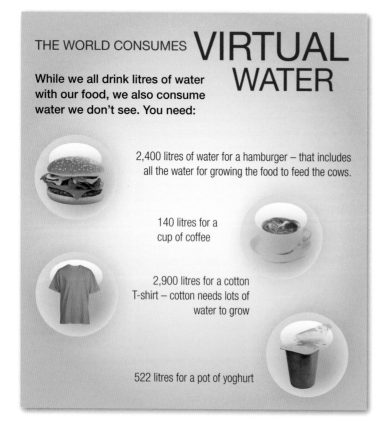

THE WORLD CONSUMES **VIRTUAL WATER**

While we all drink litres of water with our food, we also consume water we don't see. You need:

2,400 litres of water for a hamburger – that includes all the water for growing the food to feed the cows.

140 litres for a cup of coffee

2,900 litres for a cotton T-shirt – cotton needs lots of water to grow

522 litres for a pot of yoghurt

Reading

3 Read the article on page 27 quickly. Afterwards, discuss these questions as a class.

   1 Why is life difficult for Aylito Binayo and the women in her village?

   2 What will help her? How could her life change?

4 Read the article again and write in the four missing sentences from A to F. There are two extra sentences.

   A There is a terrible shortage of clean water in Foro.

   B Very young boys fetch water, but only up to the age of seven or eight.

   C The water is dirty and unsafe to drink but it is the only water Foro has ever had.

   D Aylito Binayo wants the men to help carry the water.

   E Then gravity would carry the water back down to taps in the village.

   F And freedom from water slavery would mean girls could go to school and choose a better life.

Speaking

5 Here are five ways in which you can help reduce wastage of water in your school. Discuss the advantages and disadvantages of each. Then, choose the best two for your school.

   • poster campaign with information near places where water is used (toilet areas, cafeteria, etc.)

   • pay a plumber to check all the taps and pipes in the school for leaks

   • fine students who waste water

   • install water barrels or a rainwater tank to catch water from roofs and gutters. Use the water on green areas of the schools (gardens, sports field, etc.)

   • include lessons for students about the importance of water

 Watch a video about a village making a difference. Turn to page 136.

Our thirsty world

Aylito Binayo can walk up and down the mountain with her eyes closed. Even at four in the morning she can run down the rocks to the river and climb the steep mountain back up to her village with 25 litres of water on her back. She has made this journey three times a day for nearly all her 25 years. So has every other woman in her village of Foro in south western Ethiopia.

> 'Dirty water kills 3.3 million people around the world annually, most of them children under age five.'

Binayo dropped out of school when she was eight years old, partly because she had to help her mother fetch water from the Toiro River. (**1**) _____ The task of fetching water defines life for Binayo. She must also help her husband grow cassava and beans in their fields, gather grass for their goats, dry grain and take it to the mill for grinding into flour, cook meals and take care of her three small sons. None of these jobs is as important or as consuming as the eight hours or so she spends each day fetching water.

In wealthy parts of the world, people turn on a tap and clean water pours out. But nearly 900 million people in the world have no access to clean water. Dirty water kills 3.3 million people around the world annually, most of them children under age five. Here in southern Ethiopia, and in northern Kenya, a lack of rain over the past few years has made even dirty water elusive.

Fetching water is almost always women's work. (**2**) _____ 'If the boys are older, people gossip that the woman is lazy,' Binayo says. 'If I sit and stay at home and do nothing, nobody likes me. But if I run up and down to get water, they say I'm a clever woman and work hard. When we are born, we know that we will have a hard life.'

When you spend hours hauling water long distances, you measure every drop. The average American uses 400 litres of water just at home every day. Aylito Binayo makes do with 10 litres. Binayo washes her hands with water 'maybe once a day.' She washes clothes once a year. 'We don't even have enough water for drinking – how can we wash our clothes?' she says.

If Binayo and the people in her village had taps with clean water, all the hours she spends on carrying water could be used to grow more food and raise more animals. Her family would spend less time sick from diseases in the water. (**3**) _____

One charity called WaterAid is trying to bring water to the villages like Foro. They build dams to capture rainwater and provide water pumps. WaterAid's work also includes training so the local people learn about hygiene and how to maintain the technology. Before beginning any project, WaterAid asks the community to form a WASH (water, sanitation, hygiene) committee of seven people – four of them must be women. The committee works with WaterAid to plan projects and involve the village in construction. Then it maintains and runs the project.

In Aylito Binayo's village, WaterAid is planning to pump water from a deep well up the mountain into a reservoir. (**4**) _____ Aylito Binayo would have a tap with safe water just a three-minute walk from her front door. 'If it works, I will be so happy, so very happy.'

Women in northern Kenya walk for up to five hours a day to get water.

Case Study 1 〉 The good earth

THE SECRET IS IN THE SOIL

Everything we eat comes directly or indirectly from the soil beneath our feet. Soil is made up of rock, **organic** matter, water and air. The mixture (and the balance of chemicals in it) varies, depending on where you are and the type of rock and organic matter. Food growers know that they can grow better food if we get this balance right. They also know that they can add chemicals to the land (in the form of **fertilisers** and compost) to make the soil more productive and to hold water better.

Some problems

With intensive farming, where crops are grown year after year on the same piece of land, the goodness is eventually taken out of the soil and it no longer holds together, so it turns to dust. Heavy rain and wind can then completely remove the **topsoil**, leaving only the poor quality soil below. Deforestation in order to grow food for cattle can have a similar effect because the roots of the trees no longer hold the soil in place. When the first heavy rains come, all the **nutrients** in the soil can end up in the nearest river. Bad water management can sometimes introduce salty water to the land. Plants can't grow well in salty water and within a few years this can lead to **desertification** – rich, **fertile** land literally turns to desert. Today, many people are looking to **bio fuels** as a way to solve our energy crisis. Growing plants for fuel may stop us depending on fossil fuels. However, critics suggest that using land in this way means that we'll soon run out of places to grow food.

Soil solutions

Clearly, good land management is essential if we want to keep growing food. We simply can't afford to **misuse** something that takes hundreds of years to form. And we need to keep looking at renewable sources of energy because we are unlikely to find an alternative to growing food in the soil – something we have been doing successfully for thousands of years.

An argument in favour of vegetarianism!

If every person in the world ate meat every day, we could only feed 2.5 billion of the world's population. If we all became vegetarians, we could feed everyone. Also, to feed one meat-eating person for a day, we use around 15,000 litres of water to grow the food to raise the cattle. In contrast, to feed someone who does not eat any animal products for one day, we need just over 1,000 litres.

---

1 Match the words in bold in the text to the definitions.

1 something which helps plants grow _____

2 to treat something badly _____

3 plants which we grow for energy _____

4 able to support life _____

5 made from plants or animals _____

6 important chemicals that we need in food

_____

7 when the soil becomes unusable _____

8 the part of the earth on the surface _____

2 Answer the questions in your own words.

1 Explain what the writer means by **indirectly** in the sentence: *Everything we eat comes directly or indirectly from the soil beneath our feet.*

2 How can the weather affect soil quality?

3 Why do we have to be careful with the way we water the plants we grow for food?

4 What is the writer's objection to bio fuels?

3 In pairs, discuss the following questions.

- What kind of food is grown in your country?

- What do you know about bio fuels? Do they grow them in your country?

- Would you consider eating less meat after reading the information above?

- What would you suggest as a way to help feed the world's population?

Review > Unit 1

Grammar

1 Read this explorer's blog. Write the verb in brackets in the present simple, present continuous or present perfect simple.

{ explorer's blog }

Hi! Welcome to my blog.
April 20 | Uncategorized

It (**1**) _____ (**rain**) non-stop for three days but – finally – today the sun (**2**) _____ (**shine**) and the sea is blue! I (**3**)_____ (**not / talk**) to anyone for two weeks, so I (**4**) _____ (**feel**) a bit lonely for the past few days. Of course my family and friends (**5**) _____ (**email**) me since I left the port in Sydney but it isn't the same. The only life I (**6**) _____ (**see**) recently is a blue whale. It was enormous! My other friends (**7**) _____ (**be**) a group of dolphins. At the moment, they (**8**) _____ (**follow**) the boat. They're amazing animals and they always (**9**) _____ (**seem**) so happy! Oh! I think the wind (**10**) _____ (**increase**). I must go! Will write more tomorrow.

Add Comment

Vocabulary

2 Change the form of the word in CAPITALS and complete the sentence with it.

1 Why are you so <u>disorganised</u>? You can never find anything in your room. ORGANISE

2 My cousin is very clever. He has lots of _____ from university. QUALIFY

3 People with lots of _____ usually get what they want. DETERMINE

4 Don't be so _____! The bus will arrive in a minute. PATIENT

5 Artists and musicians have to be very _____. CREATE

6 I tried to get into the school football team but I was _____. The coach told me to try again next year. SUCCESS

3 Write in the missing vowels (a, e, i, o, u) in the words.

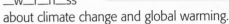

1 The dodo is an __xt__nct type of bird.

2 Be careful of this snake. It is v__n__m__ __s.

3 The Amazon j__ngl__ is the largest rainforest in the world.

4 It's important to raise everyone's __w__r__n__ss about climate change and global warming.

5 I think it's terrible that p__ __ch__rs kill elephants for their tusks.

6 Scientists have found a lot of dinosaur f__ss__ls in parts of South America.

7 Sharks are probably the most dangerous pr__d__t__rs in the ocean.

Functions

4 Match the two halves of the sentences.

1 He looks like
2 They've both got
3 You look
4 I think you're wearing
5 Is that your brother? I didn't know he

a blue eyes.
b a famous film star.
c was so handsome!
d my coat.
e guilty. What have you done?

Now I can ...

☐ describe people
☐ talk about exploring the world
☐ write an informal email
☐ use reflexive and reciprocal pronouns
☐ use the present simple, continuous and perfect tenses

Review > Unit 2

Grammar

1 Match the two halves of the sentences.

1 My father eats a lot of
2 You don't get enough
3 I'd just like a
4 There are too few
5 He doesn't take

a sugar in his coffee.
b protein in your diet.
c vegetables on your plate.
d little sugar in my tea, please.
e bread and cheese.

2 Underline the correct verb in this conversation.

A Is that chocolate on your mouth? (1) *Have you eaten / Have you been eating* sweets?

B Yes. I found those boxes in the cupboard.

A How many boxes (2) *have you eaten / have you been eating*?

B Only one box. There were only two. I (3) *'ve left / 've been leaving* the other one for you.

A But this is the one with soft centres. I (4) *'ve looked / 've been looking* forward to eating the ones with nuts in all week!

Vocabulary

3 Delete the incorrect word in each set.

1 DAIRY milk, butter, ~~fish~~, cheese
2 FAST FOOD beefburgers, salad, French fries, chicken nuggets
3 PROTEINS beans, oranges, meat, nuts
4 FRUITS melon, banana, grape, corn
5 GRAINS cheese, pasta, bread, rice

4 Complete this article with these words.

> renewable   runs out   electricity   alternative
> global   environment   fossil

Nowadays, lots of companies are using wind power to produce (1) _____. It supplies lots of homes with power and avoids the use of (2) _____ fuels. Another type of (3) _____ energy which is good for the (4) _____ and helps to fight (5) _____ warming is wave power. The oceans may be able to provide a great deal of energy. It could even be a better (6) _____ than wind power because the waves in the sea never stop, so it never (7) _____.

Functions

5 Write these expressions in the instructions below.

> Then   The first thing you need   Finally
> ~~thanks for~~   Do you have any questions
> Today I'd like   You'll also need to

Magic trick: the floating pencil!

Good morning and (1) *thanks for* coming.
(2) _____ to explain how to do a magic trick called the floating pencil.
(3) _____ is a bottle, a pencil, some tape and black cotton thread.
(4) _____ tape the black cotton to the end of the pencil. After that, tie the other end to a shirt button. (5) _____, put the pencil in the bottle.
(6) _____ remember to put the end with the cotton in first. So, now you're ready to make the pencil float. Try moving the bottle forward and backwards. The pencil moves up and down! So that's it. (7) _____?

Now I can ...

- [ ] talk about diets
- [ ] talk about environmental issues
- [ ] present information
- [ ] write an opinion essay
- [ ] use quantifiers
- [ ] use the present perfect continuous

Global opinion

3

In this unit you will learn

- **Communication:** discussing advantages and disadvantages, agreeing and disagreeing, public speaking, giving your opinion
- **Vocabulary:** politics / global issues, countries, nationalities and people, arguing for and against, synonyms
- **Reading and Listening:** the history of the European Union, cultural diversity, the spoken word
- **Writing:** a for and against essay
- **Grammar:** narrative tenses, *used to* and *would*

Let's get started

1 Answer the questionnaire. If you don't know the answers, try to guess.

Test your world knowledge

How many …
1 countries are there in the world?
2 continents are there?
3 countries do you think there are in each continent?
4 people are there in the world?
5 world currencies (e.g. dollars, euros) can you name?
6 world leaders (e.g. presidents, prime ministers, kings, queens) can you name?

2 Read the text and check your answers.

It is not easy to put an exact number on how many countries there are in the world, although 195 is a figure agreed on by many. The Olympic™ symbol, of five rings, was understood to represent the continents of Europe, Asia, Africa, Australasia (also called Oceania) and America (North and South combined). Today we often talk of Antarctica as a continent, and we often view North America and South America as separate continents, so there could be five, six or even seven continents. They have the following number of countries: Africa – 54; Europe – 50; Asia – 48; North America – 23; South America – 12; Oceania – 14. As for the number of people in the world, we know that the world population reached seven billion in 2011, and it was rising by about 74 million per year.

Vocabulary

3 Complete the sentences using the words in brackets.

1 You'll need to change _____ if you _____ to a _____ country. (*foreign / currency / travel*)

2 The _____ of the _____ is often the _____ minister. (*prime / government / head*)

3 You have to be 18 to _____ in a(n) _____. (*vote / election*)

4 The _____ of a European _____ can _____ an MEP (Member of the European _____). (*Parliament / elect / state / citizens*)

5 There is a _____ in our _____ that the _____ should be the oldest son of the king or queen. (*monarch / tradition / culture*)

6 The cost of _____ into our country is a _____ to trade. (*imports / barrier*)

4 Complete the sentences using the words in the box.

> policy   president   nation   abroad   border   export

1 Billy lived _____ for 20 years.

2 They didn't use to let us go across the _____ but it's easy these days.

3 The tragedy affected everyone in the _____.

4 They make computers here and _____ them all over the world.

5 Do you think this new _____ is a good idea?

6 He was _____ of the country for eight years.

Listening

1 Look at the headlines below. What do you think they mean?

1 **MEPs adopt new free trade agreement.**

2 **Economic and political recovery may take years.**

3 **Food producers unite to increase their influence.**

4 **Treaty for free movement of goods comes into effect.**

2 Look at the different periods in the history of the European Union on the timeline. Do you know any of the important events that happened during each period? Discuss as a class.

3 1.12 Listen to six extracts from a television documentary about the history of the EU. The parts are not in the correct order. Write the number of the extract (1–6) next to the correct title on the timeline.

1945–1959
A peaceful Europe and the beginning of cooperation ___

1960–1969
A period of economic growth ___

1970–1979
The first enlargement ___

1980–1989
The Berlin Wall comes down ___

1990–1999
Europe without frontiers ___

2000–Present
Greater enlargement and a single, common currency ___

4 🎧 1.13 Listen to the documentary again but this time the extracts are in the correct order. Write the missing words in these notes.

1945–1959	In 1950, Belgium, France, Germany, Italy, Luxembourg and the (1) _____ formed the European Coal and Steel Community. It was the first step towards a (2) _____ _____.
1960–1969	There was a cultural revolution with groups like The Beatles. It was also a good period for economies and freer trade between many (3) _____ _____. There were also agreements over (4) _____ _____, so that everybody would have enough to eat.
1970–1979	Denmark, Ireland and the United Kingdom joined on (5) _____, so the European Parliament was able to increase its influence. By (6) _____ all EU citizens could, for the first time, elect their own MEP.
1980–1989	In 1981, Greece became the (7) _____ member. Spain and Portugal followed (8) _____ _____ later. The Berlin Wall came down on (9) _____.
1990–1999	EU leaders signed a treaty at Maastricht in (10) _____ guaranteeing the free movement of (11) _____, services, people and money. Austria, Finland and Sweden joined in 1995.
2000–Present	12 member states adopted the euro as a single, common currency in (12) _____. In 2004, 10 more countries joined the EU, with another two joining in 2007. A further five countries adopted the euro as their currency. The (13) _____ Treaty came into effect in 2009.

Grammar: the past simple, the past continuous and the past perfect

5 Read these sentences from the listening. Underline the three verb forms.

The Second World War had just ended and Europe was slowly trying to recover. In 1950, Belgium, France, Germany, Italy, Luxembourg and the Netherlands formed the European Coal and Steel Community.

6 Match the verb forms to the tenses:

a the past simple

b the past continuous

c the past perfect

7 Now match the explanation 1–3 to the tense a–c in Exercise 6.

1 To talk about a completed action/event at a certain time. ___

2 To talk about an action/event before a certain moment in time. ___

3 To talk about actions/events in progress at a certain time or to give background information. ___

See **Grammar Reference, page 146**

8 Read about Robert Schuman. Underline the correct verbs in italics.

A FOUNDING FATHER OF EUROPE

Robert Schuman was born in Luxembourg but he (**1**) *became / was becoming* a French citizen in 1919. During the Second World War, Schuman (**2**) *had worked / was working* for the French Government when the Nazis invaded France and they (**3**) *arrested / had arrested* him. After the war (**4**) *had ended / was ending* Schuman returned to work in the French government. While he (**5**) *was helping / had helped* to rebuild France, he also began working on a plan to unify Europe. In 1951, six countries (**6**) *signed / had signed* the Treaty of Paris, which was the beginning of the modern EU. Schuman (**7**) *was proposing / had proposed* this treaty a year earlier on 9th May. As a result of his 'Schuman Plan' in 1950, 9th May is now known as Europe Day.

9 Look at the timeline below. Write some significant events in your life on the line. For example: date of birth, when you started and finished primary school, moved house, bought your first bike, took important exams, your favourite holiday, etc.

Date of birth   NOW

10 Work in pairs. Tell your partner about the timeline using past tenses and expressions such as:

In …, I …

While I was …

After I had …

3B Crossing borders

Vocabulary

1 Who are your country's nearest neighbours? Is it easy to travel there?

2 Read the text and find the meaning of the following:

   1 WTO   2 ASEAN   3 AFTA   4 GAFTA

   5 CEFTA   6 NAFTA   7 ECOWAS

Just as the EU makes it easy for an Englishman or a Spaniard, for example, to travel and do business with the Germans or the Dutch, other nations have similar agreements. Most countries belong to the World Trade Organisation (WTO) but there are also regional free trade areas (FTAs) which help remove barriers between countries. ASEAN – the Association of Southeast Asian Nations – has the AFTA (the ASEAN Free Trade Agreement), and ASEAN Plus 3, which links the ASEAN members with China, Japan and South Korea. Then, there are FTAs in Central Europe (CEFTA), North America (NAFTA), and South Asia (SAFTA). GAFTA stands for the Greater Arab Free Trade Agreement. There is also USAN (the Union of South American Nations) which is working towards a common currency like the euro, and allows passport-free travel between member countries.

Members of the Economic Community of West African States (ECOWAS) do not require passports for citizens travelling between the 14 member countries. Citizens of the Cooperation Council for the Arab States of the Gulf only need ID cards to cross the borders of member countries. Many similar passport-free agreements exist, such as that between Turkey and Georgia, or between the Syrians and the Lebanese.

3 Underline all the nouns and adjectives in the text that refer to nationalities, countries or people from a particular country. Complete the table.

Country	Adjective	Person	Nation
England	English	an Englishman	the English
_____	_____	a Spaniard	_____
_____	_____	_____	the Germans
_____	_____	_____	the Dutch
China	_____	_____	_____
Japan	_____	_____	_____
South Korea	_____	_____	_____
Turkey	_____	_____	_____
Georgia	_____	_____	_____
_____	_____	_____	the Syrians
_____	_____	_____	the Lebanese

4 Now read the rules and try to think of more items to add to the table in Exercise 3.

Countries, nationalities and people

- Make nationality adjectives into collective nouns with *the* to talk about the group of people from a country: *French – the French, British – the British*. Add *–s* in some cases: *German – the Germans*

- Some nationality adjectives are also used to talk about one person: *Italian – an Italian, German – a German*

- Some nationality adjectives cannot describe one person: *a British, a Polish*. In this case, the adjective and noun form of the nationality are different: *French – a Frenchman/woman, British – a Brit, Polish – a Pole*

TIP Use a dictionary to help you check which nationalities have an adjective and a noun form.

Speaking

5 Discuss these questions as a class.

   1 How good are your country's relations with its neighbours?

   2 Does your country have trade agreements with other countries?

   3 What are the advantages and disadvantages of passport-free travel?

6 Which of these opinions do you agree or disagree with? Give reasons.

> In the past, when countries disagreed, they would go to war. Now, this is much less likely.

> It used to be more difficult to travel to another country. It's much easier now – you can work or study somewhere else and come back after a year if you want.

> In my grandparents' generation, you would have to wait weeks to get foreign currency if you wanted to travel. You used to have to order the money from the bank – and they would only let you have a certain amount.

> We used to be proud of our culture but now we have so many things from abroad that our own traditions are dying out. We used to make our own laws but now we have to follow laws from other countries.

Grammar: *used to*, *would*, the past simple

used to / didn't use to

You use *used to* to talk about past habits, states and situations: *We used to make our own laws. / I used to change money at the border.*

Notice what happens to the *–d* in negative and question form of *used to*:

*We **didn't use to** study abroad. / **Did** you **use to** change money at the border?*

would / wouldn't

You can also use *would / wouldn't* to talk about repeated actions and habits in the past.

*When countries disagreed about something, they **would go** to war. / Most people **wouldn't study** in another country.*

DO NOT use *would / wouldn't* to talk about states:

*We **used to** have more free time. ✓ / We ~~would have~~ more free time. ✗*

With state verbs (*be, believe, know*) we only use *used to*.

The past simple

You can also use the past simple to talk about past habits.

We used to make our own laws. = We made our own laws.

Use the past simple instead of *used to* or *would* to talk about:

- single past actions: *Poland joined the EU in 2004. Poland ~~used to / would join~~ the EU in 2004.*
- how long an action lasted: *I studied in France for a year. I ~~used to / would study~~ for a year.*
- the number of times a past action was repeated: *We changed money twice. We ~~used to / would change~~ money twice.*

See Grammar Reference, page 147

---

7 Read the comments on this discussion forum and underline the correct answers.

▮ I think the new treaty's great. Before we (1) ***signed*** / ***used to sign*** this agreement, it (2) ***was*** / ***would*** much harder to work abroad. Now we can work anywhere.

Posted 28 January 13.54

▮ But I (3) ***lost*** / ***would lose*** my job last year and now I can't get another. It (4) ***didn't use to*** / ***wouldn't*** be difficult. One reason is all the foreign workers coming here.

Posted 2 February 18.30

▮ I sympathise, but that's not the only reason. Besides, we need these policies and agreements to deal with global problems. In the past, governments (5) ***would talk*** / ***had talked*** about solving problems but they didn't (6) ***used*** / ***use*** to do anything. Now countries work together and things get done! I think we're better off now.

Posted 8 February 10.46

▮ I'm sorry but I disagree. In the past, we (7) ***would be*** / ***used to be*** much better off. Today, we have more crime, pollution and unemployment issues. Did we (8) ***use*** / ***used*** to have problems like that in the old days? I don't think so!

Posted 8 February 20.16

8 A government has recently changed some laws. What do you think citizens in the country would say about their past? Use *used to* or *would*.

1   The new speed limit is 100 kilometres per hour instead of 130.

Example:

There used to be lots of accidents on the road. / We didn't use to worry about driving too fast. / People would drive really dangerously.

2   Foreigners who work here must have a visa.

3   18-year-olds do not have to spend a year in the army.

4   All households must recycle glass and paper.

5   Everyone must carry an identity card at all times.

9 Which of the laws in Exercise 8 are true in your country? Do you know about any more new or recent laws in your country? What is the reason for them? What did life use to be like before the new laws?

3C Cultural diversity

Speaking

1 Read the text below and answer the questions.

> The United Nations has marked the 21st May as the World Day for Cultural Diversity for Dialogue and Development. UNESCO believes that dialogue between cultures is the best way to keep peace in the world. Although our cultures may change, we need to recognise the importance of preserving them and respecting the beliefs and cultures of others so that we can all live together in harmony. Above all, cultural diversity should be seen as a positive thing – something which makes the world a better place.

1 After reading the text, what do you understand by the term 'cultural diversity'?

2 Which different traditions or cultures in your country do you think need preserving?

3 How much do you know about cultures from outside your country?

2 Match the words in the box to the correct topic a–c. Can you think of two more words for each category?

> ~~parliament~~ heritage court
> politicians tradition policy identity
> fine illegal

a Culture

b Government *parliament,*

c Law

Reading

3 Read the article on page 37 and match each topic a–c in Exercise 2 to the correct text.

4 Match these definitions to words in the text.

Text 1

a a place to hide

b from the place or country instead of from another place or country

c places which apply the law

d against the law

e to stop (because of the law)

Text 2

f previous generations going back many years

g when everyone has the same rights

Text 3

h area of land surrounded by water

i discussions for and against

5 Tick the sentences which are true, according to the texts. You can tick more than one column.

		Sami	Chinese Australians	Isle of Man
1	They are part of a larger population.	✓	✓	✗
2	They use two languages.			
3	Their culture and traditions are under threat.			
4	They have many ways of keeping their culture alive.			
5	They live in more than one country.			
6	They aren't indigenous to the country.			
7	They make their own laws.			

Speaking

6 Discuss in groups.

1 Imagine the discussion in court between a Sami reindeer herder and a person who owns a forest. Make a list of the reasons for and against their cases.

2 Are there Chinese or other ethnic communities in your country? How much do you know about them?

3 Why do you think people on the Isle of Man might not want to be EU members? What do you think are some of the reasons against joining the European Union? Make a list.

7 Work with another group or the rest of the class. Present and compare your answers in Exercise 6.

1 The Sami

It's winter in the far north of Sweden and the reindeer are seeking refuge from the bitter wind and snow. The herds move from the open mountains into the forests where they can find shelter and dig through the snow to find food beneath. These animals move across an area which stretches from Norway across Sweden, Finland and into Russia. This region is also home to one of the largest indigenous ethnic groups in Europe – the Sami people. The Sami's livelihoods and traditions have always been connected to the reindeer and, even today, ten per cent of Sami people are reindeer herders. But in modern-day Sweden many of the forests are privately owned by people who make a living by selling the wood. If the Sami's reindeer illegally gather on their land, they can take the Sami to court and fine them. Olof Johansson, a Sami herder, says that if courts start to ban them from the forests, Sweden and Europe will lose a culture that is over 1,000 years old.

2 The Chinese community in Melbourne, Australia

Like many large cities the world over, Melbourne is a city of many cultures, but this city has often been called the 'cultural capital of Australia' because of its varied, and largely successful, mix of cultures. Chinese people first started arriving in Australia either in search of work or in search of gold. Around 1850, the Australian gold rush attracted the attention of people from all over the world, and an estimated 40,000 Chinese people came. Today, there are about 58,000 people of Chinese ancestry living in the city. Of course, many of these were born in Australia but there are various ways in which people can keep Chinese traditions alive. Language is often said to be the best way to stay in touch with your cultural heritage, and in Melbourne, the second most common language spoken at home (after English) is Chinese. Chinese newspapers and magazines are readily available and the news can be heard in Mandarin and Cantonese on the TV and radio. The city has various community groups, such as the Chinese Youth Society, which teaches Chinese Australians about their heritage and co-ordinates traditional activities. The Chinese Museum in Melbourne recognises the role that Chinese people play in the community and organises a variety of events which help to promote Chinese culture, as well as an understanding of community values, cultural identity, diversity and equality.

3 Isle of Man

Things come in twos on the Isle of Man. The small island sits between two EU countries – Ireland and the United Kingdom. It has two languages. Everyone speaks English but there is also the indigenous language of Manx, spoken by two per cent of the population. Its politics and laws are influenced by the government of Great Britain but it also has its own Parliament called Tynwald which makes decisions on domestic policy. In fact, it's the oldest parliament in the world and was started by Viking settlers over one thousand years ago. The Isle's relationship with the EU is equally split. It isn't an EU member, so money and services can't move freely, but the people can. Not surprisingly, debates about the island's status within the UK and the EU are common at Tynwald. One of the most recent parliamentary debates was to decide if they needed a permanent office in Brussels so that it can represent itself in Europe. Once again, the views of the politicians and the 80,000 people who live there are divided.

3D For and against

Vocabulary

The best of this week's TV

Business across the border – Monday 7.30 p.m.
The benefits and drawbacks of free trade and an
'open-border' policy.

Our culture – Sunday 9.00 p.m.
Tonight, presenter George Lamont focuses his
attention on some of the elements of our culture
that we might lose if we don't preserve them!

This means war! – Wednesday 9.30 p.m.
Continuing the series on the conflicts that lead to
wars – and ways in which we could avoid them.

The New World – Friday 10.30 p.m.
Has the world really become a global village? This
programme looks at globalisation and examines
the state of the world today.

1 Look at the TV guide and find words or phrases
that mean the same as those given below.

1 keep out of the way of; stop
2 worldwide
3 positive and negative things
4 parts; aspects
5 looks closely at
6 result in
7 disagreements; fights
8 look after; protect

2 Complete the opinions below with words from
the box. Do you agree with the opinions?
Which programmes from Exercise 1 interest you
the most?

> long   place   favour   argue   perhaps
> advantages   arguments   balance

I think there are more (1) _____ than
disadvantages to an open borders policy. In fact,
you could (2) _____ that we should have
no borders at all. (3) _____ that would be
a good thing.

I agree with finding out about other cultures – just
as (4) _____ as we remember our own.
Foreign cultures should not be allowed to take the
(5) _____ of the traditions we have in our
own country.

On (6) _____, I am not in
(7) _____ of the world becoming a global
village. I think there are too many
(8) _____ against it.

Listening: for and against

3 1.14 Listen to Judy, Paul and Kim discussing the
importance of some school subjects.

Which speaker …

1 would like to see a new subject introduced into
   the school timetable? _____
2 thinks studying History could save the world?
   _____
3 feels that we have to learn to understand each
   other? _____
4 believes Geography is the most important subject?
   _____
5 suggests learning more about our own culture?
   _____

4 Match the two halves of the sentences.

1 You could argue that we
2 On the one hand,
3 But on the other hand, it's
4 On the whole I tend
5 I also believe

a that modern languages play an important role.
b to agree that we should learn more about the world.
c just not important for some people.
d Geography helps us to understand the news.
e need to focus on our own culture.

5 1.14 Listen again and check your answers.

Speaking: for and against

6 Work in small groups. Read the information about
school subjects on page 142. Each person should
choose a school subject and discuss the points for
and against. Then decide which subject the group
thinks is the most important.

USEFUL EXPRESSIONS speaking for and against

For and against
I think / feel / believe …
I would argue that …
We have to admit that …
One advantage of / benefit of / reason for …
However, …
But it must be said that …
*One disadvantage of / drawback of / reason
against …*

Comparing the two sides of the argument
On the one hand … but on the other …
On balance … / On the whole …
There isn't much difference between …

Writing: a for and against essay (1)

7 A student has written an essay about studying foreign cultures in school. The essay has five paragraphs. Number them in the correct order 1–5.

A__

Another argument in favour is that we now live in a global village, so knowledge of other cultures is an advantage. One drawback is that time spent studying other cultures means less time studying our own. Perhaps we should be thinking about our own culture first.

B__

Many schools today have lessons where students can learn about foreign cultures. These lessons allow schoolchildren to find out more about the world outside their own country. The question is, do we need to teach such things in our schools?

C__

So, on balance, I believe that studying foreign cultures is an excellent idea with many benefits, just as long as it doesn't take the place of other, more basic lessons.

D__

Thirdly, you could also argue that finding out about other cultures helps us understand one another. This could mean that we avoid conflict, or even war. However, critics might say that this is not the job of schoolchildren, who are far too young to have such a huge responsibility.

E__

On the one hand, any kind of learning, including learning about foreign cultures, is educational. On the other hand, there are other subjects which we need to study, like Maths or Science, and maybe we should focus our attention on those.

8 Complete this table of expressions with the underlined words in the essay.

USEFUL EXPRESSIONS a for and against essay

Introducing the topic	
Many schools today …	1 *The question is, …?*
Introducing arguments	
for	… and against
2 _____	3 _____
4 _____	5 _____
6 _____	7 _____
Concluding	
On the whole …	In conclusion …
	8 _____

9 Work in groups. Read this essay question, discuss the points you would like to include, and then make notes in the table.

In most schools, students have to study History and Geography. Write an essay (200–250 words) discussing the arguments for and against studying these subjects.

For	Against

10 Now write your essay. Use this checklist to help you.

- [ ] Your essay has five paragraphs.
- [ ] Paragraph one introduces the topic.
- [ ] Paragraph two compares one argument for and against.
- [ ] Paragraph three compares one argument for and against.
- [ ] Paragraph four compares one argument for and against.
- [ ] Paragraph five is a conclusion and says what you think.

3E Getting the message across

Speaking

1 Read the text and discuss the questions.

Tips for speaking in public

- The contents of your speech or presentation should be like an essay – with an introduction, main body and conclusion where you may repeat the main points.
- Prepare your material and practise it with friends or in front of a mirror.
- Dress smartly and try to look calm – this will help your audience feel relaxed.
- Speak slowly and clearly and make sure everyone can hear you.
- Remember: a large percentage of your message is communicated in unspoken ways. Move around and use hand gestures and facial gestures. Maintain eye contact with members of the audience.
- Speak as if you really believe what you are saying. You need the power of persuasion.
- Pause from time to time to take a breath and let your message sink in.
- Don't talk for too long.
- Smile!

1 How useful do you think each of these tips is? Can you add any others?

2 What reasons do people have for speaking in public? List as many as you can.

3 Have you ever had to speak in public? What was the occasion? How did you feel?

Reading

2 Read the text on page 41 and fill in the gaps below.

1 People used to tell stories, sometimes as _____ _____ or _____ to help others remember them.

2 The ancient Greeks wanted to _____ people and learn how to make a _____ argument _____.

3 With radio and TV, advertisers (and the US President) spoke to listeners in a _____, less _____ way.

4 In business, getting your message across can make the difference between _____ and _____.

3 Read the text again and answer questions 1–4 according to what the writer says. Circle A, B or C.

1 What is true about storytelling before the written word?

   A It has given us an accurate picture of what daily life was like.

   B The person telling the story would include details of his own.

   C The stories remained exactly the same for generations.

2 Modern politicians …

   A have to study Ancient Greek and Roman history.

   B still use skills developed 3,000 years ago.

   C use a completely different speaking style to the Ancient Romans.

3 Two speaking styles that advertisers use involve …

   A telling us what is good and speaking to us as equals.

   B selling us things for the home and buying their own products.

   C using confusing language and advertising more products.

4 We know that President Roosevelt …

   A knew how to use radio and TV to his advantage.

   B told the people that he was an expert in politics.

   C had success using a different style of talking to the public.

5 From the last paragraph, it is clear that good speaking skills …

   A are only really needed in politics and advertising.

   B are less important than the ability to listen.

   C are needed in a number of professions.

Vocabulary

4 Good writing often involves using synonyms to avoid repetition. Look at the words and phrases from the text below, and match them to the synonyms underlined in the text.

> written language   tell   handed down
> reliable   speeches   persuading   speech
> speaking   adopted   communicate effectively

The spoken word

Oral tradition

For thousands of years before **written language**, there was a long history of storytelling among many cultures of the world. However, they didn't **tell** these stories just for the amusement or entertainment of the audience – the stories also contained useful information about culture, tradition and history, and would often take the form of action stories about brave heroes, warriors or kings from the past. In some cases, the stories would actually be the laws of the land, which people would <u>relate</u> in such a way that all the citizens could understand them – sometimes as rhyming poems, or even songs, which made them easier to remember. They **handed down** their stories from generation to generation and in this way they <u>passed on</u> their cultural identity. On the one hand, it is true to say that without these stories we would know very little about ancient people. But on the other hand, we have no way of knowing how **reliable** the information was. The storyteller often used to add details to make their stories more interesting, so fact became confused with fantasy. We cannot be sure if the events in the stories were true or if they were mostly based on myths and legends.

Ancient Greece and Rome

With <u>the written word</u> we got a more <u>accurate</u> picture. We know that 3,000 years ago public speaking, or oratory, was an important skill. The Greeks studied rhetoric, which was the way they composed and delivered **speeches**. Much of the emphasis was on **persuading** people and learning how to make a weak argument stronger. As the Roman Empire became more powerful, they took the Greek models for public speaking and this style became extremely important, especially in the area of politics. This method of <u>convincing</u> people through **speech** remained almost the same for centuries and is still the basis of the methods politicians use today.

Advertising and the mass media

With increased trade and mass production of goods, it was logical that producers needed persuasive techniques so that people would buy the products of one company, rather than those of its competitors. The popularity of radio and then television provided a new use for <u>the spoken word</u>. One style of advertisements, which we still have today, focuses on a voice of authority – supposedly an expert like a doctor or a scientist – who tells us what to buy because he knows it is good for us. But with radio and TV, advertisers soon realised that they were **speaking** to us in our living rooms at home and many advertisements became less formal as sellers **adopted** a style which spoke directly to the listener or viewer in a friendly way. The people in advertisements began to speak and act like we did and we became more likely to buy their products. Although advertisers still chose their words carefully, the message was generally simpler. Incidentally, US President Franklin D. Roosevelt <u>used</u> this 'friendly' style between 1933 and 1944 when he made a series of radio broadcasts to the nation which were known as 'fireside chats'. Instead of the formal language that politicians used to use, Roosevelt spoke to the people as though he was <u>chatting</u> to them. These broadcasts were extremely popular with audiences and had more listeners than the programmes designed for entertainment.

Speaking skills today

It is not just politicians and advertisers who need good speaking skills. The media, and television in particular, need people who can speak in a clear and convincing way. There are many other professionals who we expect to be able to **communicate effectively**, sometimes in difficult situations, such as teachers, doctors, psychologists, counsellors and people who work for the emergency services. As well as being good 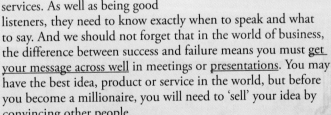 listeners, they need to know exactly when to speak and what to say. And we should not forget that in the world of business, the difference between success and failure means you must <u>get your message across well</u> in meetings or <u>presentations</u>. You may have the best idea, product or service in the world, but before you become a millionaire, you will need to 'sell' your idea by convincing other people.

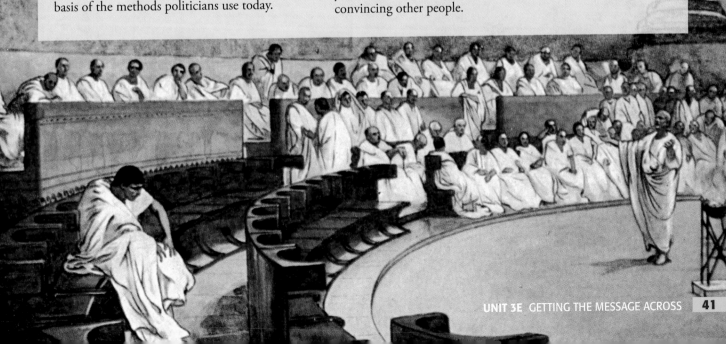

Giving your opinion

Listening and speaking

1 Do you have a debating society at your school? Which world issues do you think would benefit from discussion? Do you find it easy or difficult to give your opinion on a subject?

2 1.15 Listen to two people giving their opinions on whether or not television advertising is harmful. Note down the main points that each speaker makes. Who do you think has the strongest argument?

Speaker 1	Speaker 2

3 Work in pairs. Take turns acting out the part of the two speakers in Exercise 2. Use the notes you made and some of the Useful Expressions. You can add ideas of your own.

USEFUL EXPRESSIONS giving your opinion

Presenting an opinion
I am (strongly) in favour of / against …
I feel (strongly) that … / I (strongly) believe …
Adding points
First of all, … / Firstly/Secondly/Thirdly, …
In addition, …
Furthermore, …
… also …

Conceding a point
Although/While I understand/recognise/admit that …
Although/While it is true (to say) that …
Agreeing
I agree (with you) that / about …
You're (absolutely) right that / about …
I think what you said about … is right.
Disagreeing
I have to disagree …
I'm sorry, but I disagree / don't agree / can't agree (that / with)…
I'm afraid I disagree / don't agree / can't agree (that / with)…

4 Work in small groups. Take turns choosing a topic from the list below and giving your opinion. The rest of the group can agree/disagree and add points of their own.

1 The government should ban junk food.

2 Everyone should travel abroad at least once in their lives.

3 The spread of the English language is harmful.

4 Every student should have access to a computer and the Internet.

5 People who waste water should pay a heavy fine.

6 We should ban all cars that run on fossil fuels.

Culture and civilisations

Let's get started

1 Discuss the picture in pairs.

  1 What kind of festival is it?

  2 Which country do you think it's in? Why do you think that?

  3 Describe a festival you participated in.

2 Think about each season of the year. Can you think of one special day for each season for you, your family or your country?

3 Now work in groups. Tell each other about the special day in each season. As you present your information, tell the group about:

- the exact date or time of day
- the location
- the events
- any special details (food, clothes, presents, fireworks, etc.)

4 Look at the words in the box connected with festivals and celebrations.

> gift (or present) costume candle cake
> greetings cards fireworks lantern mask tree

Which can you …?

- decorate
- put up
- wear
- give or receive
- light

In this unit you will learn

- **Communication**: describing an event
- **Vocabulary**: festivals and celebrations, adjectives expressing emotions
- **Reading and Listening**: special days around the world, ancient civilisations, great treasures of culture, the Bering land bridge
- **Writing**: description of an event
- **Grammar**: modals for speculating, modals for obligation and ability in the past, order of adjectives

4A Festivals and celebrations

Reading

1 Read texts A–D and match them to pictures 1–4.

2 Match these sentences to the texts. Write A, B, C or D.

1 The colours on this day represent something. _A and C_
2 The food on this day represents something. _____
3 People give presents to each other on this day. _____
4 It marks a specific historical event. _____
5 Candles are important on this day. _____
6 People celebrate it differently in different parts of the world. _____
7 It is only celebrated in the USA. _____

Text A: Chinese New Year

Chinese New Year is the most important of the traditional Chinese holidays. It falls on different dates each year depending on the moon, but always between 21st January and 20th February. Visits to friends and family take place during this celebration. The colour gold is said to bring wealth, and the colour red is considered especially lucky. The New Year's Eve dinner is very large and includes fish, noodles and dumplings.

Text B: Australia Day

Australians celebrate Australia day on 26th January every year. It marks the day when the first immigrants from England arrived in Sydney Cove in 1788. Many Australians like to celebrate their national day by spending time with friends and family, or by organising parties and barbecues in their local communities. Amazing firework displays bring an end to the day when Australians reflect on their history and achievements, and look forward to their nation's future.

Text C: Kwanzaa

On 26th December, Kwanzaa is celebrated in the USA. It is a holiday to commemorate African heritage. Kwanzaa lasts a week during which participants gather with family and friends to exchange gifts and to light a series of black, red and green candles, which symbolise the seven basic values of African-American family life that are unity, self-determination, collective work and responsibility, cooperative economics, purpose, creativity and faith.

Text D: New Year's Day

New Year's Day is the first day of the year in the Gregorian calendar on 1st January. There are often fireworks at midnight to celebrate the new year. Many parts of the world celebrate this day in different ways. For example, in the southern part of the United States, black-eyed peas are thought to bring luck and prosperity for the new year and 'collard greens' bring wealth and good fortune.

Listening

3 You are going to listen to an interview with *National Geographic* photographer, Bob Krist. Here are two of his pictures.

  1 Which festival is it?

  2 What is happening in each picture?

4 🔊 1.16 **Listen to the interview and answer questions 1–4. Circle A, B, C or D.**

  1 The main topic of the radio show is …

     A good holiday destinations.

     B taking good pictures on holiday.

     C cultural festivals.

     D what to pack on holiday.

  2 The presenter mistakenly thinks that Bob …

     A was in China.

     B is a photographer.

     C is American.

     D is the man in the picture.

  3 Bob arrives early at festivals …

     A to avoid the crowds.

     B to take pictures of the crowds.

     C so no one is in his way.

     D so that he can leave early.

  4 The problem with taking photographs at night is that …

     A you can't take pictures.

     B you only see the main image.

     C the camera flash might not work.

     D the crowd is in front of you.

Grammar: modals for speculating (1): the present

5 **Read sentences 1–3 from the listening and match them to meanings a–c.**

  1 It's summer, so it must be time for the holidays.

  2 That might be a problem.

  3 It can't be easy with so many people in front of you.

  a It's not likely or possible.

  b It's very certain or likely.

  c It's possible.

6 **In which sentence could you also use the modal verbs *may* and *could*?**

See Grammar reference, page 147

7 **Rewrite sentences 1–4 using a modal verb.**

  1 There's no doubt that it's his birthday because I can see candles on the cake.

    It _____ because I can see candles on the cake.

  2 It's impossible that this is Paris because that tower is the Empire State Building!

    It _____ because that tower is the Empire State Building!

  3 The man in this picture is possibly related to the family. I'm not sure.

    The man in this picture _____. I'm not sure.

  4 I'm not certain but I think it's in Japan because of the writing on the road signs.

    It _____ because of the writing on the road signs.

8 **Work in pairs. Turn to page 142 and look at the pictures of different festivals around the world. Make speculations about:**

- the country and location
- the reason for the festival

Use different modals depending on how sure or unsure you are.

Speaking

1 Archaeologists found these artefacts from some ancient civilisations. What do you think each object is? What was its purpose? Discuss as a class.

Listening

2 (•) 1.17 Listen to an archaeologist describing five of the objects. Match the description to the object. There is one extra object.

Description 1: ___   Description 4: ___

Description 2: ___   Description 5: ___

Description 3: ___

3 (•) 1.17 Listen to the five descriptions again. Decide if these statements are true or false.

	The archaeologist …	True	False
1	doesn't think the owner used the vase much.		
2	thinks the civilisation possibly used metal.		
3	is sure the owner was the wife of someone important.		
4	guesses he was aged between 16 and 17.		
5	is very certain the soldier fought in a lot of battles.		

Grammar: modals for speculating (2): the past

Modals for speculating about the past

You can use *must / might / may / could / can't / couldn't + have + past participle* to speculate about whether something was true in the past.

*They **might have attached** it to a longer piece of wood.*

*This civilisation **couldn't have discovered** metal at this stage in history.*

*She **may have been** the wife of someone wealthy and important.*

*The soldier **must have fought** a lot …*

*This civilisation **can't have discovered** metal because it's made of stone.*

See Grammar Reference, page 147

Pronunciation: 've

4 (•) 1.18 Listen to someone saying the sentences in the grammar summary. How do they pronounce *have*?

5 (•) 1.18 Now listen again and repeat.

6 Work in pairs. Look at these cave paintings from an ancient civilisation. Speculate about this civilisation in the past. Make sentences about their:

- transport
- food and hunting
- written language
- the organisation of their society (system of government, king or queen, etc.)

Example:

They must've had transport because they knew about wheels.

Grammar: order of adjectives

7 Read the grammar summary below about the order of adjectives. Complete the table with the words in bold from these sentences in the listening.

*This first piece is a **beautiful, old Greek vase**.*

*You can see the **small, golden fruit bowl**.*

*He was a **handsome, older man**.*

*It's an **ancient Roman metal relic**.*

8 Work in pairs. Complete and say these sentences with two or three adjectives and a noun where necessary.

Example:

Today I'm wearing a stylish, white cotton T-shirt.

1 Today I'm wearing a … shirt.
2 Our lesson is in a … classroom.
3 In my bag I have a …
4 My favourite possession is a …

Order of adjectives

You can use more than one adjective before a noun. However, you normally use them in this order:

opinion	size / shape	age	colour	origin / nationality	material	noun
beautiful		old		Greek		vase

When you use more than one adjective, you normally use two or three at most. If you use more adjectives, use *and* or a new sentence:

This first piece is a beautiful, old, Greek, ~~clay~~ vase. → *This first piece is a beautiful, old Greek vase and it's made of clay. / This first piece is a beautiful, old Greek vase. It's made of clay.*

See Grammar Reference, page 148

An ancient civilisation

Reading

1 There are five different texts about the Maya civilisation on page 49.
Match these titles to each text.

    a THE MAYA MYSTERY   **b** AGRICULTURE   **c** NUMBERING SYSTEM

    d THE CALENDAR   **e** ARCHITECTURE

2 Match the underlined words in the article on
page 49 to pictures 1–4.

3 Read paragraphs 1–5 and decide if these
sentences about the Maya are true or false.

		True	False
1	The pyramids were used for burials and no one lived in them.		
2	The Maya began counting from the number zero.		
3	The Mayan month was longer than our months.		
4	Farmers increased the level of the fields because the land was too wet.		
5	Mayan farmers only produced enough food for their families.		
6	Mayan culture disappeared very suddenly.		
7	Everyone agrees on how the Maya civilisation died out.		
8	Experts believe we can still learn from the ancient Maya.		

Grammar: modals of obligation and ability in the past

4 Underline the correct verb in these sentences.

    1 The Maya ***must / had to*** bury their kings in the pyramids.

    2 Mayan farmers ***have to / had to*** grow crops on wet, swampy land.

    3 For many years they ***didn't have to / don't have to*** worry too much about the problem.

    4 The large Mayan cities ***can't / couldn't*** survive as the food and water ran out.

Modals of obligation and ability in the past	
PRESENT	PAST
must	→ had to
have to / don't have to	→ had to / didn't have to
can	→ could
can't	→ couldn't

See Grammar Reference, page 148

5 Here are some laws from the Maya in the present.
Rewrite them in the past.

    1 People must pay for something if they break it (even by accident).

       People had to pay for something if they broke it (even by accident).

    2 Thieves have to pay for anything they take.

    3 If a thief can't pay for it, he has to work as a slave.

    4 Musicians can't make mistakes when they play.

6 Think of three rules you have at home or at school
now and three rules you had when you were
younger. Write them down (six rules in total).
Tell your partner.

 Watch a video about the Maya. Turn to page 137.

1: _____

During the Classic Period from around AD 250 to AD 900, the ancient Maya civilisation was one of the greatest groups of people in the world. They built cities with thousands of buildings including <u>pyramids</u> for kings, and <u>huts</u> where poorer people lived. The Maya used pyramids as <u>tombs</u> where they also had to bury their kings.

2: _____

The Maya people had an unusual and advanced numbering system. At the time, most of the world had no concept of the number zero. The Maya, however, were using a flat, round shape as a symbol to represent this amount. Their counting system had only three symbols: a dot, which represented one, a bar for five, and the round shape for zero. The Maya also thought that certain numbers were very important. For example, the number 20 was special because of the total number of fingers and toes. The number 52 represented the number of years in a Mayan century.

3: _____

Mayan farmers had to grow crops on wet, swampy land. They could do this because of their system of 'raised fields'. They dug <u>canals</u> around areas of land and put the soil onto these fields. This increased the level by 0.6 to 1.2 metres and avoided flooding. The soil from the canals was very fertile and so extended the season for growing crops. This produced enough food for the local community and a little more to sell to other communities. Today, agricultural researchers and farmers are learning from the ancient Maya. In dry areas of Central and South America with poor soils, local farmers and governments have gone back to using the raised-field system that worked so well 1,500 years ago.

4: _____

How the Maya viewed the passage of time is different from many other cultures. They didn't use a chart with rows of numbers representing days and months. They used several different calendars at the same time. One calendar contained 13 months consisting of 20 days each for a total of 260 days. It was for religious purposes and planting their fields. Another calendar had 365 days and followed the movement of the planets. When the Maya referred to both calendars, they matched their 20-day months with the 365 days in the planetary calendar.

5: _____

Around 800 AD, the Maya were at the peak of their history and were among the great ancient civilisations. Then, almost in an instant, a society of nearly 15 million people disappeared. All that was left were empty cities, trade routes and immense pyramids in ruins. Many archaeologists now go along with the theory that climate change ended the Mayan society. By studying soil in the region, scientists believe there were three serious droughts within a decade and so the large Mayan cities couldn't survive as the food and water ran out. Experts say that the Maya collapse could serve as a valuable lesson to the modern world today as it faces a shortage of water.

4D Describing an event

Speaking: describing an event

1 Work in pairs. Describe the picture and discuss these questions.

- What does the picture show?
- Where might it be?
- What do you think is happening?
- How do the people in the picture feel?
- Do you have anything similar in your country?
- Have you ever dressed up for a special event or a parade?

2 You can use the expressions (a–h) for talking about pictures. Read them and put them into the categories (1–3).

1 Describing the picture *a*
2 Speculating about what is happening
3 Speculating about a person's feelings

a The picture shows …
b There are four people in it …
c It might be at a festival.
d This person looks excited.
e They must be in a parade.
f Maybe they're dancers.
g The person in the middle …
h This person seems a bit nervous!

Vocabulary

3 Match an adjective from the box with the feelings in situations 1–7.

> nervous   cheerful   impatient   overjoyed
> fascinated   frustrated   excited

1 You don't want to wait any longer for your friend to arrive.
2 You are about to find out your exam results.
3 You have just found out your exam results and got the results you needed!
4 Your friend is telling you some really interesting news about someone at school.
5 There is only one more day to go before you see your favourite group play live.
6 You keep trying to answer a question in maths and you keep making the same mistake.
7 You wake up and think that today is probably going to be a good day.

4 Work in pairs and look at two more pictures. Take turns to describe the pictures. Speculate about what is happening and how the people feel.

USEFUL EXPRESSIONS describing places and events

Describing the picture

The picture shows … / I can see …
There is … / There are some …
The person in the middle / on the right / at the top/bottom …

Speculating about people

She looks …
He seems …

Speculating about what's happening

It might / could / must be … -ing
Maybe / Perhaps / Possibly …

Writing: describing an event

5 Work in pairs. Look at these pictures from the city of New Orleans. Compare them and describe the differences. What do you think has happened in the second picture?

6 A student is preparing an essay about the festival of Mardi Gras in the city of New Orleans. She has planned her essay with a 'mind map'. Write these missing headings on the mind map:

- During the festival
- New Orleans celebrations
- Why is it important?
- The history and background

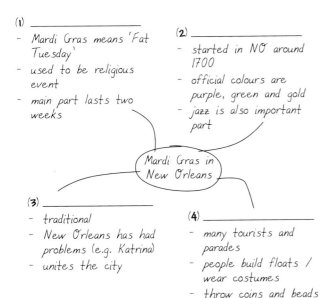

(1) _____
- Mardi Gras means 'Fat Tuesday'
- used to be religious event
- main part lasts two weeks

(2) _____
- started in NO around 1700
- official colours are purple, green and gold
- jazz is also important part

Mardi Gras in New Orleans

(3) _____
- traditional
- New Orleans has had problems (e.g. Katrina)
- unites the city

(4) _____
- many tourists and parades
- people build floats / wear costumes
- throw coins and beads

7 Now read her essay. Underline where the writer includes the notes from the mind map.

8 Write a description of an annual event in your country or culture. First plan your essay, using the mind map technique above. Brainstorm your notes under four similar headings. Then use your plan to write a description of 200–250 words.

The word 'Mardi Gras' means Fat Tuesday. Originally it was a religious event and today Mardi Gras is still very important in many countries around the world. One of the most famous is in the city of New Orleans.

The first Mardi Gras celebrations probably happened in New Orleans around 1700, when it was a small town. As the city grew, the parties also became bigger and bigger with large parades down the streets. It became known as 'Carnival' and purple, green and gold became the official colours. In the twentieth century, New Orleans also became famous for the music of jazz, so nowadays that's also an important part of the celebrations.

The main events last for about two weeks and tourists come from all over the world to join the party. The most popular parts of Mardi Gras are the parades. Groups of local people build and decorate 'floats'. They wear colourful costumes and ride on the floats through the centre of the city. As they go past, they throw coins and beads to the people watching.

Mardi Gras in New Orleans has a long tradition but it has become even more important in recent years. In August 2005, Hurricane Katrina destroyed many parts of the city and people's homes. But Katrina didn't stop Mardi Gras, and the following year the people of New Orleans were united once again!

9 Swap your descriptions with a partner and check if their description answers these questions.

1 When does it happen? ☐
2 Where is it? ☐
3 Who is involved? ☐
4 What do you prepare? ☐
5 What happens on the day? ☐
6 Why is it important? ☐

4E Cultural treasure

Speaking

1 Discuss as a class.

1 How often do you visit museums or art galleries? Do you think they are important? Why? Why not?

2 Which period of your country's history do you think is the most interesting? Why?

3 What types of artefacts do you like looking at most? For example, paintings, statues, rare antiques, etc.

Reading

2 Read the article on page 53 and answer questions 1–5. Circle A, B, C or D.

1 In the first two paragraphs, the writer says …

A he thinks museums behave like criminals.

B some people think museums behave like criminals.

C museums must stop the criminals.

D museums buy their artefacts from criminals.

2 When Lord Elgin took the marble statues, …

A they weren't in Greece.

B Greece was part of the Ottoman Empire.

C Greece didn't want them.

D he paid for them.

3 Museums don't want to return any artefacts because they might …

A get stolen.

B get damaged.

C lose money.

D have to give many other artefacts back.

4 The Amber Room …

A never existed.

B has never been returned.

C was definitely destroyed.

D is now back in Russia.

5 The writer …

A thinks museums should return all their treasure.

B thinks museums should keep the treasure.

C wants to visit Greece and Egypt.

D doesn't express his opinion.

3 Write a different form of the words below. You can find the correct words in the text.

adjective	noun	person
(1) _____	nation	nationalist
cultural	(2) _____	▬▬▬▬▬
artistic	(3) _____	(4) _____
fake	(5) _____	▬▬▬▬▬
civilised	(6) _____	civilian
(7) _____	history	historian
smuggled	(8) _____	smuggler
stolen	(9) _____	thief
▬▬▬▬▬	crime	(10) _____

4 Read about a famous crime. Use the correct form of the word in brackets and complete the text.

No one could believe it when one of Norway's most famous (1) _national_ (nation) treasures, *The Scream* painted by the (2) _____ (art) Edward Munch, (3) _____ (steal) from the walls of the Munch Museum in Norway. Two (4) _____ (thief) with masks pulled the painting from the wall and escaped in a car. It only took them 50 seconds and they even had time to leave a postcard which said: 'Thanks for the poor (5) _____ (secure).' An international search began in case the painting was smuggled out of the country. Finally, after two years of police (6) _____ (investigate), the painting was found undamaged and still in Norway.

The great treasures of culture

Since the beginning of civilisation, artists have created works of beauty. And since that time these pieces of national culture have also vanished from the nations that created them. Sometimes, private individuals are responsible. Smuggling and trading in illegal art and treasure is big business and worth billions of dollars a year. The dealers buy stolen goods from a country and quickly ship them abroad. Then, to sell them, they must have historical documents for the objects which say where they were made, who made them, when they were made and who owned them. If the artefact is stolen, then they have to create a fake history for it.

However, there are also many examples of rare objects which are on display in famous museums but were also taken from their original country. Many people believe there is little or no difference between these museums and the criminals who trade in stolen works.

One of the most famous cases is between Greece and Great Britain. For years the two countries have been arguing over marble statues which were taken from the Parthenon temple in Athens. They are called the 'Elgin Marbles' because Lord Elgin was the British Ambassador in 1799 in Constantinople (now Istanbul). At that time, the huge Ottoman Turkish Empire included Greece. While there, Elgin paid a group of men to remove some of the statues from the site of Acropolis and he transported them back to Britain. In 1821, the Greeks defeated the Turks and gained independence. Soon after, they officially requested the return of the artworks. The British Museum, which keeps the priceless objects, has refused ever since.

Egypt is another country which has been the target for lots of cultural theft over the centuries. Statues and artefacts taken from the region are on display in museums in different countries all over the world. Now, the Egyptian government wants them back. The problem for many of the museums is that if they return one piece of treasure to a country, they worry that they will have to return hundreds of pieces collected over decades.

There is also a long history of armies taking cultural treasures as they invaded countries. The longest list of stolen treasure probably

> 'As Hitler invaded countries, he also took their most famous works of art.'

belongs to Nazi Germany. During the Second World War, as Hitler invaded countries, he also took their most famous works of art. Many of these eventually vanished and were never returned. The biggest mystery for art historians is the Amber Room which was stolen from a town near St Petersburg (then Leningrad), in 1941. The room was made completely of amber and belonged to Peter the Great. The Nazis took the whole room back to Germany but just before the end of the war it disappeared and has not been found since.

Case Study 2 〉 The people of the north

THE BERING LAND BRIDGE

Thousands of years ago, the continents of North America and Asia were linked in the far north by what we call the Bering land bridge. This was a large area of land which connected Siberia and Alaska after a dramatic fall in the sea level. Between 10,000 and 20,000 years ago humans used this opportunity to migrate to the Americas. When the sea level rose, the continents were separated again.

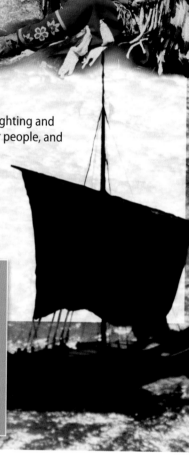

The first Americans

It is believed that Native Americans crossed the land bridge from Siberia and then travelled south by river to North America and Canada. Others may have sailed down the Pacific coast to South America. After their time in the far north, they were skilled hunters and fishermen. Today's Native Americans have a similar appearance to people from Mongolia and China, which supports the theory that they walked across the land bridge from Asia. But discoveries in Chile in 1996 revealed a skeleton which had similar facial characteristics to Aboriginal Australians, suggesting that the first settlers came from there, perhaps by sea. The lifestyle of the Eskimo, or Inuit people of the far north of Canada, is probably the closest we can get to imagining how the early settlers lived. They survived mostly by hunting sea mammals.

The Vikings

The Vikings were a successful civilisation from Denmark, Norway and Sweden. They existed between AD 700 and 1100. A great sea-faring people, they had a reputation for fighting and conquering. They began travelling in search of better farmland to grow food to feed their people, and they settled in eastern England, Ireland, and Scotland, particularly on the islands around Scotland's coast. Many people believe that they went to North America but did not stay long there. Some Vikings settled in an area of France known today as 'Normandy', which means *the land of the north men*. They also reached Iceland and Greenland. Some archaeological discoveries suggest that the Vikings met the Inuit in Greenland and lived happily side by side for some time.

What have we inherited from the Vikings?
* **Language**: the Viking influence can still be found today in words like *sky*, *skin*, *husband*, *sister* and *happy*.
* **Laws**: many Viking laws were adopted in Britain, and the Tynwald in the Isle of Man, which began in Viking times and still exists today, is the oldest parliament in the world.
* **Shipbuilding**: the Vikings had excellent ships and their shipbuilding skills were passed down in the places where they settled.
* **Stories**: Viking stories had terrible monsters and strange creatures such as trolls and dragons. Some of these creatures lived in 'Midgard' (or Middle Earth) – a thousand years before it was mentioned in *The Lord of the Rings*!

1 Read the text and answer these questions.

1 What created the Bering land bridge?
2 Which two routes were taken by the people who originated in Siberia?
3 Why is a study of the Inuit useful in our understanding of early settlers?
4 Why did the Vikings leave their native land?
5 What is the connection between the Vikings and the Inuit?

2 Mark these statements *True* or *False*.

1 The Bering land bridge is still there today. _____
2 Native Americans look a little like Mongolian people. _____
3 People from Australia also used the land bridge. _____
4 The Vikings fought with the Native Americans. _____
5 The influence of the Vikings is still present today. _____

3 With a partner, take turns telling each other about the information in the text. Use narrative tenses.

e.g. *The Bering land bridge <u>had gone</u> long before the Vikings <u>went</u> to America.*

Review 〉 Unit 3

Grammar

1 Underline the correct tense.

> Herman Van Rompuy is the first full-time President of the European Council. Originally, Rompuy (**1**) *had been / was being* a Belgian politician and while he (**2**) *had worked / was working* in the Belgian parliament, the European Council elected him to be their President.
> At university, Rompuy (**3**) *had studied / was studying* many different subjects but he soon (**4**) *became / was becoming* interested in politics and, after jobs in banking and universities, he (**5**) *joined / was joining* the Belgium government in the nineties. Although he is a busy man, Rompuy recently published a book of poetry which he (**6**) *had written / was writing* over many years.

2 Complete the questions about the text in Exercise 1.

1 Q What _____ before he became President of the European Council?

   A A Belgian politician.

2 Q Where _____ when the European Council elected him?

   A In the Belgian parliament.

3 Q What _____?

   A Many different subjects.

4 Q When _____?

   A In the nineties.

5 Q What _____?

   A A book of poetry.

3 Underline the correct verb. In some sentences both forms are possible.

1 Our country didn't *use / used* to be part of the EU.

2 We *used to / would* walk this way to school every day when we were kids.

3 There was a time when only men *used to / would* vote in elections.

4 Many countries in Europe used to *have / had* a monarchy.

5 Greece *joined / used to join* the EU in 1981.

Vocabulary

4 Write the missing word in each sentence.

1 The b_____ between the two countries is 200 km long.

2 The g_____ runs the country.

3 The c_____ of the USA is the dollar.

4 Every four years we have an e_____ and we vote for our MPs.

5 Some countries have a Prime Minister and some countries have a P_____. And some countries have both!

6 Ted couldn't c_____ his mum that he was right.

7 If you drive too fast, you might get a f_____.

Functions

5 Replace the words in bold with a similar word (or words) in the box.

> I agree   first of all   I disagree   hand
>   while   I think

1 **You're absolutely right** that there needs to be a change.

2 **Firstly**, we need to find out how serious the problem is.

3 **Although** I see your point, I think you're wrong about that.

4 **In my opinion**, the situation is serious.

5 On the one **side**, people will be able to travel, but on the other, they may not find work when they come back.

6 **It's not true** that things used to be better in the past.

Now I can ...

- [ ] talk about global issues
- [ ] discuss politics
- [ ] talk about the history of the EU
- [ ] discuss international organisations and relations
- [ ] talk about nations and nationalities
- [ ] discuss cultural diversity
- [ ] talk about points for and against a subject
- [ ] write a *for and against* essay
- [ ] give my opinion
- [ ] use narrative tenses, *used to* and *would*

Review 〉Unit 4

Grammar

1 Underline the correct modal verb. In one sentence both words are possible.

1. This tradition *might / must* be over 100 years old. No one really knows.
2. That picture with Josh *can't / mustn't* be in Japan because he didn't travel with us there.
3. We had 900 people last year so the event *could / can* attract over 1,000 visitors this year.
4. This *may / must* be the place because we've been everywhere else.
5. We have an ancient coin. It *might / may* be from Roman times but it's impossible to say for sure.

2 Rewrite these sentences using the modal verb in bold.

1. There's no way this is the right direction.

    can

    This _____ the right direction.

2. There's a possibility we'll meet someone famous.

    might

    We _____.

3. The fossils show that dinosaurs certainly lived here.

    must

    The fossils show that dinosaurs _____ here.

4. The Romans possibly made this statue.

    could

    The Romans _____ made this statue.

5. In the past, it wasn't obligatory for school children to stay at school until they were 16.

    have

    In the past, school children _____ at school until they were 16.

Vocabulary

3 Read these descriptions of different festivals and celebrations. Write in the missing words.

> ~~masks~~   greetings cards   fireworks   lanterns
> candles   costumes

Halloween is really popular in the USA. Children wear scary (1) ___masks___ and (2)_____. They walk from house to house and ask for sweets.

I love birthdays because in the morning you receive (3)_____ and presents in the post. For the party, you eat a big cake with (4)_____ on. Each one represents one year.

November the fifth is important in the UK because it's bonfire night and lots of (5)_____ go off around the country.

At the festival of Shang Yuan, Chinese children carry (6)_____. It is at the end of Chinese New Year.

4 Add the missing letters at the end of the words.

1. My national___*ity*___ is British.
2. Who is the art_____ of this painting?
3. My father is a local histor_____. He knows everything about our village's past.
4. In the summer, London has lots of cultur_____ events.
5. The Maya were an ancient civilis_____.

Functions

5 Write in the missing words.

1. It's some k_____ of knife.
2. It's a s_____ of museum.
3. The picture s_____ three teenagers.
4. The person in the middle l_____ excited.
5. I'm not sure but m_____ they're dancers.
6. This person s_____ a bit nervous!

Now I can ...
☐ talk about festivals around the world and cultural heritage
☐ describe an event
☐ write a description of an event
☐ use modal verbs for speculating
☐ use modal verbs of obligation and ability in the past
☐ use the correct order of adjectives

A new home

In this unit you will learn

- **Communication**: renting a flat, asking for information
- **Vocabulary**: homes and furnishings, phrasal verbs
- **Reading and Listening**: living in space, a new home on Mars, cultural trips
- **Writing**: description of a place
- **Grammar**: *will, be going to*, the present continuous, modals for speculating about the future

Let's get started

1 Discuss these questions in pairs.

1 What type of home can you see in the picture? Compare it with your home.

2 Would you like to live in this kind of house? Why? Why not?

3 What is the worst place you've stayed in? Describe it to your partner.

Vocabulary

2 Put these words into the correct category in the table.

~~kitchen~~ hall conservatory bedroom living room
semi-detached terraced pictures tiles flat desk
~~carpet~~ curtains armchair apartment sofa
bookshelves ~~dining table~~ mansion ~~detached~~
cottage bathroom blinds log cabin

type of house	rooms	furniture	furnishings
detached	kitchen	dining table	carpet

Note! flat (BrE) = apartment (AmE)

3 Look at these pairs of words connected with homes and houses. What is the difference? Use a dictionary to help you.

detached / semi-detached   carpet / rug
terrace / flat   desk / table   tile / carpet
fireplace / heater   curtains / blinds

4 Tell your partner about where you live. Describe your ...

- home (type? number of rooms? garden?)
- bedroom (furniture? furnishings?)

Friedrich Stowasser (1928–2000), an Austrian architect who designed this house, rejected straight lines and was fascinated by onion towers

5A Home obsessions

Reading

1 Look at the pictures of three unusual homes. What do you think makes them unusual?

2 Now read about three people and their obsessions. Match them to the pictures.

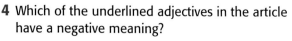

A Tony Alleyne has transformed his one-bedroom apartment into the inside of a **state-of-the-art** spaceship. He based the original design on the spaceship from the hit seventies TV show, *Star Trek,* but later he decided the interior was a bit too **out of date**, so he created a more **futuristic** look. He says: 'My whole life has gone into this. I have given up absolutely everything. Some people might think I'm a bit of a sad individual but I'm not … I always wanted to live somewhere like this.'

B A movie fan has spent two years converting his garden shed into a pirate ship. Reg Miller, 65, was inspired by the *Pirates of the Caribbean* films, starring actor Johnny Depp. To get the **historic** look, Reg collected bits and pieces from junk shops. The shed includes swords, a hammock, an **old-fashioned** chest and even a parrot.

C From the outside, Anthony Toth's house looks like an ordinary **modern** house. But step inside the garage and you enter the passenger cabin of an **eighties** Pan Am Boeing 747 aeroplane. Anthony has spent thousands of pounds over 20 years to complete the **retro** airline look which comes complete with a departure board, aircraft seats, luggage racks, oxygen masks and safety manuals. 'I became obsessed with flying Pan Am because of the amazing cabin interiors,' said Mr Toth.

3 Match the sentences to the texts (A, B or C). There are two possible answers for sentences 5 and 6.

This person …

1 has changed the entire living area.
2 has changed part of the house.
3 hasn't changed the house.
4 has based the interior on something real.
5 has based the interior on something from TV or film.
6 has based the design on the past.
7 wonders what other people think about his obsession.

4 Which of the underlined adjectives in the article have a negative meaning?

5 Which can you use to describe …?
- your clothes
- the architecture in your town / city
- the music you listen to

Listening

6 1.19 Listen to a radio documentary about a woman and her house. Afterwards, discuss these questions as a class.

1 What has she done to her house?
2 What other plans does she have?
3 Would you like to change your house? Would you make it similar to a film or a particular period in history? Which one?

7 🔊 1.19 **Listen again. Circle answer A, B, C or D.**

1 Julia has made her home look like the inside of …
  A a medieval castle.
  B a house in the suburbs.
  C a house from the seventies.
  D a house in Birmingham.

2 All the furniture in the house is …
  A original.   B fake.
  C wooden.   D metal.

3 The dining room …
  A isn't finished yet.
  B is going to be changed.
  C was built by her husband.
  D is still used as a dining room.

4 Julia likes …
  A traditional clothes.
  B old films.
  C romantic people.
  D anything connected to the medieval period.

5 Julia is worried about changing the front of the house because …
  A it costs a lot of money.
  B she can't buy original furniture.
  C the neighbours are jealous.
  D the council might not give her permission.

Grammar: future forms (1): *will*, *be going to*, the present continuous

8 **Work in groups. Compare sentences a and b. Answer the questions about each pair.**

1 What is the tense? Which sentence refers to the future?
  a We're meeting the owner this morning.
  b We're standing in your hallway.

2 Which sentence describes an intention? Which is a prediction?
  a I'm going to start decorating my bedroom this year.
  b That'll be expensive.

3 Which is a question about a prediction? Which is about someone's decision?
  a What will you do?
  b Do you think they'll give you permission?

4 Which is an intention? Which is a prediction based on evidence?
  a It's going to cost a lot of money to build the house.
  b I'm going to build the house.

Future forms (1)

- We use the present continuous to talk about arrangements between people (e.g. to meet)
- We use *will* + infinitive for predictions and spontaneous decisions.
- We use *be going to* to talk about intentions and predictions based on evidence.

See Grammar Reference, page 149

9 **Work in pairs and follow the instructions using the future form given in bold.**

1 Explain your plans for when you leave school: college? university? a job? (**be going to**)

2 Explain your plans for this weekend: meet friends? go away? (**present continuous**)

3 Make a prediction about your future: (**will**)

10 **Work in groups of three. You are a group of students and you are going to live in this flat. Discuss how you plan to decorate and furnish it so that you can live there.**

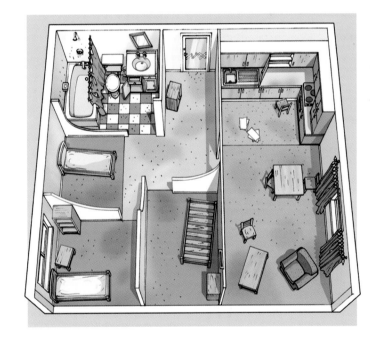

Remember to discuss:
- the style of decoration and the colour of the walls
- furniture and furnishings

Afterwards present your plans to the class.

Example:

We are going to paint this room yellow and add curtains …

Living in space

Speaking

1 Discuss these questions in groups. Then report your opinions back to the class.

1 Do you think global warming is a possibility or a certainty? Why? / Why not?

2 How do you think we will solve the problem of climate change?

3 Do you think the human race will leave Earth and live on other planets? Why / Why not?

Reading

2 Read the article. Decide if these statements about the author's opinion are true or false.

	The author thinks …	True	False
1	the human race will possibly need to look for a new home.		
2	we will possibly fit on the moon.		
3	we probably won't live on Venus.		
4	we'll almost definitely have to look outside our solar system for a new home.		
5	we'll possibly move to Gliese 581 d in the near future.		
6	the whole human race definitely won't be leaving Earth in the near future.		

If climate change forces us to leave Earth, will we find another life-supporting planet?

Our little planet has an ecosystem of enormous variety. This certain combination of temperature, terrain, vegetation, gravity and atmosphere supports millions of species of creatures including humans. But if climate change affects that balance, the human race might need to look for a new home. But is Earth the only planet with the right conditions to keep us alive?

Lunar living

Our closest option is the moon but it isn't ideal for humans. Despite being the easiest of extra-terrestrial locations to reach, there's no air to breathe and the temperature can reach a peak of over 100°C during the day and minus 150°C at night. These extreme conditions don't mean lunar living is impossible but you would need to supply air and maintain temperatures at a human-friendly level. The other problem is that the moon is just one fiftieth the size of Earth, so it's too small for the whole human race.

Life in the solar system

What are the other options? Venus is roughly the same size as Earth. However, you also have volcanic temperatures and some dangerous clouds of sulphuric acid, so it's an unlikely home. Mars, on other hand, may be a possibility. It's further from the Sun than Venus or Earth so the red planet has cold but reasonable temperatures (around minus 50°C). The other advantage is that in 2008 NASA*. confirmed that water existed (in ice form) and there might be more below the planet's surface. However, if we want a planet exactly like Earth, then we need to travel further abroad – to planets beyond our own Solar System.

Extrasolar planets

Since the 1990s, astronomers have discovered more than 300 planets orbiting distant stars. Telescopes have observed many 'extrasolar' planets and the most likely alternative for Earth is the strangely-named Gliese 581 d. It's the right distance from its sun, so not too hot and not too cold. Scientists also believe that Gliese 581 d could have water on the surface.

Space travel

The first mission to Mars is scheduled for sometime in the next decade, so moving large numbers of people there is a long, long way off. At this stage of history, you can only read about the kind of space travel technology you need for trips to places like Gliese 581 d in science fiction novels.

*NASA: National Aeronautics and Space Administration

Grammar: future forms (2): *will* (+ adverb) for prediction

3 We often use adverbs with *will / won't* to make predictions. Underline the adverbs in sentences 2–5 in Exercise 2 and write them on the scale in the grammar summary.

Example:

We'll <u>possibly</u> have to look for a new home.

4 How does the word order change with *won't*?

will + adverbs for predictions

will certainly … (or)   100%
will definitely

_____

_____

possibly won't

_____

almost definitely won't
certainly won't … (or)

_____   0%

See Grammar Reference, page 149

5 Put these words in the correct order to make predictions. Afterwards, rewrite any predictions you disagree with.

1 humans probably on Mars won't land

2 Earth the get certainly warmer will

3 be one possibly there'll global language

4 read won't almost definitely people books

5 it become won't easier definitely to learn a language

Grammar: future forms (3): modals for speculating about the future

6 Read the grammar summary below and underline three sentences with *may*, *might* and *could* for speculation about the future in the article on page 60.

Modals for speculating about the future

We use the modal verbs *may*, *might* and *could* to say that something is possible in the future but you are not 100% certain:

*The human race **will possibly** need to look for a new home. = The human race **might / may / could** need to look for a new home.*

Use *may not* or *might not* to say something possibly won't come true or is unlikely to happen:

*We **possibly won't** find water on Mars. = We **may / might not** find water on Mars.*

Note!

You can't use *could not* with the same meaning:

*We **could not** find water on Mars. = We **weren't able to** find water on Mars.*

See Grammar Reference, page 149

7 Work in groups. In the past, writers have made predictions in their novels. Read about three famous books and make a list of their predictions. Then discuss:

- which predictions will or won't happen? How certain are you?
- which are probable or may happen?

H. G. Wells, *The Time Machine* (1895)

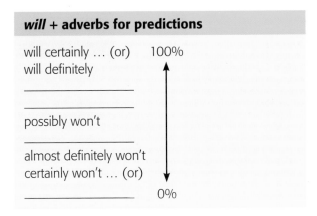

A scientist invents a machine that travels through time. The hero visits the future and eventually he arrives in AD 802,701. He finds a community of people called Eloi who do not have to work and they seem to live in peace. There is no war and everyone is equal. Then he discovers Morlocks, another race of people below the ground who use the Eloi as their food. Eventually the time traveller travels to the end of the Earth's history and finds giant crabs living on it.

Philip K. Dick, *Do Androids Dream of Electric Sheep?* (1968)

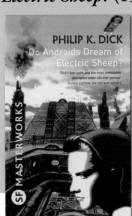

Many people haven't heard of this story but they know the famous film called *Blade Runner* which was based on it. The story is about a private detective in the future where cars can fly, giant advertisements float in the sky and humans live with androids. Then one day the androids get angry!

Pierre Boulle, *Planet of the Apes* (1963)

Three astronauts travel at the speed of light and arrive in a new star system on a planet very similar to Earth. However, the humans are like animals and apes rule the planet. The apes live in houses and dress in clothes. They capture the humans and use them as slaves.

5C A new home on Mars

Reading

1 Look at these pictures. Do you think they are on Earth or on Mars?

2 Read the article on page 63 and check your answers in Exercise 1. Match pictures 1–5 to paragraphs A–E.

3 Read the article again and choose an answer for questions 1–5. Circle A, B, C or D.

1 In the past, who has lived on Devon Island?

   A Canadians

   B the Inuit

   C NASA scientists

   D no one

2 Mars is _____ Devon Island.

   A identical to

   B similar to

   C easier to live on than

   D totally different from

3 The space suit …

   A works properly.

   B needs completely changing.

   C needs improvements.

   D is too small.

4 Which statement is true?

   A They are trying to build a greenhouse.

   B The greenhouse doesn't need any energy.

   C They are trying to grow plants in the greenhouse.

   D They have successfully grown plants in the greenhouse.

5 What is the team's conclusion?

   A That they need a new Martian Rover.

   B Many of the tests have failed.

   C Humans can live on Devon Island.

   D Humans can live on Mars.

4 Match words from each paragraph to the definitions.

Paragraph A:

no people live there _____ (adj)

the type of education and work experience you have had _____ (n)

Paragraph B:

the top part or the outside of something (e.g. a planet) _____ (n)

things that could hurt you _____ (n)

Paragraph C:

something right for a particular purpose _____ (adj)

clothing for a particular activity or purpose _____ (n)

Paragraph D:

operate _____ (v)

Paragraph E:

area of land with many different physical features (e.g. mountains and rocks) _____ (n)

very important _____ (adj)

5 Work in groups and discuss these questions.

1 Do you think other planets are inhabited or uninhabited?

2 What do you think are some of the dangers of living on another planet?

3 Do you think space exploration is crucial? Why? Why not?

Mars on Earth

A ___
Devon Island has always been a cold and uninhabited place in the Canadian Arctic. Day after day there are high winds and the temperature is below freezing. But for the first time, despite the terrible weather conditions, Devon Island is the new home for a group of explorers from NASA. They are living here for a few months in order to train and learn how to live and work on Mars. The group's members come from various backgrounds and nationalities, but they all have the same purpose: to find out how people can live on Mars in the future.

B ___
They have chosen Devon Island because the environment and landscape is similar in many ways to Mars. The surface is freezing cold and the ground is rough. However, there are some differences: on Mars, the atmosphere is poisonous to breathe. Devon Island is easier to travel to and it has its own dangers that you won't find on Mars. For example, you might meet a hungry polar bear on Devon Island!

> ' ... the environment and landscape is similar in many ways to Mars'

C ___
One thing the team wants to develop is suitable clothing for Mars. This includes a space suit. The suit they are testing at the moment is strong enough but it's too difficult to put on and take off. It's very big and bulky, which means that just walking around is very difficult and tiring. In addition, people will need to do experiments on Mars while wearing the suit so they have to be able to move around easily. One team member, Addy Overbeeke, specialises in space suit engineering. He explains: 'You have to think about what they're really going to be operating in.'

D ___
Another part of daily life on Mars will be meals and food. Creating a new home on Mars requires a lot of food. So the big question is: can you grow plants in order to survive? Scientists believe that growing plants on Mars might be possible. Mars and Earth have many similarities. They both have about the same amount of dry land and a 24-hour day. However, the atmosphere on Mars is totally different, so Canadian scientist Alain Berinstain is attempting to grow plants in a special greenhouse that you could also build on Mars. The greenhouse needs to run 365 days a year, so it uses a combination of solar energy and wind power.

E ___
People living on Mars will also want their own transportation. For this, the team on Devon Island have built the 'Martian Rover'. It's a huge heavy vehicle that can travel over rocks and rough terrain. This kind of testing takes many days but so far the work has been valuable and effective. As a result, the whole team now believes their work is crucial and that it's possible for humans to land on the planet Mars and create a home there. Addy Overbeeke adds: 'We know that it's man's destiny to go out and do space exploration. It's always time to think about what you want to do in the future.'

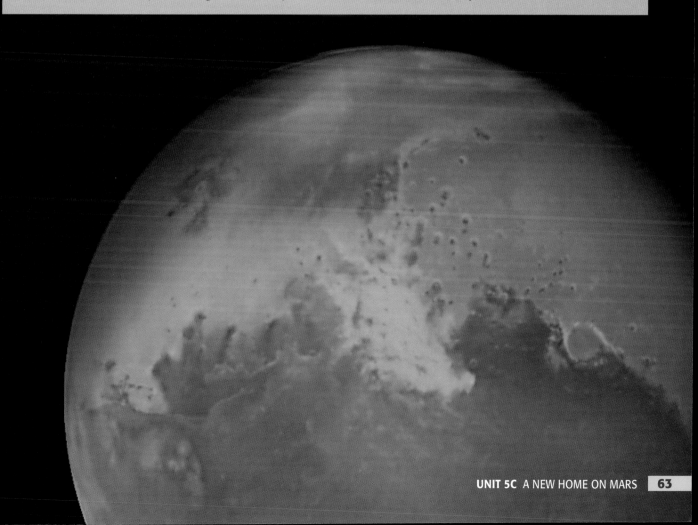

5D Renting a flat

Reading: asking for information

1 Look at these advertisements A–C. Which accommodation …?

1 is the cheapest
2 is the nearest to public transport
3 is close to amenities
4 would suit someone with a car
5 includes furniture
6 has the most space
7 is the most expensive

A

Unfurnished two-bedroom flat in Grove Towers. Full air-conditioning and heating. State-of-the-art kitchen. Marble bathroom. Short walk to underground station. On 30th floor with panoramic view over London and the River Thames. Five minutes to shops, restaurants and cafés. Sports centre on ground floor! 950 pcm*.

B

Detached family house with three bedrooms and two bathrooms. Newly decorated master bedroom and en-suite. Fitted wardrobes. Wood flooring. Garage attached. 1100 pcm.

C

Small terraced house in friendly street. Two-bedroom house but downstairs living room could also be a bedroom. Seconds from Wimbledon station and town centre. Modern bathroom with shower. Furnished. 600 pcm.

*pcm: per calendar month

Listening: asking for information

2 🔘 1.20 A student wants to rent some accommodation. Listen to his conversation with a landlord. Which accommodation in Exercise 1 is he visiting?

3 🔘 1.20 Listen again and make notes for each heading.

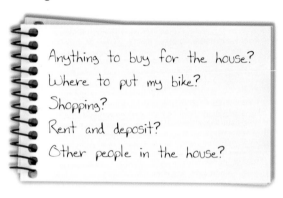

Anything to buy for the house?
Where to put my bike?
Shopping?
Rent and deposit?
Other people in the house?

Speaking: asking for information

4 Work in pairs. Role-play a conversation between a tenant and a landlord about the flat at Grove Towers.

The tenant: Ask questions about the flat. You can also use questions from the list below.

The landlord: Answer questions using the information in the advertisement and create any other information you need.

5 Now change roles and repeat a similar conversation about the detached family house.

USEFUL EXPRESSIONS questions for renting

Rent
How much is the rent per week / month?
Does the rent include utilities (e.g. water, electricity, gas, council tax)?
Is there a deposit?
How much notice do I give if I want to leave?

Furnishings
Is it furnished?
Is the kitchen equipped? What kitchen appliances are there (e.g. fridge, dishwasher)?
Do the bedrooms have linen / pillows / blankets / a desk?
What will I need to buy before I move in?

Location
How close is it to the train station / bus stop / shops?
What are the neighbours like?
Is there a place to put my bike / park my car?

Other
Can I paint the walls / put pictures on the walls?
What day do they collect the rubbish?
Who are the other people in the house?
Is the kitchen / bathroom shared?

Writing: describing a place

6 The student writes an email to a friend who is interested in sharing the flat. Read his description of the place. Make notes about the accommodation in this table.

The house	Good points	Bad points
Location and transport		
Living room and kitchen		
Garden		
Bedrooms		
Bathroom		
Overall impressions		

Hi!

I think I might have found somewhere we can both live! I've just been talking to the landlord about it. It isn't luxury but it'll suit us for a few months. I've attached a picture of the outside.

First of all, it's close to the shops and underground, so it isn't far to walk. Also, I saw about three buses go past while I was there. This means the road is a bit noisy but at least there's plenty of public transport.

One thing I really liked was the living room and kitchen. Some old houses in London can be very dark but the sun shines in through some large glass doors at the back of the kitchen. They lead into a small garden with a shed. Great for summer barbecues!

Upstairs there are two bedrooms. Each one has a single bed, a wardrobe and a desk with a lamp. The walls need a coat of paint, really. I asked the landlord and he said we were free to paint it whatever colour we like.

The worst part about the house is the bathroom. It's more like a cupboard and the shower looks like something from the Stone Age! It really needs updating but I tested it and hot water came out. ☺

Anyway, apart from needing a big clean (I don't think the previous tenants bothered), it would be perfect for us. The rent is 300 each per month and you'd need the deposit (another 300).

What do you think? Are you interested?

7 A friend from England wants to study in your country. You are trying to find a room for him/her. Today you looked at some accommodation and made these notes.

	Good points	Bad points
Location and transport	On a quiet road Regular buses to the centre	Three miles from the city centre Shops 20 minutes away
Living room and kitchen	Furnished and clean. Internet. Has got a balcony with space to sit	Very small No TV No garden
Bedroom and bathroom	Sofa bed so you can sit and sleep Huge modern bathroom	Dirty rugs – need clean
Overall impressions	Share with two other (friendly) students Good price per month	Kitchen equipment out of date Maybe too quiet!

Now write an email to your friend and describe the place. Use all the notes above.

5E Visiting someone's home

Reading

1 Work in pairs. Where are these famous cities? Name the country.

- Rio de Janeiro
- Beijing
- Bangkok
- Delhi
- Prague

2 Now read the article on page 67. Try to match the city to each description 1–5. Afterwards, check your answers on page 142.

3 Which of the cultural tips give advice on the following? There might be more than one answer for each category.

- What to wear 3
- Presents for your host
- What to remove
- Table manners (use of hands, cutlery, etc.)
- Polite body language (for greeting someone)
- What time to arrive and eat

4 Match the underlined words in the article to the definitions.

1 (correct) behaviour in public *manners*
2 person who invites you
3 when two people put hands together when they meet
4 feelings or opinions about something
5 lower your head when you meet someone
6 shared between a group of people

5 Work in pairs. Test your knowledge of correct cultural behaviour in other parts of the world with the quiz below. At the end, look at page 142 to check your answers.

6 Work in groups. Make a list of guidelines for foreign visitors visiting someone's home in your country. Use the categories in Exercise 3 to help you. Afterwards, present your ideas to the class.

1 Bangkok
Don't forget to remove your _____ at someone's house in Bangkok.
A shoes **B** socks **C** belt

2 Rio
You arrive for dinner in Rio. Do you kiss your host on ...?
A one cheek
B both cheeks
C their hand

3 Egypt
You are eating in Egypt. Your host offers you a second helping. You should ...
A not accept any more. It's rude.
B accept more. It's polite.
C ask what's for dessert and then decide.

4 Scotland
Do NOT refer to your host as being _____. They will be very upset.
A Scottish **B** British **C** English

5 USA
You are in a restaurant. You normally tip the waiter _____ of the price.
A 5–9% **B** 10–14% **C** 15–20%

6 Germany
You go to a party. Take the host _____
A flowers.
B chocolates.
C either A or B.

Cultural tips*

1 _____

When you receive an invitation to a private home, it's a good idea to take <u>a gift</u> such as sweets or flowers. Remove your shoes when you enter. It's also considered good <u>manners</u> to wash your hands before and after eating. One last thing – remember to eat using your right hand.

2 _____

Modern Thais will <u>shake hands</u> when they meet someone from the West but they prefer the traditional *wai* where you put the palms of hands together and bow. Your clothes don't need to be too formal in most homes but be quite smart. Thais usually share the dishes and drinks. Plates of food are <u>communal</u>, and you should use communal cutlery when serving, not your own.

3 _____

When you arrive, don't be surprised if your <u>host</u> asks you to remove your shoes at the door. So make sure your socks are clean – and match! If you are eating out, your host will probably offer to pay but you could leave a tip. Tips* are not usually included in the price of the meal. Ten per cent is considered standard.

4 _____

People are very physical here and body contact is essential. When greeting people, women kiss women, (two kisses, right cheek first) and men exchange a firm handshake. Other guests will dress fashionably, casually and comfortably. <u>Attitudes</u> to time are relaxed, so don't be surprised if other guests arrive later, and be prepared to eat after midnight!

> 'You might receive a knife and fork but typically, you'll have to eat using chopsticks.'

5 _____

Traditionally people <u>bow</u> but in modern cities people will shake hands. If you are a foreigner here, people will really like it if you try to speak a few words in their language. You might receive a knife and fork but typically, you'll have to eat using chopsticks. Between bites, keep your chopsticks together and place them horizontally on your plate or across the top of your bowl. Never stand chopsticks upright in your rice bowl: this is very impolite.

Tip has two meanings:

tip advice

tip money you leave for the waiter (not part of the main bill)

Find a flatmate

Listening and speaking

1 Look at this picture. These people share a flat.

- What kind of problems do you think might happen when people share a flat?
- How could you find the right kind of flatmate?
- What kind of person would you share with?

2 Read the advert. What kind of flatmate is Gerard looking for?

> Hi!
>
> I've got a two-bedroom house in Wimbledon but I need someone to share the rent. It's furnished and is close to shops, buses, etc. I am looking for a non-smoker, student or professional. Must be friendly, easy-going and someone who likes a clean house!
>
> I am 21, from France, and I'm spending a year in London learning English and doing part-time work. Your rent is £300 per month plus bills.
>
> Call 077 756 7456 if you would like to know more or come and look.
>
> Gerard

3 1.21 Two people telephone Gerard. Listen to each conversation and tick the table.

Who …	Barry	Gavin
introduces himself at the beginning of the call?		✓
explains why he is calling?	✓	✓
makes mistakes with names?		
says what he does? (e.g. studying, employed)		
arranges to visit?		
sounds polite and friendly?		

4 Discuss as a class. Who do you think Gerard will choose as a flatmate? Why?

Pronunciation: sounding friendly

5 1.22 Listen to five expressions. Tick if you think the speaker sounds friendly ☺ or less friendly ☹.

I'm calling about your advert.	☺ ___	☹ ___
What do you do?	☺ ___	☹ ___
Would you like to come and take a look?	☺ ___	☹ ___
Perhaps I can help you?	☺ ___	☹ ___
Let me give you my address.	☺ ___	☹ ___

6 1.23 Listen to the expressions in Exercise 5 again but this time the speaker sounds friendly every time. Listen and repeat.

7 Role-play a similar conversation. One of you is Gerard and one of you is interested in his advertisement for a flatmate. Follow these stages and remember to sound friendly and polite!

- start the telephone call
- introduce yourself
- explain your reason for calling
- say what you do / why you live in London
- arrange to visit

Afterwards, swap roles and repeat the roleplay.

Sports and competition

Let's get started

1 Work in pairs. Describe the picture.

1 What is the event? Would you like to be there? Why?

2 How important do you think sport is in your country?

3 Tell your partner about a sporting event you participated in.

2 Which of these sports do you like to take part in?
Do you like to watch any of the others?

> javelin long jump tennis football hockey boxing
> show jumping ski jumping table tennis marathon
> basketball archery swimming ice skating relay race

In this unit you w

- **Communication**: compa
  contrasting
- **Vocabulary**: sports and
- **Reading and Listening**:
  disabled sportspeople, C
  unusual competitions, s
- **Writing**: a for and again
- **Grammar**: articles, com

Vocabulary

3 Answer questions for these sports.

Which sports …?

1 do you	A play	B go	C do		
2 have	A a pitch	B a court	C a ring	D a track	
3 have	A a goal	B a net	C a target	D a hoop	
4 use	A a ball	B gloves	C an arrow		
5 use	A a racket	B a bat	C a stick		
6 are controlled by	A a referee	B an umpire	C a judge		
7 have	A two halves	B rounds	C lengths	D sets	E laps

Grammar: articles

1 Discuss as a class.

  1 Do you watch the Olympic Games? Why? Why not?

  2 Have you ever heard of the Paralympic Games? What do you know about them?

2 Read about the Paralympics. Underline the correct article (*the*, *a*, *an* or no article) in 1–14. Use the language summary to help you.

Since (**1**) – / *the* ancient Greeks first held the Olympic Games, winning (**2**) *a / an* gold medal represents (**3**) *a / the* highest achievement for (**4**) *a / an* athlete. The Paralympic Games are for (**5**) *an / –* athletes with physical disabilities and they follow (**6**) – / *the* Olympic Games every four years. (**7**) *An / The* earliest official Paralympics were in 1960 with (**8**) – / *the* 400 athletes. Nowadays, there are over 4,000 athletes and currently 22 different sports. Wheelchair basketball is (**9**) *a / the* popular competition at the games and even though all (**10**) *a / the* players are in wheelchairs, the court and rules are virtually the same. Swimming is also (**11**) *a / an* exciting event at the Paralympics with few changes. One Paralympic sport that only exists for athletes with (**12**) *a / –* disability is boccia. Individuals, pairs or (**13**) *the / –* teams of three play the game with red or blue balls. They take turns to move the balls as close as possible to another ball called (**14**) *the / –* jack.

JAVELIN THROW
ATHENS 2004

Articles

Use *a / an* to talk about	Use *the* to talk about	Use *no article* to talk about
- a person or thing in a general way: *I've never met an Olympic medallist.*	- a specific (or unique) title or thing: *The Queen … It's the Olympic Games.*	- plural and uncountable nouns in a general way: *I love horses.* (= horses in general) *He's good at sport.* (= any type of sport, not a specific one)
- something for first time: *Boccia is a sport for athletes with disabilities.*	- something mentioned earlier: *Pairs or teams of three play the game (of boccia).*	Special cases with no article: - *play* + sport: *play tennis* - home, work, school as part of your daily life: *go home, at work, in school*
- singular countable nouns	- singular, plural countable and uncountable nouns: *Pass the ball. The athletes … Swim in the water.*	- *by* + transport: *by bicycle, by car*

Also note common differences between using *the* or no article:

Use *the* with:

deserts, rivers, mountain ranges, oceans and seas: *the Sahara, the Amazon, the Himalayas, the Atlantic*

countries whose name includes a common noun / plural: *the United States, the United Kingdom*

groups of people: *the unemployed, the French*

some buildings: *the White House*

periods of time: *the sixties*

We don't use an article before:

proper names of people, cities, countries, continents: *Caroline, Madrid*

languages, school subjects: *Greek, geography*

single mountains/islands/lakes: *Lake Geneva, Mount Olympus*

See Grammar Reference, page 150

3 What similarities and differences are there between the Olympics and Paralympics? Find answers in the article above.

Pronunciation: *the*

4 We pronounce *the* in two different ways:

/ðiː/ before a vowel sound: the athlete /ðiː æθliːt/

/ðə/ before a consonant sound: the team /ðə tiːm/

2.02 **Listen to the pronunciation.**

5 **Say these words with *the*.**

> the Olympics   the highest   the competitor
> the medal   the ancient Greeks   the umpire
> the ball   the arrow   the skier

2.03 **Now listen and check.**

Listening

6 2.04 **Listen to a sports documentary about a famous Paralympian. Complete this profile about her.**

SPORTS PROFILE

Name: _____

Born: _____

Nationality: _____

Sport: _____

Paralympic Winter Games medals:

_____ *Japan:* Two silver medals

2002 Salt Lake City: Two _____ and two bronze medals

2010 Vancouver: _____ medal

7 2.04 **Listen again and answer questions 1–5.**

1 Karolina Wisniewska started skiing to …

   A win medals at the Olympics.

   B beat other children with no disability.

   C help her feel better and stronger.

   D cure her cerebral palsy.

2 When she started competitive skiing …

   A she used standard skiing equipment.

   B she would win against other skiers.

   C she focused on winning.

   D Answers A, B and C are all correct.

3 When she won four medals in 2002, …

   A no Canadian skier had ever done it before.

   B no skier had ever done it before.

   C no athlete had ever done it before.

   D no Paralympic skier had done it before.

4 How many times has she been injured?

   A once in 2004

   B twice

   C never until this moment

   D many times

5 She thinks winning requires …

   A mental strength.

   B physical strength.

   C mental and physical strength.

   D good equipment.

Choosing an Olympic city

Reading

1 Discuss as a class. What do you think is important when choosing a city for the Olympic Games? For example, transport or the size of the city? What else?

2 Choose a city for the Olympic Games in 2024. Read about the shortlist on page 73 and write the correct city name in the sentences below.

1 _____ is a bit bigger than Atlanta in terms of population.

2 _____ is by far the biggest city in terms of population.

3 _____ and _____ aren't as experienced as London with hosting international sporting events.

4 In terms of climate, _____ has much warmer weather than the other cities.

5 Warsaw will have a bit more space for spectators than _____.

6 Spectators in _____, compared with Atlanta, won't be able to travel quite as quickly as to the Olympic Park.

7 _____ has by far the most airports and transport links.

Grammar: the language of comparison

Comparative and superlative forms

We add *-er / -est* to short adjectives and adverbs.

We put *more/most* or *less/least* before long adjectives or adverbs.

We often put *the* before a superlative adjective.

Modifiers for comparisons

We use *a little, a bit, slightly* for comparing small differences.

We use *much, a lot, far* for comparing big differences.

We use *easily* or *by far* for superlatives.

Similarities and differences

We use *as + adjective / adverb + as* to compare two things and show they are similar.

We use *not as + adjective + as* to compare two things and show they are different.

See Grammar Reference, pages 150–151

3 Say or write full sentences about the three cities with the words given. Change the form of the words where necessary. See the first example.

1 London is / far / biggest city.
   London is by far the biggest city.

2 Atlanta has / easy / small / population.

3 Warsaw's average summer temperature / warm / London's.

4 London / lot / experienced at hosting sporting events.

5 Atlanta / much / hot / Warsaw and London in the summer.

6 London's area for spectators will have / slight / few / seats / Warsaw.

Speaking

4 Work in groups. You are the International Olympic Committee (IOC). Discuss the pros and cons of each city, including:

- size, location, climate
- experience as a place for sport
- transport
- accommodation and entertainment
- benefits to the city

At the end of the discussion, choose one of the cities and prepare a short presentation which explains your choice.

5 Present your final choice to the class with your reasons.

6 Work in pairs. Look at these headlines from a city newspaper after it hosted the Olympic Games:

BILL FROM OLYMPICS HITS 1 BILLION – AND STILL RISING!

CITY SHOP OWNERS SAY THEIR PROFITS DOUBLED DURING GAMES

SCHOOL CHILDREN ENJOY USING NEW OLYMPIC SPORT FACILTIES

PROPERTY PRICES DOUBLE AFTER OLYMPICS – LOCAL FAMILIES CANNOT AFFORD TO BUY

What were the pros and cons for the city after the Olympics? Do you think international sporting events like the Olympics or the World Cup are good for local people?

City: **London**

Population (approximately): 8 million
Average temperature in the summer: 23°C
Experience of hosting other sporting events: London held the summer Olympic Games before in 1908, 1948 and in 2012. It also hosted the football World Cup in 1966 and the European Football Championship in 1996.
Transportation: London already has an extensive underground, hundreds of bus routes and five international airports. A new train line will be specially built from central London to the Olympic Park taking 45 minutes. There will also be cycle paths around the Olympic Park.
Accommodation: The Olympic village will offer accommodation to thousands of athletes and visitors.
Other entertainment: London already offers the best in international theatre and live entertainment.
How the Olympic Games will help London: The city will build an Olympic Park with facilities for 180,000 spectators. The area for the Olympics is an unused area of London with old factories. By hosting the Olympics, London can reuse this area and improve it. After the Olympic Games, local schools can use the sports facilities.

City: **Atlanta**

Population: Over 0.5 million
Average temperature in the summer: 30°C
Experience of hosting other sporting events: Atlanta held the Olympic Games in 1996. It is also a city with sports stadiums and it is home to successful baseball and football teams.
Transportation: It has a subway and bus routes. There is a good road system and plenty of parking in the centre. Atlanta international airport is the busiest in the world. Transport from the centre to the Olympic Park will take 30 minutes.
Accommodation: Good hotels and special accommodation will be built at the Olympic site.
Other entertainment: Theatres, international restaurants, regular outdoor concerts and live music.
How the Olympic Games will help Atlanta: Atlanta is one of the fastest growing cities in the USA. It has a busy commercial centre and a long tradition of sport. The city will build the Olympic city on an area with old and poor housing. Residents living here will be put in temporary accommodation during the games and then will return to new houses afterwards.

City: **Warsaw**

Population: 1.8 million
Average temperature in the summer: 23 °C
Experience of hosting other sporting events: European Capital of Sport in 2008 and joint host of the European Football Championship in 2012.
Transportation: Warsaw is easy to travel around by bus, tram, metro and taxi. Flights from all over the world land at its airport.
Accommodation: The city centre has plenty of hotels at different prices with new ones built for the event.
Other entertainment: Poland and Warsaw have a long artistic tradition and are famous for their museums, galleries, music and theatre.
How the Olympic Games will help Warsaw: In recent years, Warsaw has improved its infrastructure and by hosting the Olympic Games they will continue this work. They will build new sports facilities in the city centre, which their national football and athletics teams can use. The planned centre will have space for 185,000 spectators.

A real winner

Vocabulary

1 Look at these forms derived from the root word *compete*. Match the word to the form.

compete   NOUN (PERSON)

competing   NOUN

competitive   ADVERB

competition   VERB

competitor   ADJECTIVE

competitively   PRESENT PARTICIPLE (verb)

Reading

2 Read this text about the girl in the picture. Complete the text with correct answers from 1–6. Circle A, B, C or D.

Dog sledge racing is a (**1**) ___ sport. In it, the dog (**2**) ___ try to be the first to reach the finish line with a team of 12 dogs. These races can last for many days and with the dog teams (**3**) ___ tall mountains in below-zero temperatures and heavy snow. It's a difficult sport for even (**4**) ___ adult. It's even more difficult if you have a (**5**) ___. Rachael Scdoris is a 16-year-old who races dogs and is (**6**) ___ blind …

1 **A** competitively   **B** competitive
    C competition   **D** compete

2 **A** sledge   **B** sledging
    C sledger   **D** sledgers

3 **A** crossing   **B** running
    C chasing   **D** pulling

4 **A** as experienced   **B** the most experienced
    C experience   **D** the experience

5 **A** ability   **B** disability
    C disable   **D** disabled

6 **A** legalise   **B** legal
    C legally   **D** illegally

3 Look at the words you didn't use in Exercise 2. What types of words are they? (verb, adjective, noun, etc.)

4 Read the article on page 75 and choose an answer for sentences 1–4.

1 The first paragraph makes you think that Rachael …
    A would prefer going to high school dances.
    B would prefer the Atta Boy 300 to be shorter.
    C would prefer to be like the other people in her class.
    D prefers to be racing with her dogs.

2 Because she is blind, Rachael must rely …
    A only on the sense of touch.
    B on hearing and taste.
    C on a snowmobile.
    D on all her senses.

3 According to the text, Rachael completes her races with help from …
    A a number of other people.
    B one other person.
    C the race organisers.
    D no one.

4 Many people consider that …
    A she should have won the race.
    B she won by managing to complete the race.
    C she only won because of her dogs.
    D she lost the race.

5 Write five questions about the text. Swap them with another student. Check the questions are grammatically correct and try to answer them. Then give them back and check the answers to your questions. See if your partner corrected any of your questions.

A real winner

It's winter in the Cascade mountains of the northwestern United States. Most of 16-year-old Rachael Scdoris' classmates are getting ready for a high-school dance, but Rachael has different plans. She's where she'd rather be. That's leading her team of 12 dogs through one of the more difficult dog sledge races around – the 'Atta Boy 300' race. The Atta Boy is a staged race that lasts for seven days and goes through the Cascade mountains. It is divided into seven timed legs, or sections, that total 480 kilometres.

Being a dog sledge competitor would be difficult enough for any 16-year-old. However, it's an even bigger challenge for Rachael. Rachael is legally blind and has been since birth. She sees a world of unclear shapes without form or colour. She can't see past her lead dog and depends a lot on her other senses, particularly touch.

As Rachael sets off on the fifth day of the race, her father, Jerry Scdoris, explains: 'Rachael never gives up. She always accomplishes her goals and she works hard at them. That's an inspiration to me as a dad.' Jerry is a world champion in dog sledging and taught his daughter to lead dogs when she was only three. She started competing when she was 11 and now, at 16, she is competing in international events against some of the top competitors in the sport.

During the fifth day of the race, Rachael runs into trouble. The dogs on her sledge are tied together with special ropes but these ropes have become tangled. She has to stop and get them straight. Because she can't see them she follows the ropes with her hands. She gets help from Matt, who is allowed to assist her during the race. He moves the dogs into position and she is able to continue the race. The delay means she finishes last on day five but at least she didn't give in.

The next morning it's snowing but Rachael has a lot to do before day six of the race. She carefully packs her sledge with all the supplies she will need. Rachael's friends and family help her to check and recheck her sledge and equipment. She also needs to study the route for day six. The race organisers give out a map but Rachael cannot read it. She'll rely on her dogs to follow the way and Matt who will ride closely by on a snowmobile. He can use a radio to communicate with Rachael and warn her about any problems ahead. But Matt comments: 'It really surprises me how little Rachael needs my help.'

Day six ends and Rachael finishes the sixth leg of the race with a good time for the day. She has moved ahead in the competition, but there's only one more day of the race, so she can't relax. She gets up early for day seven to examine her dogs for any cuts and bruises. She has to feel their paws carefully and make sure each one can run. The dogs are in good shape and ready to go. It's a clear, beautiful winter's morning at the starting line. Rachael can't see the scenery but she can smell the fresh pine trees, feel the snow, and hear the excited barking of her dogs. She can also hear her fans cheering as she sets off.

Rachael really appreciates the support she receives: 'I expected to come here, do my best, have my dogs do their best, and hopefully finish in the top 15 or 20. The worst thing you can do is to give up. It doesn't matter what your disability is, you can overcome it.' Today Rachael crosses the finishing line in 23rd place (out of 27 racers) but many people are very proud of her. She successfully completed seven days of hard racing and crossed 300 miles guided by her alternative senses and love of racing. In many people's opinion, this is what makes her a real winner.

6D A question of sport?

Listening: comparing and contrasting

1 Describe what you can see in the pictures. What are the similarities and differences between the three sports?

2 2.05 **Ritchie (from Scotland) and Mark (from the USA) are watching TV.**

1 Which sport in Exercise 1 are they watching?

2 How do they compare American football and soccer? What are the similarities and differences?

3 How do they compare American football and rugby? What are the similarities and differences?

3 2.05 **Listen again and complete these expressions from the listening.**

1 How _____ _____ it to our kind of football?

2 Apart from that, they are _____ _____.

3 So, it's _____ _____ rugby than soccer.

4 Yes, you're right. It's _____ physical _____ rugby.

5 Is _____ of them more dangerous than the other?

6 _____ do they _____ for the number of injuries?

7 I'd say _____ can be fairly dangerous. But _____ of them is as dangerous as soccer.

8 There are _____ injuries in soccer _____ in any other sport.

9 They look _____ more dangerous to me!

Speaking: comparing and contrasting

4 Work in pairs. Compare and contrast the things in each topic below. Take turns to ask and answer about similarities and differences, using the language in the Useful Expressions box.

Sport: *basketball, volleyball, football*

Pets: *rabbits, cats, horses*

Entertainment: *computer games, cinema, TV*

Types of English: *British English, American English*

Cities: *London, Paris, New York*

USEFUL EXPRESSIONS similarities and differences

Asking about similarities and differences
How similar is …?
How do they compare?
Is either of them more …?
Is there much difference between …?
Comparing differences
They are entirely different.
It's more like … than …
There are more … than …
They aren't as … as …
Describing similarities
It's as … as …
Both are … / Neither is …
It looks fairly similar to …
There isn't much difference between them.
They are more or less the same.

Writing: a for and against essay (2)

5 Look at these headlines from newspapers in Great Britain.

  1 What do you think the news story was about?

  2 Why do you think people had different opinions?

  3 Do you have any similar sports in your country?

> ## COUNTRYSIDE PROTESTERS OUTSIDE PARLIAMENT

> ## GOVERNMENT BANS FOX-HUNTING

> ## ANTI-CRUELTY CAMPAIGNERS CELEBRATE NEW LAW!

6 Read this essay giving arguments for and against this statement: 'The sport of fox-hunting should be allowed in Great Britain.' Write these missing expressions in the essay.

> In conclusion
> There are a number of arguments for
> The issue of   However   Firstly
> On the other hand   In my opinion
> Another point to add is

For many years, the traditional sport of fox-hunting took place in the countryside of Great Britain. People dressed in red coats and rode on horseback with dogs after foxes. **(1)** _____ fox-hunting was always controversial in Britain and eventually it was banned. **(2)** _____, the debate has never gone away. Many people still enjoy riding their horses in the traditional clothes of fox-hunters, though they are not allowed to kill the fox.

(3) _____ allowing people to hunt foxes. In the countryside, foxes attack and kill farm animals. It is also natural for dogs to chase the fox. **(4)** _____ that when the government made fox-hunting illegal, lots of people connected with the sport lost their jobs.

(5) _____, there are many arguments against this kind of sport. **(6)** _____, the sport is cruel and nobody has the 'right' to be cruel. Besides, foxes can be killed more humanely. If people enjoy riding across the countryside, that is fine but why is it also necessary to kill something at the same time?

(7) _____, I don't think it is necessary to make fox-hunting legal again. **(8)** _____, there are many other civilised ways to enjoy sport in the countryside.

7 Do you agree with the arguments in the essay? What do the rest of the class think?

8 Work in groups. You are going to write an essay giving arguments for and against this statement: 'The sport of fishing is cruel and unnecessary and should be made illegal.' Plan your essay by thinking of two or three arguments for and against the statement.

9 Choose the best arguments for and against on the board and write the essay (200–250 words) using some of the expressions.

10 Afterwards, check that your essay …

  • introduces the topic in paragraph 1 ☐
  • gives arguments for in paragraph 2 ☐
  • gives arguments against in paragraph 3 ☐
  • gives an opinion in the conclusion in paragraph 4 ☐
  • is 200–250 words in total ☐

USEFUL EXPRESSIONS a for and against essay

> **Introducing the topic**
> *The issue of … is very controversial.*
> *There is no easy answer to the question of whether …*
> **Comparing arguments for and against**
> *There are a number of arguments for / against …*
> *One view is that …*
> *On the one hand … on the other hand …*
> *Firstly, … / Secondly, … / For example, …*
> **Adding and contrasting information**
> *Also / In addition / Moreover / Another point to add is that …*
> *However / On the other hand / Although*
> *I agree that … but I don't believe that …*
> *I also believe that …*

Unusual competitions

Reading

1 Are there any competitions and contests at school or where you live? For example, sports competitions or general knowledge quizzes? Do you take part in the competitions? Why or why not?

2 Read the article on page 79. Which would be the best title?

  1 Pumpkin-rolling Contest

  2 Delaware's Interesting Contest

  3 People like Pumpkins

  4 Confusing Contest Rules

3 Read the article again and choose A, B, C or D.

  1 The people who attend the contest are people …

    A who like to be inside.

    B who know nothing about machines.

    C from all over America.

    D from all over the world.

  2 How many people watch the contest?

    A 80

    B over 20,000

    C 20,000

    D less than 20,000

  3 The most important part of the throwing machine is the _____.

    A size B weight C design D colour

  4 Why is 'the King of Spring still in charge'?

    A because his team won

    B because everybody knows him

    C because his machine broke

    D because he organises the contest

  5 What is the purpose of this story?

    A to show how far pumpkins can fly

    B to convince other countries to hold similar contests

    C to describe building an invention

    D to introduce an unusual event

4 Label the pictures below with the underlined words in the text.

5 Work in pairs. Cover the text and try to explain the importance of each of the objects in this competition.

6 Work in groups. Your local council wants you to design a new and unusual competition for your town to attract more tourists in the summer. Your competition must use some or all of the following items:

- a skateboard
- a long piece of rope
- goal posts
- something your local area or town is famous for, e.g. a type of food, a special type of clothing or ornament.

You can also add more objects. Prepare a list of rules for the competition and explain how someone is the winner. Afterwards, present your competition to the rest of the class.

Every year in the US state of Delaware, a group of people who enjoy the outdoors have a very interesting competition. It's a pumpkin-throwing contest! The rules of the competition are easy. First, the <u>pumpkins</u> must weigh at least four kilograms. Second, no explosives, or dangerous materials, are allowed. Other than that, competitors can do anything they want to do! People come from all over the country to see the competition. Some of them take it very seriously. The people who compete in the event tend to have two things in common: they all love the outdoors, and they all love inventing.

There are several teams that take part in the contest. Mick Davies is part of a group which has taken part in the competition for many years. Mick talks about his team, and how they've improved since they began. 'We started out with a little contraption with about 14 garage door <u>springs</u> on it', he says. 'We threw 387 feet* that first year – and we've progressed from there.'

The aim of the competition is simple: to make a machine that can throw a pumpkin through the air. The unusual sport began over 20 years ago. In those days, there were only three teams and a few of their friends who came to watch. But now, more than 20 years later, this strange contest has really grown. It's become very popular. Today, the competition attracts more than 80 teams, and more than 20,000 people come to watch it!

‘**The competition attracts more than 80 teams, and more than 20,000 people come to watch it.**’

The inventors have to think carefully about the design of the machine if they want to win. All of the teams in the contest think that they've created just the right one. John Huber is one of the members in a team named 'Team Hypertension'. He talks about their machine: 'It's probably one of the few machines on this field that's really engineered.' Team Hypertension started seven years ago. It used garage door springs to throw its first pumpkin from a <u>bucket</u>. Since that time, the competition has become much more advanced. Nowadays, the machines can be anything from a simple <u>catapult</u> to an actual <u>cannon</u>. A good design isn't everything, though. If a team really wants to win, they need to practise. To do this, they throw many things, not just pumpkins. A member of one team explains: 'We throw pumpkins, <u>watermelons</u>, <u>kegs</u>, toilets, <u>refrigerators</u>, microwaves, tyres … anything we can get our hands on!' Unfortunately, even with a lot of practice, things don't always go perfectly. Accidents can still happen! One competitor tells the story of an accident that happened at one of the contests. During the competition, his machine threw their pumpkin backwards! It destroyed some coffee tables but fortunately missed members of the crowd. He says regretfully: 'Maybe if we'd practised a bit more before the event, we would have won.'

It's not just the pumpkins that can break. This year, Team Hypertension's pumpkin is very big and it breaks part of their machine. Luckily, despite this difficulty, their machine throws a pumpkin over 1,728 feet! Team Hypertension wins the contest again. After the event is over, John Huber happily announces, 'The King of Spring is still in charge!' The event is over for another year. But if you happen to be in Delaware at the right time, remember to look up at the sky. You just might have your own chance to see a real flying pumpkin.

* 387 feet = approx. 118 metres

Case Study 3 〉 Is our future in the stars?

GET READY!

For $200,000, you could book a place now with Virgin Galactic to travel into space. You will need to have three days of astronaut training before you and five other passengers travel over 100 km up in the air. Although your journey will only last two and a half hours, it will certainly give you a good idea of what life is like in space.

Space stations and space hotels

At the moment, most of the people on board the International Space Station (ISS) are fully-trained scientists and astronauts, but we think that space tourism is going to play an important role in their use in the future. There are several plans to build space hotels but the costs involved mean that it will be a long time before we will be holidaying in space. However, a holiday in space may not be the relaxing holiday you're looking for. Just to give you an idea of your daily routine, astronauts have to exercise for two or three hours a day to keep themselves fit!

An island in space

The Space Island Group (SIG) has plans for an 'island' in space which will be able to hold up to 20,000 people. Shaped like a giant wheel and in many ways similar to a space station (but much larger), they say that they will be able to grow their own food and get valuable resources from other planets and asteroids. They are keen to see what it will be like for people who are born in space, or even on Mars, and if there is life beyond our Earth.

SETI

Maybe we don't need to travel into space if all we want to do is to discover new life forms. The SETI project (the Search for Extra-Terrestrial Intelligence) uses radio telescopes to try to detect signals that are being sent to us from outer space. Most of the people involved in SETI believe that we will one day make contact with other life forms and it is only a matter of time. To increase their computing power, SETI invites ordinary people to join their SETI@home project, which began in 1999. Volunteers on the project download a SETI program which runs in the background while the computer is not being used.

---

1 In small groups, look at some of the problems linked to space travel and discuss them. Which ones would bother you the most?

- Space exploration is very expensive
- Accidents happen – you might be killed
- Living in space means living in a weightless environment
- Space travel means being separated from your loved ones
- Travelling deep into space means never coming back
- Living conditions on a spaceship are not what we're used to

2 Read the article above and complete the sentences.

1 The cost of a trip to space _____
2 The number of passengers on the Virgin Galactic space flight _____
3 The height Virgin Galactic passengers reach _____
4 The duration of the Virgin Galactic space flight _____
5 The number of hours a day astronauts exercise _____
6 The year when SETI@home was started _____

3 Read all the information above and answer these questions.

1 How is the use of the ISS going to change?
2 Why are space hotels still a long way in the future?
3 What do the people behind the planned space island hope to do?
4 How can volunteers help SETI?

Review 〉Unit 5

Grammar

1 Underline the correct *will* or *be going to* form.

1 That book on the top shelf looks dangerous.
It *'ll / 's going to* fall on someone's head.

2 Don't worry about your homework. I *'ll / 'm going to* help you with it.

3 They said on TV that it *'ll / 's going to* freeze tonight.

4 Jack rang. He's got a problem at home, so he *'ll / 's going to* do his homework here.

5 Let's go this way. It *'ll / 's going to* be quicker.

6 Sorry, I can't help you now but I promise I *'ll / 'm going to* help you later.

2 Underline the correct future form.

Peter Hi Steve. It's Peter.

Steve Hi. Where are you?

Peter I (1) *'m being / 'm going to be* about 15 minutes late. My bike has a flat tire. Anyway, my dad (2) *may bring / is going to bring* me instead so don't worry.

Steve OK. So where (3) *will we meet / may we meet?*

Peter Outside the cinema – as we planned.

Steve (4) *Will anyone come / Is anyone coming* with you?

Peter I'm not sure. Mark (5) *might / will* come, too.

3 Rewrite the first prediction using the word in bold.

1 It'll snow tonight for certain.
   definitely
   It _will definitely_ snow tonight.

2 There's no way we'll get there on time.
   certainly
   We _____ get there on time.

3 He doesn't think the car will be ready for tonight.
   probably
   He thinks the car _____ for tonight.

4 Humans might land on Mars in the next 20 years.
   possibly
   Humans _____ on Mars in the next 20 years.

Vocabulary

4 Delete the word which <u>isn't</u> possible in these sentences.

1 I live in a *semi-detached / terraced / carpet* house.

2 I really like the *pictures / curtains / blinds* on your windows.

3 This *armchair / tile / sofa* is very comfortable.

4 I live in *a flat / a mansion / an apartment* on the fifth floor.

5 We're putting down *a new carpet / new tiles / a new table* on the hall floor.

6 He's working *in his office / at his desk / in his shelf*.

Functions

5 Write in the missing question words.

> How much   Is   Can   Who   How close
> What   Does

1 _____ is the rent per week?
2 _____ the rent include utilities?
3 _____ it furnished?
4 _____ kitchen appliances are there?
5 _____ is the flat to the shops?
6 _____ I paint the walls?
7 _____ are the other people in the house?

Now I can ...

☐ describe houses
☐ make plans
☐ rent a flat
☐ write a description of a place
☐ use *will, be going to,* the present continuous to talk about the future

Review 〉 Unit 6

Grammar

1 Write *a / an, the* or no article (-).

1 I'm looking for _____ seat in the stadium but it's full!

2 That's _____ athlete I was telling you about. He's the fastest in the world.

3 They love _____ sport. They'll watch anything.

4 She's _____ member of our team.

5 _____ only team to win the football World Cup more than three times is Brazil.

6 _____ Europe has the highest paid players in the world.

7 The children aren't going to _____ school today. It's a bank holiday.

8 How big is _____ Baltic Sea?

2 Compare these three popular sports in the United Kingdom and tick the correct sentences in 1–9. Make untrue sentences correct.

	Football (Soccer)	Rugby	Cricket
Size of a team	11	15	11
Length of a match	90 minutes	80 minutes	1–5 days
Income per year for top professional players (approximate)	£1.5 million a year	£350,000 a year	£350,000 a year

          bigger than
1 Rugby teams are ~~as big as~~ cricket teams. (✗)

2 Football teams aren't as big as rugby teams. (✓)

3 Football teams are smaller than cricket teams.

4 A rugby match is slightly shorter than a football match.

5 Football players are much better paid than rugby players.

6 Cricket players are paid a little less than football players.

7 Rugby players are paid as much as cricket players.

8 Football players are by far the best paid.

Vocabulary

3 Complete the sentence using the word in CAPITALS. Change the form of the word.

1 Do you like to go _swimming_? SWIM

2 In _____ you fire a bow and arrow. ARCH

3 Football is a game of two _____. HALF

4 The _____ lasts two weeks with the final on the last Sunday. COMPETE

5 Her _____ doesn't seem to affect her skill. DISABLE

6 Hitting below the belt is _____ in boxing. You have to hit above the belt. LEGAL

7 In doubles tennis there are four _____ on the court. PLAY

8 Michael Phelps is an Olympic gold _____ with 14 in total. MEDAL

Functions

4 Match the two halves of the expressions.

1 Is there much difference

2 Is either of them

3 They are more

4 They are entirely

5 They aren't playing as

6 Neither side

a or less the same.

b between them?

c different.

d more experienced?

e well as the other team.

f is playing very well.

Now I can …

☐ talk about sports and sporting events

☐ write a for and against essay

☐ use articles and language of comparison

7

Careers and education

In this unit you will learn

- **Communication**: interviewing, negotiating
- **Vocabulary**: careers, education
- **Reading and Listening**: TV correspondent, butler school, Charles Dickens' *Nicholas Nickleby*
- **Writing**: letter of application
- **Grammar**: relative pronouns, relative clauses

Let's get started

1 Describe the picture in pairs.

1 Do you think this kind of job is hard work?

2 In your opinion, what are the most dangerous jobs?

3 Tell your partner about the most unusual job you have ever heard of.

Vocabulary

2 Look at these pairs of words with different suffixes. Discuss what you think the difference is between the pairs of words.

Example:

A journalist is a person. Journalism is the activity.

1 journalist / journalism

2 cook / cooker

3 employee / employer

4 management / manager

5 waiter / waitress

6 trainer / trainee

7 reception / receptionist

8 technician / technology

3 Guess the name of the occupation. See the example.

A person who …

1 cleans houses – *cleaner*

2 plays the guitar

3 works in politics

4 writes novels

5 fixes electrical problems

6 manages a company

7 works voluntarily (for no money)

4 The words in the box can describe a job. Think of one job (either from Exercise 3 or a new job) that each adjective describes.

> physically hard   flexible   mentally hard
> manual   creative   skilled   unskilled
> repetitive   challenging

Listening

1 2.06 Listen to the beginning of a recording and guess …?

- where it is
- who is involved
- what is the purpose

2 2.07 Now listen to the rest of the recording. Decide if the following statements are true or false.

		True	False
1	The whole show is about people before they became famous.		
2	Harrison Ford's first occupation was as a carpenter.		
3	We find out three of Brad Pitt's jobs before he became famous.		
4	We don't find out about Leonardo DiCaprio's previous occupations.		
5	Rochester Boys' School team is certain that Johnny Depp sold pens.		

Pronunciation: intonation in questions

3 2.08 Listen to these questions. Does the intonation rise or fall at the end? Write ↑ or ↓.

1 Do you think it was Brad Pitt? ↑
2 Which Hollywood actor starred in Indiana Jones? ___
3 Who sold pens over the phone? ___
4 How did you know that one? ___
5 Are you sure? ___

4 Complete these rules for intonation on questions with the word *rise* or *fall*:

Yes/No questions usually _____ at the end.

Wh- or *How* questions usually _____ at the end.

5 2.08 Listen again and repeat the five questions.

6 Write four general knowledge quiz questions for your partner. Write two *Yes/No* questions and two *Wh-* or *How* questions. Then ask your partner the questions using the correct intonation.

Grammar: relative pronouns

7 Read these sentences from the listening and write in the missing words: *whose, who, where, when, which, why* or *whom*.

1 I'm not going to ask you about their lives in Hollywood _____ they all became millionaire actors.

2 This actor, _____ film roles include the infamous Captain Jack Sparrow in *Pirates of the Caribbean*, originally sold pens over the phone.

3 Which Hollywood actor, _____ starred in the films *Star Wars* and *Indiana Jones*, began his career as a carpenter?

4 This actor dressed as a chicken for a company _____ sells fast food.

5 I want to know about a time in their lives _____ they all had other jobs.

6 It's hard to understand the reason _____ anyone would want to dress as a chicken.

7 I'm going to ask questions about some men _____ we all know as famous actors.

HOLLYWOOD

8 Now complete the language summary. Write in the missing pronoun.

Relative pronouns
We use _____ for things (and animals).
We use _____ for locations.
We use _____ for possessions.
We use _____ for time.
We use _____ for reasons.
We use _____ for people. You can also use _____ for people but it sounds more formal and is not commonly used.

See Grammar Reference, page 151

9 Read about Mireya Mayor's job and what she did before. Fill the gaps 1–6 with A, B, C or D.

Speaking

10 Work in groups. You are going to compete in a classroom quiz. Prepare six definitions of different nouns. Start each definition using the words in the table below and completing the sentence.

Example:

It's a place where people go to work.

It's a(n)	object	where	
	person	which	
	place	when	...
	time	who	
	reason	why	
		whose	

11 Now join another group. You are going to compete against each other in the quiz. Each team takes turns to read a definition. The other team has three guesses at the answer.

Example:

Team 1: *It's a place where people go to work.*

Team 2: *A factory.*

Team 1: *Incorrect.*

Team 2: *An office.*

Team 1: *Correct.*

If they guess correctly after three guesses, they receive 1 point.

TV Correspondent
Mireya Mayor

How does a city girl and cheerleader (**1**) _____ had never been camping and (**2**) _____ family thought being a Girl Scout was too dangerous now find herself living and working amongst snakes, gorillas and sharks? It all started (**3**) _____ Mireya began studying primates at college. She was learning about animals (**4**) _____ are close to extinction and wanted to find out more about them. Now she is the lead correspondent on National Geographic TV series Ultimate Explorer. The TV series highlights places (**5**) _____ animals around the world are in danger. It's the reason (**6**) _____ Mireya has earned the nickname 'female Indiana Jones'.

	A		B		C		D	
1	who		whose		who's		which	
2	who		whose		who's		why	
3	where		which		why		when	
4	where		who		which		whose	
5	when		where		which		whom	
6	which		whom		where		why	

Madeleine is a typical 15-year-old girl living in Philadelphia. She is interested in clothes and music and plays soccer twice a week. But unlike the other children on her street, who head off to their daily routine of school bus, morning assembly and busy class timetables, Madeleine is home-schooled.

She sits down with her older brother in the family living room where her mother – an ex-schoolteacher – tells them to take out their books and begins the lesson. Her mother explains: 'Most kids spend around eight hours a day at school but the actual amount of time that they spend in class is about four hours in total. And when you have around twenty-five pupils per class, a lot of that time is spent just on classroom management and discipline issues.'

Over three million children are now home-schooled in the USA and the number is growing. Parents are taking their children out of the 'normal' state-funded schools system believing that they can provide a better learning environment. Madeleine adds: 'It's better than normal school. We do all the same kind of work which other kids my age do, but we finish by lunchtime and then we have time for a trip somewhere in the afternoon like a museum or an art gallery.'

Reading

1 Read the article above and answer these questions.

1 How is Madeleine's daily life different to other teenagers'?

2 Why do Madeleine and her mother think home-schooling is better?

2 Read eight arguments for and against home-schooling and regular school. Decide which type of school they refer to and complete the table.

	Home-school	Regular school
For		1
Against		

1 You learn how to work with other people.

2 There are a lot of students for one teacher.

3 The class size is smaller and you get personal attention.

4 There is less social interaction.

5 You have more flexibility and personal choice with the curriculum.

6 There are lots of after-school activities as well.

7 Your teacher might not be qualified in every subject.

8 There is less flexibility with the curriculum.

3 Discuss as a class. Which arguments do you agree with in Exercise 2? Do you think home-schooling is a good idea? Why? Why not?

Grammar: defining relative clauses

4 Read the grammar summary below and find examples of defining relative clauses in the text.

Defining relative clauses

A defining relative clause …

- comes after a noun.
- tells the reader more important information about the noun (e.g. a place, thing or person).
- can appear in the middle or at the end of a sentence.
- begins with a relative pronoun (e.g. *where, which, who, that**).

* we use the relative pronoun *that* instead of *which* or *who*. It is less formal and often used in speech.

See Grammar Reference, page 152

5 Combine these sentences to make one sentence. Use a defining relative clause with the relative pronoun in brackets.

Example:

1 That's the teacher. He teaches us physics. (*who*)
   That's the teacher who teaches us physics.

2 In Britain, an independent school is a school. You pay for it. (*which*)
   In Britain, an independent school is a school

3 In other countries, a public school is a school. It's funded by the government. (*that*)
   In other countries, a public school is a school

4 This is the classroom. We have maths here. (*where*)
   This is the classroom _____

6 Work in pairs. Explain the difference between these pairs of words. Use relative clauses in your explanation.

Example:

A state school is the type of school where most pupils go but a home-school is a school where your parents teach you.

1 state school / home-school
2 teacher / head teacher
3 maths / English
4 pen / keyboard
5 school uniform / ordinary clothes

7 Complete this text about another type of school with the correct answer in 1–6.

In Britain, independent schools receive none of the money which the government gives to state (1) _____. Instead, these schools charge fees to parents who in return expect very high (2) _____ of education for their children. Many are boarding schools where pupils live for the whole (3) _____ and only see their parents at weekends or during the holidays.

One of the most famous independent schools is Eton, where generations of the royal family have (4) _____. It has also produced 18 Prime Ministers. The school, which was founded in 1440, has many ancient (5) _____ including its famous black and white uniform. The class size can be as small as 10 pupils per teacher and over a third of the pupils usually (6) _____ Oxford and Cambridge, which are Britain's two oldest universities.

1 A education   B taxes
   C occupations D people
2 A passes   B scores
   C exams   D standards
3 A timetable   B term
   C class   D night
4 A learned   B studied
   C educated   D been studied
5 A classrooms   B teachers
   C traditions   D clothes
6 A attend   B attended
   C have attended D had attended

8 Look at sentences a and b and underline the relative clause in each sentence.

a *Independent schools receive none of the money which the government gives to state education.*

b *The school, which was founded in 1440, has many ancient traditions.*

9 Answer 1–3 with sentence a or b.

1 Which sentence needs the relative clause? (It has essential information.)
2 Which sentence would make sense without the relative clause? (The information is extra but not essential.)
3 What is the difference between the punctuation in the two sentences?

10 Underline the other examples of relative clauses in Exercise 7. Are they all defining?

Grammar: non-defining relative clauses

11 Compare this grammar summary with the one on page 86. What are the similarities and differences between defining and non-defining relative clauses?

Non-defining relative clauses

A non-defining relative clause …

• comes after a noun, pronoun or noun phrase.
• gives extra information about the noun (but is not important or essential to its identification).
• begins and sometimes ends with a comma.
• cannot use the relative pronoun *that*.

See Grammar Reference, page 152

12 Write the missing relative pronoun in these sentences and insert the two commas.

1 My class , which already has 25 pupils , is increasing in size to 30 next year.
2 The job pays about 10 euros an hour is good for a student or someone at school.
3 Julia has a degree in physics wants to become an actress and is going to drama school.
4 My uncle has worked as a teacher all his life is retiring this year.

7C Butler school

Reading

1 Read this text. Which English tradition is Ivor Spencer trying to save? Why?

People often imagine that England is still a land with rich ladies and gentlemen who live in large houses with a butler and servants to help with cleaning and cooking. This might be a stereotypical image but there are still a few large houses and people (such as kings, queens and lords) who need butlers. Nowadays, a good butler is hard to find, so the Ivor Spencer International School for Butler Administrators teaches people how to do the job. At the school, students have a full **timetable**. It includes classes on knowing titles, such as 'Sir' or 'Madam' or how to carry heavy trays properly. At the end of the **course**, the school's **head**, Ivor Spencer, **assesses** each student's new **skills** and successful **graduates** receive a **certificate** that says they are ready to work as a butler.

2 Match the words in bold to the definitions 1–7.

1 abilities that let you do something well
2 makes a judgement on the quality (often using tests)
3 a series of lessons
4 a plan for each week with times of lessons
5 official piece of paper to say you have completed a course or passed a test
6 people who complete school
7 the person in charge of a school

3 These five pictures show activities or skills the butler must learn. Read the article quickly on page 89 and number the pictures 1 to 5 in the order they are mentioned.

A  B

C

D  E

4 Read the article again and decide if these statements are true or false about the school and the course.

		True	False
1	The school is in a beautiful location.		
2	It offers many different subjects.		
3	Each course lasts just over a month.		
4	All the students are English.		
5	The main tutor expects that everyone will be successful.		
6	There is a special day for successful students at the end.		

5 Discuss in pairs. How many of the statements in Exercise 4 are true for your school? Rewrite any false statements to make them true. Tell the class your new sentences.

A school for butlers

These days, if you ask an average English person about butlers, they say things like: 'Butlers? I haven't seen a butler for a long time.' It's true that there aren't many butlers in England these days. Seventy years ago, there were an estimated 30,000 butlers in England; now there are fewer than 200. So in modern England, where does one find a good butler? More importantly, where does one learn how to become one?

The Ivor Spencer International School of Butler Administrators is located in the grounds of a beautiful country house. It specialises in teaching men and women how to be butlers. The aim of the school's founder and main tutor, Ivor Spencer, is to bring back the butler and save a dying tradition.

The course lasts five weeks and consists of 86 lessons. Students come from all over the world and, if they graduate, they may work for a rich businessman, an important world leader, or even royalty. On the first day of class, the students quickly learn how to refer to employees, guests and visitors correctly. For example, butlers should say, 'Good morning, Your Excellency', when they are answering the door to ambassadors or rulers. However, they must use 'Your Highness' when talking to a king or queen.

Another important skill is to be able to carry food and drinks properly. For a new butler, carrying a tray can be very difficult. They must walk with a very straight back, keep their eyes ahead and carry the tray carefully. It takes a lot of concentration and practice. One classroom exercise involves walking around the room with glasses on their heads, tray in their hands, and smiles on their faces. As they walk, the future butlers repeat the same phrases:

'Good evening, sir.'

'It's a pleasure, sir.'

'No problem, sir,'

'I'll fetch it immediately, sir.'

If they make a mistake, the glasses go crashing to the ground from everyone's heads, but for those who persevere, practice makes perfect. Ivor Spencer says that on every course there are about two people that don't make any progress and drop out after the first two days. It's important for students to keep their hopes up and to keep trying.

As the course continues, students move on from the basic exercises to the 'higher arts', or the more specialised parts of the job. There are a lot of secrets to being a good butler who gets everything just right. For example, when doing the ironing, a butler must iron a newspaper to make it look nice and avoid leaving ink everywhere. If you see a burnt newspaper it probably means the butler was reading it too long.

Butlers need other unusual skills. For example, they might need to deal with unwelcome guests such as burglars. The Ivor Spencer School teaches them how to protect themselves and defend the house. Butlers must also acquire the skill of recognising good quality products, or 'the finer things in life'. To learn more about this, the students go out to different shops and find out about products such as expensive shoes and suits.

For those who complete the course, graduation day arrives and everyone is proud to receive their certificates. Before they came to the school, many of these young men and women made a living by doing things like driving buses, working with computers, or even working in restaurants and shops. Now, they are butlers and part of an old English tradition. Ivor Spencer has done his job well.

Vocabulary

6 Write the correct form of the verbs *make* or *do* in these sentences. Then check your answers in the text.

1 If they _____ a mistake, the glasses go crashing to the ground.

2 There are about two people that don't _____ any progress.

3 When _____ the ironing, a butler must iron a newspaper to make it look nice.

4 Before they came to the school, many of these young men and women _____ a living by _____ things like driving buses.

5 Ivor Spencer has _____ his job well.

7 Match *make* or *do* to these nouns: homework, a timetable, your best, an essay, a test, friends, a course, an exercise.

Work in pairs. Make sentences with your combinations about your school and education.
Example:
I have to do homework every night for two hours.

 Watch a video about difficult food preparation. Turn to page 138.

7D Life after school

Listening: interviewing

1 Discuss with the class. Does your school have someone who advises students about their careers? Have you ever spoken to a careers counsellor?

2 2.09 A careers counsellor is interviewing a student. Complete her notes.

Name: Peter Howarth

Time of meeting: _____

Career the student is interested in:

_____

Particular subjects interested in:

_____

Free-time interests: _____

Recommendations of the careers counsellor:

_____

3 Complete these questions with the words in the box.

> Have you   Do you   Are you   Do you know
> How   Which   What about   Can I

1 _____ here for your careers interview?

2 _____ have an appointment?

3 _____ ask you a few questions?

4 _____ what kind of career you're interested in?

5 _____ subjects do you enjoy studying?

6 _____ do you like to spend your free time?

7 _____ thought about applying to university after you leave school?

8 _____ something like engineering?

4 2.09 Now listen again and check the questions.

Speaking: interviewing

5 Work in pairs. Role-play the interview between the careers counsellor and a student.

Student A: Turn to page 141.

Student A: Turn to page 141.

Student B

1 You are the careers counsellor. Interview Student A and make notes in this form. Try to recommend a possible career.

* Career the student is interested in:

_____

* Particular subjects he/she is interested in:

_____

* Free-time interests:

_____

* Recommendations of the careers counsellor:

_____

2 Now you are the student. You don't know what you are going to do in the future. You like history at school. In your free time, you work on the school newspaper. Answer the careers counsellor's questions.

6 Discuss in pairs. Imagine you both visit the careers counsellor in the listening. How would you answer each of her questions in Exercise 3?

USEFUL EXPRESSIONS interviewing

Are you here for your interview?
Do you have an appointment?
Can I ask you a few questions?
Do you know what kind of career you're interested in?
Which subjects do you enjoy studying?
How do you like to spend your free time?
Have you thought about …?
What about something like …?

Writing: a letter of application

7 A student has written a letter of application for this advert. Match the purpose of each part of the letter a–e to each paragraph 1–5.

a Your current situation

b Why you are applying

c What you are applying for

d Your availability for an interview and contact details

e Your personal qualities and any other relevant experience

SUMMER VOLUNTEERS NEEDED

Your local zoo needs young people to help over the summer. Volunteers work in the shop, sell tickets and help with feeding and cleaning some of the animals. The job would suit a caring and helpful young person who wants work experience.

---

17 Bridge Lane
Monmouth
LN13 15F
16th July

Mr R Bassett
Monmouth Zoo
Forest Road
LN13 14A

Dear Mr Bassett,

1 I am writing with reference to your advertisement on the town website for summer volunteers at your zoo. I would like to apply for one of the positions.

2 This summer I would like the opportunity to gain some work experience and to help my local community. Working for our town zoo would nicely combine these two goals.

3 I am 17 years old and currently in the sixth form of my school (Glenwood Comprehensive School). I am studying maths, biology and chemistry and hope to study biology at university.

4 I am a caring person with a strong love of animals (including my three cats). In my free time I go horse riding and look after my neighbour's horse when she is away.

5 I would be happy to come to the zoo for an interview or you can call me at home any time between 5 and 7 p.m. My number is 404 665 7382.

I look forward to hearing from you.

Yours sincerely,

Jennifer Cottrell

USEFUL EXPRESSIONS a formal letter

Starting
Dear Mr / Mrs / Ms …
Dear Sir or Madam (if you don't know the name)

Reason for writing
I am writing to … / I would like to …
I am writing with reference to …

Ending
I would be happy to …
I look forward to hearing from you.
Yours sincerely / Best regards
Yours faithfully (if you don't know the name)

Tip
Use full forms in more formal letters, not the contracted form:
I am, I'm, I would, I'd

---

8 Write a letter of application for the scholarship below. Follow the order from Exercise 7 and use some of the Useful Expressions.

Scholarship for *English language* course in London

Applications are welcome from students of English to study for two weeks at a language school in London. The Arnold Hoffman Scholarship pays all course fees and accommodation for a student. Applicants must attend an interview to apply for the scholarship.

Reading

1 Read about a famous English author and discuss as a class.

  1 Have you heard of this author? Do you know the names of any of his books?

  2 Which writers from your country (living or dead) are also famous for writing about social injustice?

Charles Dickens was the most popular English novelist during the Victorian Age and, since his death in 1870, his books have never gone out of print and many have been made into films. Aside from his detailed characters and fascinating plots, what makes his books particularly interesting to the modern reader is that they show the social injustices of the period he was writing in.

The Life and Adventures of Nicholas Nickleby was his third novel and includes many of Dickens' typical themes: the unfair class system, poor working conditions, lack of education and poverty.

After the death of his father, Nicholas Nickleby must earn money to keep his mother and sister. His first job is as a teacher at a boys' boarding school. Dickens based the lives of the boys at the terrible school on real schools. The violent headmaster in the book is also based on a real headmaster called William Shaw who was infamous at the time for his abusive methods.

2 Now read part of *The Life and Adventures of Nicholas Nickleby* on page 93. It is Nicholas' first day at the school. As you read, match each of these characters from the book to their situation.

Example:

The boys = D

Character	Situation
The boys	**A** His father didn't pay all his fees, so he is punished.
Bolder	**B** His grandmother has just died.
Cobbey	**C** He isn't interested in the boys' education – only in their parents' money.
Nickleby	**D** They live in fear of the schoolmaster.
Squeers	**E** He's optimistic about the job until he enters the classroom.

3 Read the text again and answer questions 1–6.

  1 What does 'it' refer to in line 4?

    A his cane   **C** the schoolroom

    B the door   **D** the house

  2 In paragraph 3, Nickleby thinks a classroom should be a place where …

    A pupils enjoy themselves while they learn.

    B pupils learn because of discipline.

    C silence and sadness are good for learning.

    D pupils eat and talk.

  3 What does 'one' in line 23 refer to?

    A a place   **C** a chair

    B a book   **D** a pen

  4 In line 25, 'jump out of their boots' means …

    A jump because they are excited.

    B put their boots on.

    C jump because they are scared.

    D take their boots off quickly.

  5 After Squeers has read out the letters, he …

    A teaches them.

    B falls asleep.

    C leaves the school.

    D tells Nickleby to teach them.

  6 What does 'This' in the last sentence mean?

    A the lesson   **C** the whole situation

    B the darkness   **D** the school

Speaking

4 Discuss in groups. From what you have read about education in Dickens' time, what was the approach of schools towards …?

- discipline
- the relationship between the teacher and the student
- how pupils learn best

Afterwards, discuss the approach of modern education and your school to these three areas. Do you agree with it? What would you change about it?

'Come!' said Squeers, 'Let's go to the schoolroom.' He picked up his cane and led the way to a door at the back of the house. 'There,' said the schoolmaster as they stepped in together; 'this is it, Nickleby!'

It was a bare and dirty room, with a couple of windows. It was impossible to tell whether the walls had ever been painted. There were a couple of long,
10 old, wooden desks and two other desks for Squeers and his assistant.

But worse than that, as he looked at the pupils, any ideas that Nicholas might do them some good disappeared from his mind. They were children who looked like old men. There were little faces which should have been handsome. There were vicious-looking boys and there were lonely young pupils. This place was Hell! He could see how silent and sad the boys were. There was none
20 of the noise of a schoolroom, none of the play or joy of learning.

The boys took their places and their books, although there was only one for eight learners. 'Now,' said Squeers, hitting the desk with his cane, which made half the little boys nearly jump out of their boots. Immediately, there was a deathlike silence. The lesson began.

> **'There was none of the noise of a schoolroom, none of the play or joy of learning.'**

'Boys, I've been to London and I have seen the parents of some boys. They're so glad to hear how their sons are
30 getting on. However, I have some disappointing news', said Squeers.

'First of all, Bolder's father didn't pay me enough. He was two pounds short. 'Come here, Bolder.' An unhealthy-looking boy stepped from his place to the master's desk and raised his eyes. Mr Squeers hit him a few times with his cane until his arm was tired out.

'Now, let us see,' said Squeers. 'I have
40 a letter for Cobbey. Stand up, Cobbey.' Another boy stood up. Squeers announced: 'Cobbey's grandmother is dead.'

Squeers passed on to the next boy 'Graymarsh,' said Squeers, 'he's the next. Stand up, Graymarsh.' Another boy stood up, and the schoolmaster looked at another letter as before.

And so it continued in this way with Squeers reading out letters from parents to each boy. Afterwards, Squeers left for a rest after his hard work and he told Nicholas to
50 continue the lesson.

He taught and took care of the boys until dark. Bread and cheese was served in the evening and Nicholas sat down by the only heater in the room. This was so depressing.

cane a long thin stick a person uses to help them walk

schoolmaster headmaster

Talking to parents

Listening and speaking

1 Discuss as a class.

1 What is the relationship between the people in the picture?

2 Why might they argue? What could they argue about?

3 What's a good way to avoid arguments?

2 Discuss in groups.

1 Which of these topics do your parents or guardians often discuss with you?

- your career plans
- the type of people you are friends with
- your plans for future education (e.g. going to university)
- your choice of clothes
- household jobs (e.g. helping to clean)
- where you can go at the weekend
- how you spend your free time

2 Are there any which you often disagree about?

3 How do you solve any disagreement?

3 2.10 **Listen to a conversation between a mother and her son.**

1 Which topics from the list in Exercise 2 do they discuss?

2 Do they reach an agreement? Do both sides get what they want?

4 2.10 **Listen again and tick the correct answer.**

	Who …	Son	Mother
1	wants the other person to do something?		
2	has a deadline?		
3	isn't sure about something?		
4	hasn't got any money?		
5	makes a deal by offering something in return?		

5 **Work in pairs. Practise two role plays. Take turns to be the parent or the son or daughter. Include all the points in the bullets below.**

Role play 1

The parent doesn't like a particular friend of the son or daughter. Discuss:

- reasons for disliking the friend
- why the son or daughter should not see them
- what the parent will do if the son / daughter agrees
- a final agreement

Role play 2

The son or daughter thinks he/she should be allowed to visit a friend in another country. Discuss:

- what the son or daughter wants to do on the visit
- what the son or daughter will do, if their parent agrees
- a final agreement

What's on your mind?

In this unit you will learn

- **Communication**: expressing preferences and interests
- **Vocabulary**: senses, learning styles, languages
- **Reading and Listening**: endangered languages, talking animals, British accents, the Welsh language
- **Writing**: a report
- **Grammar**: verb patterns, passive voice, phrasal verbs

Scientists test a man's brain activity.

Let's get started

1 Look at the list below. What kind of information do you usually find easy to remember? Number the items from 1 (the easiest to remember) to 7 (the most difficult to remember).

a new telephone number ___

how to ride a bike ___

where I've put things from the day before ___

new words in English ___

my friend's birthday ___

how to pronounce words in English with the letters *-ough* ___

when my teachers want my homework ___

2 Compare your list with the rest of the class.

3 Read the text about the brain. Which part of the brain (A, B or C) do you use for each item in 1? (e.g. a new telephone number = A)

Vocabulary

4 Work in pairs. Look at these pairs of verbs and explain the difference. Use a dictionary to help you if necessary and say them in a sentence.

imagine / see

touch / feel

hear / listen

sniff / smell

eat / taste

5 Our brain gets information from the five senses. Which parts of the body do we use for the senses? Match them to the verbs in Exercise 4.

6 Discuss as a class. Which sense or senses do you think are most important for …?

- learning a language
- riding a bicycle
- deciding if you like someone

The brain stores different types of information and memories in different places.

A Facts and Events
This is the first place we memorise new facts.

B Habits and Skills
We store skills here which are habitual or things we do every day, like driving a car.

C Language Area
The two main languages areas are here. One helps use to understand language. The other produces speech.

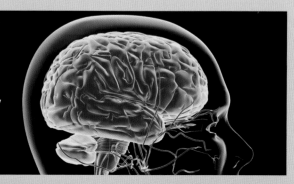

How do I learn?

Listening

1 These five people need good memories.
What do you think they have to remember?

Saskia, theatre actress

Martin, taxi driver

Jenny, web designer

Barry, neurologist*

Neurologist: a medical
doctor who deals with
nerves and the brain.

2 ◎ 2.11 Listen to the five people talking about
how they remember. Write the names of the
people in the order you hear them.

Speaker 1 _____

Speaker 2 _____

Speaker 3 _____

Speaker 4 _____

Speaker 5 _____

Pilar, translator and interpreter

3 ◎ 2.11 Look at the techniques a–h. Listen again
and write the letter of the technique each person
uses. One technique isn't mentioned.

	Techniques
1 Speaker 1	a
2 Speaker 2	
3 Speaker 3	
4 Speaker 4	
5 Speaker 5	

a – spend many hours learning and studying

b – use visual techniques like colours and pictures

c – get help from other people

d – know where to find the information

e – say the words many times

f – use music

g – write things down

h – predict what is important to remember

4 Discuss with the class. Which of the techniques
do you use for learning English? What other
techniques do you use?

Vocabulary

5 Write the words *remember*, *forget* or *remind* in
sentences 1–5.

1 What's your favourite way to _____ new
words?

2 Do you often _____ words and have to
look them up in your dictionary?

3 Do mental images _____ you of words?

4 Which English grammar rule is the most difficult to
_____?

5 Do you ever _____ to do your homework?
How often does your teacher have to
_____ you?

6 Work in pairs. Take turns to ask and answer
the questions in Exercise 5.

Grammar: verb patterns

7 Read these sentences from the listening. Match the underlined verbs to the correct pattern (1–4) in the grammar summary.

1 I <u>need</u> to know common programs like HTML.
2 I <u>imagine</u> seeing the building in my mind.
3 I <u>begin</u> by highlighting all my lines with a coloured pen.
4 I <u>like</u> to read the script with other actors.
5 I <u>like</u> writing notes to myself.

Grammar: verb patterns (1)

You often follow the main verb in a sentence with another verb. This verb can be a *to-infinitive* or an *–ing* form. For example: *I learnt to speak French in Paris. / We dislike studying after school.*

Pattern 1: Verbs followed by the *to-infinitive* include: *agree, decide, learn, manage, need, plan, promise, want, would like …*

Pattern 2: Verbs followed by *–ing* include: *consider, dislike, enjoy, imagine, keep, practise*

Pattern 3: When a preposition follows the main verb, the next verb is in the *–ing* form: *I learn by repeating words.*

Pattern 4: Some main verbs can be followed by the verb in the *to-infinitive* or *–ing* form with no change in meaning:

I prefer to start work at 9. = I prefer starting work at 9.

Verbs followed by either form include: *begin, hate, like, love, prefer, start*

See Grammar Reference, pages 152–153

8 Underline the correct verb form in italics. In some sentences both forms are possible.

What type of learner are you?

1 I need *to use* / *using* mental images to remember. ☐
2 I love *to listen* / *listening* to songs in the language. ☐
3 I practise *to speak* / *speaking* English by talking to other students. ☐
4 I remember by *to use* / *using* different colours to help learn new words. ☐
5 I want *to listen and learn* / *listening and learning* from other students during the lesson. ☐
6 I like *to stand* / *standing* up and move around in class. ☐
7 I learn by *to draw* / *drawing* pictures and diagrams. ☐
8 I enjoy *to listen* / *listening* to the CD recordings in class. ☐
9 I prefer *to find out* / *finding out* a grammar rule myself (instead of the teacher telling me). ☐

9 Now complete the questionnaire for you. Tick the sentences that describe your learning styles. Compare your answers with a partner.

Listening

10 🔊 2.12 Listen to someone explaining what the questionnaire means. Write the missing words in these notes.

Visual learners learn by looking at things and they tend to _____ or watch images on _____.

Auditory learners learn by hearing a _____ or a _____.

Kinaesthetic learners learn by _____.

Sentences _____, _____ and _____ are for visual learners.

Sentences _____, _____ and _____ are for auditory learners.

Sentences _____, _____ and _____ are for kinaesthetic learners.

11 What do your answers in the questionnaire say about you? Do you have a particular learning style? Tell the class.

Watch a video about a man with a special memory. Turn to page 139.

Save our language

Reading

1 In which part of the world are there large communities of people from your country? Do they use their native language as their first or second language?

2 Read this article. Decide if the statements are true or false.

		True	False
1	The aim of the 'Enduring Voices Project' is to save languages which are dying out.		
2	Native American children aren't talking to their parents any more.		
3	Some Aboriginal languages have always been spoken, not written.		
4	In Central South America, there is only one rare language left called Kallawaya.		
5	The author contrasts the loss of plants with the loss of languages.		

Vocabulary

3 Match these definitions to the underlined words in the article.

1 no longer existing
2 existing for a long time
3 not common
4 started or created
5 common or over a large area
6 naturally existing in a region or country
7 put in danger or threatened

Saving the World's Languages

English and Spanish are spoken all over the world. But as these global languages grow, other local and minority languages are being made <u>extinct</u>. It's estimated that one dies every two weeks. But now, the _Enduring Voices Project_ has been <u>set up</u> to try and save many of these 'smaller' languages which are being <u>endangered</u>. Language 'hot spots' have been identified as places which are in need of particular help. Here are the stories about three 'hot spots'.

North America

The USA is normally associated with the language of English and increasingly with Spanish as its unofficial second language. However, it might surprise you that there are 165 <u>indigenous</u> languages across the country. Many of these are spoken among native American communities. However, because English is the language of TV, Internet and day-to-day communication, the children are not speaking the language of their parents and grandparents anymore.

Australia

Some ancient Aboriginal languages were first spoken over 50,000 years ago. They were never written down but now, with modern recording equipment, members of the _Enduring Voices Project_ are interviewing older people in the tribes. The team has already met the last three speakers of Magati Ke and the last woman who speaks Amurdag – a language which they thought was extinct.

Central South America

Like the many <u>rare</u> plants in the jungles, the region also has some languages that cannot be found anywhere else in the world. One of these is Kallawaya. Native speakers of Kallawaya have used these plants for medicinal purposes since the time of the Incas. But if their language is killed off by the <u>widespread</u> use of Spanish and Portuguese, then the information about thousands of these plants will also be lost for ever.

Grammar: the passive form

4 Read these sentences. The underlined verbs are in the active form. Find the sentences in the text with the same verb in the passive form. Underline the verb.

1 People <u>speak</u> English and Spanish all over the world.

2 Global languages <u>are making</u> local and minority languages extinct.

3 An organisation <u>has set up</u> the 'Enduring Voices Project'.

4 The Aborigines <u>never wrote</u> some of their languages down.

5 Humans <u>cannot find</u> many rare plants in the jungles of this region anywhere else in the world.

6 We <u>will lose</u> information about thousands of these plants for ever.

5 Look at your answers to Exercise 4 and match the verbs to 1–6 below.

1 present simple: *is spoken*

2 present continuous:

3 present perfect:

4 past simple:

5 future *will*:

6 modals:

The passive form

We use the passive form when we want to focus on the person or thing affected by the action expressed by the verb. The object of the active verb becomes the subject of the passive verb. To form the passive use *to be + past participle*.

	verb	object
ACTIVE: People	**speak**	English all over the world.

	subject	verb
PASSIVE:	English	**is spoken** all over the world.

See Grammar Reference, pages 153–154

6 Complete this article with correct verb form in 1–7.

The Cornish language

Cornwall is on the south western tip of England. Every year it (**1**) _____ by hundreds of holidaymakers because of its long beaches and warm summers. However, it's less famous for having its own language. That's probably because the Cornish language (**2**) _____ fluently by about 2,000 people. People (**3**) _____ Cornish since the sixth century. Over the centuries, the language (**4**) _____ as the English language spread. But in 1904, a book (**5**) _____ about Cornish and people became interested once more. Nowadays, the language (**6**) _____ on road signs and some children (**7**) _____ the ancient language once again.

Welcome to
CORNWALL
KERNOW
a'gas dynergh

CORNWALL

1 A visits   B is visit   C is visited
  D are visited

2 A only speak   B is only speaking   C is only spoken
  D only spoke

3 A used   B have used   C were used
  D have been used

4 A die out   B died out   C is died out
  D was died out

5 A published   B has published   C was published
  D has been published

6 A can see   B can to see   C can been seen
  D can be seen

7 A is learning   B are learning   C is being learnt
  D are being learnt

8C What's on your pet's mind?

Speaking

1 Discuss as a class. Do you have a pet? Why do you think people have pets? What are the pros and cons of pets?

2 Work in pairs. Look at the information below and discuss these questions.

1 Which pets in the list would you choose? Which wouldn't you want? Why not?

2 What do you think about people who spend lots of money on their pets?

3 Which do you think are the most intelligent species of animals? Why?

How much do you spend on your pets?

Pet shops have reported their biggest profits ever. The multi-million pound industry says humans are spending more and more money on their animals. One reason is that couples are having children later in life and buying a pet before they have children …

Reading

 Dogs — 7.3
 Hamsters — 0.5
Estimated no. (m)
 Cats — 7.2
 Horses and Ponies — 0.3
 Rabbits — 1.4
 Gerbils — 0.14
 Birds (Indoor) — 0.8
Tortoises/Turtles — 0.12

3 Read the article on page 101 and answer questions 1–5. Circle A, B, C or D.

1 Irene wanted to find out …
   A if parrots could speak.
   B if parrots could speak English.
   C what a parrot thinks.
   D what parrots like to eat.

2 The article tells us that most scientists nowadays believe that …
   A Pepperberg is crazy.
   B chimpanzees talk better than parrots.
   C animals do have thoughts.
   D their pets love them.

3 Alex learnt new words by …
   A repeating them.
   B reading them.
   C writing them.
   D hearing them once.

4 The two dogs mentioned in the article could …
   A understand words.
   B say words.
   C make up new words.
   D communicate with two-year-old children.

5 The article concludes that …
   A dogs might speak to humans one day.
   B humans are related to chimpanzees and apes.
   C our pets understand what we say.
   D mental ability can evolve in species.

What's on your pet's mind?

In 1977, Irene Pepperberg of Harvard University began studying what was on another creature's mind by talking to it. Her first experiments began with Alex. Alex was a one-year-old African grey parrot and Irene taught him to produce the sounds of the English language. 'I thought if he learned to communicate, I could ask him questions about how he sees the world.'

At the time, most scientists didn't believe animals had any thoughts. They thought animals were more like robots which reacted to stimuli (e.g. the smell of food) but didn't have the ability to think or feel. Of course, if you own a pet you probably disagree. But it is the job of a scientist to prove this and nowadays more scientists accept that animals can think for themselves.

'That's why I started my studies with Alex,' Pepperberg said. 'Some people actually called me crazy for trying this,' she said. 'Scientists thought that chimpanzees were better subjects, although, of course, chimps can't speak.' Chimpanzees and gorillas have been taught to use sign language and symbols to communicate with humans but this is not the same thing as having an animal look up at you, open his mouth, and speak.

Nowadays, we have more and more evidence that animals have all sorts of mental abilities. Sheep can recognise faces. Chimpanzees use a variety of tools and even use weapons to hunt small mammals. Dolphins can imitate human postures. And Alex the parrot became a very good talker.

Thirty years after the Alex studies began, Pepperberg was still giving him English lessons up until his recent death. For example, if Alex was hungry he could say 'want grape'. Alex could count to six and was learning the sounds for seven and eight. 'He has to hear the words over and over before he can correctly imitate them,' Pepperberg said, after pronouncing 'seven' for Alex a few times in a row. Alex could also tell the difference between colours, shapes, sizes, and materials (e.g. wood or metal). Before he finally died, Alex managed to say 'seven'.

Another famous pet that proved some animals have greater mental skills was a dog called Rico. He appeared on a German TV game show in 2001. Rico knew the names of 200 different toys and easily acquired the names of new ones. When scientists studied his skill they found he could learn and remember words as quickly as a two-year-old child. When Rico became famous, many other dog owners wanted to show how clever their pets were. Another dog called Betsy could understand 300 words. This is surprising because it's more than most chimpanzees or apes – our closest relative in the animal world – can.

One theory for dogs' ability to learn a language is that they have been close companions to humans for many centuries and so their ability to understand us is constantly evolving. While animals cannot do what humans do yet, some scientists believe that examples like Alex, Rico and Betsy prove that evolution develops intelligence, as well as physical appearance.

4 Think about your opinions of the information in this article. Complete these sentences with your own words about the article and then compare them in groups.

1 *One thing that surprises me is that …*
2 *One interesting thing was that …*
3 *If animals could answer our questions, my first question would be …*

Harvard University, Cambridge, Massachusetts

8D Taking a break

Speaking: preferences and interests

1 Discuss these questions.

1 What do you do at school when you're not in class? Are you a member of any teams or clubs?

2 Look at the information on a school noticeboard. Would you do any of these activities? Why is it important to have these kinds of activities at school as well as lessons?

Listening: preferences and interests

2 🔘 2.13 Listen to two pupils discussing the noticeboard. Which do they choose?

3 🔘 2.13 Listen again and underline the expression in italics you hear.

1 *I'd like to do / I'd hate to do* art club but I already have a piano lesson on Wednesdays.

2 *How about / What about* joining the chess club?

3 *I really enjoy / I can't stand* playing games like that.

4 *I'd prefer to do / I prefer doing* something active after sitting in class all day.

5 *Why don't you / You should* come, too?

6 *I'm not very keen on / I'm not very interested in* standing up in front of people.

7 *You're good at / You're not bad at* making things.

8 *I'd rather do / I'd prefer to do* something like that.

9 *Let's / We could* do that then.

4 Read the questionnaire on page 142. What does the school want to find out?

Speaking: preferences and interests

5 Work in pairs. Take turns to interview each other with the questionnaire. Use the Useful Expressions box. If you have time, interview more than one person and report your findings back to the class. Find out what everyone in the class would prefer.

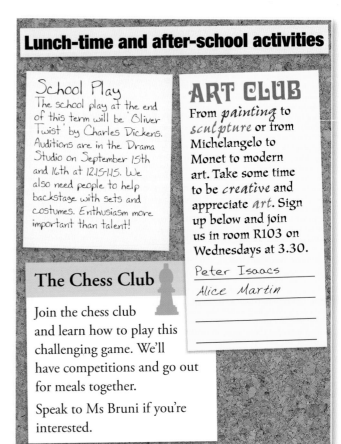

Lunch-time and after-school activities

School Play
The school play at the end of this term will be 'Oliver Twist' by Charles Dickens. Auditions are in the Drama Studio on September 15th and 16th at 12.15-1.15. We also need people to help backstage with sets and costumes. Enthusiasm more important than talent!

ART CLUB
From *painting* to *sculpture* or from Michelangelo to Monet to modern art. Take some time to be *creative* and appreciate *art*. Sign up below and join us in room R103 on Wednesdays at 3.30.

Peter Isaacs
Alice Martin
_____
_____

The Chess Club
Join the chess club and learn how to play this challenging game. We'll have competitions and go out for meals together.
Speak to Ms Bruni if you're interested.

USEFUL EXPRESSIONS preferences and interests

Asking about preferences and suggesting
Would you like to / be interested in …?
How / What about …?
Why don't you …?
You should / You could
Let's …

Talking about likes / dislikes / general preferences
I like / love / enjoy …
I don't like / hate / can't stand …
I prefer …

Talking about preferences in a specific situation
I'd like to / prefer to / rather … because …

Talking about interests and abilities
I'm good at / keen on / interested in …

Writing: a report

6 Work in groups. Read the results of a school survey about extra-curricular activities*. Then discuss the information.

1 What conclusions can you make about pupils' preferences and interests?

2 Make a list of recommendations for the school based on the information.

> **extra-curricular activities**: activities in school that happen in addition to the official lessons and timetable.

Preferred time of day for activities

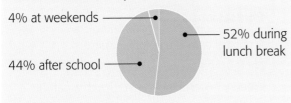

4% at weekends
52% during lunch break
44% after school

Most popular choices

Activity or club	Pupils showing interest
Football club	66
Chess club	31
Art club	15
Canoeing and camping club (weekends only)	7
Drama club	57

Other comments:

'We have so much homework, how can we do extra activities?'

'I'd like more activities for people who aren't interested in sport or outdoor activities.'

'How about having a music club? People who play musical instruments could practise and then give a performance at the end of term.'

7 Now read this report about the information in Exercise 6. Are the conclusions and recommendations in the report similar to your own?

Report on school survey

Introduction

The aim of this report is to summarise the findings of the survey into extra-curricular activities for the pupils.

Procedure

We sent out a questionnaire to 200 pupils in years 7, 8 and 9 in the school. 120 were returned.

8 Find expressions in the report with similar meanings to 1–7.

1 This report sets out to …
The aim of this report is to …

2 We distributed … _____

3 With reference to … _____

4 Most pupils … _____

5 Just under 50% of the pupils … _____

6 We especially … _____

7 Overall … _____

9 Imagine your local town has been given a large amount of money to improve something in the community. The council sent out 500 questionnaires to local people for their opinions. Write a report based on this information below.

Number of questionnaires returned: 299

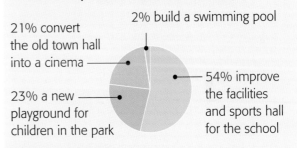

21% convert the old town hall into a cinema

2% build a swimming pool

54% improve the facilities and sports hall for the school

23% a new playground for children in the park

Other comments:

'Instead of building something with our money, maybe you should reduce our taxes.'

'If we improve the school sports hall, then local people could also use it at weekends and in the evening.'

'There's another cinema five kilometres away in the next town. Why build another one?!'

Findings

With regard to the best time of day for most activities, the majority of pupils requested lunchtimes. There is one hour at lunch and pupils would like some activities to do either before or after they have eaten lunch. Nearly half the pupils are also interested in activities after school.

Secondly, the most popular choices were football and drama. Chess is also popular. Art club and canoeing received less interest.

A few students also added comments. In particular, we liked the suggestion for a music club.

Conclusions and recommendations

In general, there was positive interest in our suggestions for activities and clubs, so we should offer these if possible both during lunch and after school. Football and drama should begin as soon as possible. We also think the suggestion for a music club was a very good idea and that it could be very popular.

Where are you from?

1 English is now spoken all over the world with many different accents. But even in England itself, there are many different accents. Read the article on page 105 and decide if the statements are true or false.

		True	False
1	There are big differences in accents between people from the cities and from the countryside.		
2	Most people in England still want to speak like the Queen.		
3	Lots of people in the southeast of England would say 'ouse' instead of 'house' or 'fought' instead of 'thought'.		
4	People in Manchester and Liverpool sound identical.		
5	Doctor Workman believes his study shows that intelligence is connected to where you come from.		
6	The study didn't prove that people who speak the Queen's English are more intelligent.		

Grammar: phrasal verbs

2 Look at the phrasal verbs from the article. Replace the words in bold in sentences 1–6 with the correct phrasal verb.

> grew up   look up   came across   come from
> put on   work out

1 I **became an adult** in the city of Liverpool.
  grew up
2 All my family **were born in** the south east of England.
3 **Find** the words in your dictionary.
4 Let's try to **find** the answers to this exercise.
5 Today I **discovered by accident** a new word in my dictionary.
6 Some people like to **use** a false accent when they meet other people.

3 Read the grammar summary. Then decide which phrasal verbs in Exercise 2 are:

transitive: _____

intransitive: _____

separable: _____

inseparable: _____

A good dictionary will also give you this information about a phrasal verb so look up these phrasal verbs in your dictionary to help you.

Phrasal verbs

A phrasal verb is a verb + particle:

Look up the words in your dictionary.

When you combine the verb with a particle, it creates a new meaning:

Look after this book. (= take good care of it)

Look up the word. (= try to find it)

Some phrasal verbs need a direct object. They are TRANSITIVE:

I came across this word in my dictionary.

Some phrasal verbs do not take a direct object. They are INTRANSITIVE:

I grew up in Liverpool.

Some TRANSITIVE phrasal verbs can be SEPARABLE. The direct object can go before or after the particle:

Look up the word in your dictionary. = Look the word up in your dictionary.

Some transitive phrasal verbs are INSEPARABLE. The direct object can only go after the particle:

I came across this word in my dictionary. ✓
~~*I came this word across in my dictionary.*~~ ✗

See Grammar Reference, page 154

4 Discuss these questions as a class.

- Which part of your country do you come from?
- Do people from this region have a strong accent?
- Are there any other regions in your country with accents you can easily recognise?
- How different are accents in the city compared with the countryside?
- Do you make any associations with certain accents?
- Do you ever put on an accent?

What does your accent say about you?

Our environment and the world around us greatly affects the language we use. One famous example says that certain Eskimo tribes have between five and ten different words for snow. Which word you use depends on the type of snow. Conversely, in parts of Africa, there is no word at all to describe white stuff that falls from the sky when it's very cold – because it never happens!

The English language is also typical of many languages for having more than one word to refer to the same thing. If you look up the word 'rain' in your dictionary, you might also come across synonyms such as 'drizzle', 'shower', 'sprinkle', 'downpour', 'spitting' and so on. In this case, the range of words describing rain reflects the weather conditions of England.

And like many other countries, the English have an incredibly diverse range of accents. If you listen to an English person speak, you will usually be able to work out which part of the country they grew up in, especially if they come from one of the major population areas, or a rural area with an especially strong accent. The one accent which is rarely heard today is the traditional 'BBC' accent or so-called Queen's English and a few – usually older – people complain that young people don't speak 'properly'.

You can still hear the Queen's English in some richer parts of London, but most of the city speaks quite differently. Parts of London and the South East still use a form of speech in which the 'h' is missed off the start of words; so the word 'home' might sound like 'ome'. And 'th' is often replaced by 'f' or 'v' sounds, depending whereabouts it appears in the word. So the word 'thought' might actually be pronounced 'fought'.

> 'each individual city has its own accent, and they are all very distinctive'

The most populated areas of England outside London are the large cities such as Manchester, Birmingham and Liverpool. Although there are some similarities between the northern accents in these cities, each individual city has its own accent, and they are all very distinctive.

In Birmingham, which is England's second biggest city, you often hear words such as 'you' pronounced as 'yow'. The bad news for Birmingham is that a new study published by psychologists at Bath University found that people associate a Birmingham accent with criminals and low intelligence. Dr Workman from Bath University added: 'These are of course stereotypes that are not based in any way on how intelligent people actually are.'

In the tests, different people looked at the same photograph of someone but heard that person speaking with a different accent. They graded the speaker differently. Surprisingly, the speaker using the Queen's English didn't score the highest. The northern Yorkshire accent has overtaken it as the accent people most associate with intelligence.

If the results from these tests are true, then it explains why people often put on an accent in order to be accepted when they move to a new place in the same way they might learn a new language in a new country.

Case Study 4 〉 The Welsh language

Wales, which is part of the United Kingdom, has a population of just under three million. Of these, about 20% speak Welsh, although most people also speak English. Welsh is a compulsory subject at school and students must study it up to the age of 16. There are also schools which teach exclusively **through the medium of** Welsh.

Welsh is a language with a long history which can be traced back to the 6th century. It has a rich **literary** tradition and the first book in Welsh was printed in 1546, although many texts have survived from before that time.

However, during the 18th and 19th century, when Wales became more industrialised, many people migrated there from England and the traditional language **became diluted** by English. The Welsh began to fight for their language which, until the middle of the 20th century, was in danger of dying out completely, as the number of Welsh-speakers dropped dramatically.

Then, in 1962, the Welsh Language Society was **founded**. They successfully **campaigned** to have Welsh on all road signs as well as English, to establish a Welsh-language TV channel, and to make sure that children can learn Welsh in schools. Although the language is still threatened, a lot of work has been done to help it to **flourish**. In 2009, two companies, Samsung and Orange™, combined forces to produce the first mobile phone service using the Welsh language.

Just as the English migrated in large numbers into Wales, many Welsh people have emigrated over the years. Because of this, you might find it surprising to read that a large number of Welsh speakers can be found in Patagonia, Argentina, and this number is believed to be rising. As well as this, there are significant numbers of speakers of the language in Australia and in the USA, where around two million people have Welsh **ancestry**.

- The longest place name in Wales is:
  Llanfairpwllgwyngyllgogerychwyrndrobwllllantysiliogogogoch (58 letters).
  It means *Saint Mary's Church in a hollow of white hazel near the swirling whirlpool of the church of Saint Tysilio with a red cave.*
  For obvious reasons, it is often written on maps in its shortened form, Llanfair P.G.

1 Read the text and choose the most likely meaning for the words in bold.

1	through the medium of	**A** using	**B** reading
2	literary	**A** related to history	**B** related to writing
3	became diluted	**A** was made stronger	**B** was made weaker
4	founded	**A** discovered	**B** started
5	flourish	**A** be successful	**B** be unsuccessful
6	ancestry	**A** roots	**B** friends

2 Read all the information and note down:

1 how many people in Wales speak the language.

2 how old the Welsh language is.

3 the situation before the Welsh Language Society.

4 the achievements of the Welsh Language Society.

5 a recent development for the Welsh language.

6 places outside Wales where Welsh is spoken.

Review 〉 Unit 7

Grammar

1 Write the missing relative pronoun in these sentences. There is more than one answer in two sentences.

1 This is the person_whose_desk you are currently using.
2 There's a problem with your work we need to discuss.
3 It's a town lots of students come because of the university.
4 Isn't he the teacher taught us at school?
5 Ten thirty is the time everyone takes a break.
6 My sister, has worked here for over five years, is leaving.
7 This course in business, also includes work experience, lasts three years and gets you a good job afterwards.
8 Bryan, degree was in astronomy, became a famous rock star!

2 Decide if the relative clause in each sentence is defining (D) or non-defining (ND). Add commas to sentences with non-defining clauses. See the examples.

1 That's the same man who we saw on TV last night. (D)
2 Scotland, which is to the north of England, is one of my favourite places. (ND)
3 Mary who is my youngest sister has just started school. ( )
4 Mr Langston is the teacher that you need to talk to about chess club. ( )
5 My cat whose name is Felix caught a mouse yesterday. ( )
6 This house which was built in the seventeenth century is absolutely freezing! ( )
7 Our cousin whose birthday is next week has passed his exam and is going to Oxford University. ( )
8 It's a restaurant where you can get fantastic pizza. ( )

Vocabulary

3 Add a suffix to the word in CAPITALS at the end and complete the sentence.

1 _Journalists_ have to ask lots of difficult questions. JOURNAL
2 My _____ won't pay me any more money. EMPLOY
3 After university I'd like to work as a _____ for a large company. MANAGE
4 Have you heard of Jimi Hendrix? He was an amazing _____. GUITAR
5 The people for the job of a _____ are all waiting for an interview. RECEPTION
6 I'm sorry about the mistake. We have a new _____ who is learning the job at the moment. TRAIN
7 Where's the _____ with my soup? He was here a minute ago. WAIT
8 My brother earns lots of money as an _____. ELECTRIC

Functions

4 Match questions 1–6 to the responses a–f.

1 Are you here for your interview?
2 Do you have an appointment?
3 Can I ask you a few questions?
4 Do you know what kind of career you're interested in?
5 Which subjects do you enjoy studying?
6 How do you like to spend your free time?

a Sure.
b Yes, at three. I'm slightly early.
c Yes, I am.
d No, not really.
e With friends.
f None in particular.

Now I can …

- [ ] describe jobs
- [ ] talk about career choices
- [ ] write a letter of application
- [ ] negotiate
- [ ] use relative pronouns and relative clauses

Review 〉 Unit 8

Grammar

1 Underline the correct verb forms in italics. In some answers, both options are possible.

Humans like (1) *to talk / talking* to their pets but can you imagine (2) *to listen / listening* to your pet's reply? Here are two animals which have learnt (3) *to understand / understanding* a range of vocabulary.

Kanzi started (4) *to developed / developing* his language skills by watching scientists teaching his mother and he began (5) *to copy / copying*. Now he regularly communicates by (6) *to use / using* the keyboard of a computer.

Don White wants (7) *to find out / finding out* how dolphins communicate. He puts a mother dolphin and her child in separate swimming pools and they communicate by (8) *to make / making* noises through a special underwater telephone. The mother recognises her child's sounds but the question for White is: What exactly are they saying to each other?

2 Write the verbs in brackets in the passive form using the correct tense.

1 The post _____ (**deliver**) every day at ten o'clock.

2 Our new house _____ (**still / build**). It should be ready in a month.

3 *Heart of Darkness* _____ (**write**) by Joseph Conrad in 1899.

4 Cars _____ (**make**) in this town for over 50 years.

5 Your essay _____ (**mark**) by your teacher by the end of the week.

6 Your letter of application _____ (**can / send**) to 98 Malvern Road, London.

7 The subject of English _____ (**teach**) at my school since 1998.

8 The computers _____ (**switch**) off every night when everyone leaves.

9 Please note that this shop _____ (**close**) all next week until January 2nd.

10 Another satellite _____ (**launch**) today for Mars.

Vocabulary

3 Underline the correct word in italics.

1 Many species are now becoming *extinct / indigenous* because of hunting.

2 Pandas are quite *widespread / rare* in the wild but you can still see them in zoos.

3 You must *hear / listen* to this new song! It's great!

4 Did you *remember / memorise* to bring your books today?

4 Write in the missing participle. There are two possible answers in some sentences. See the first example.

        up   *OR*   *up*

1 Can you look ∧ his telephone number ∧?

2 My father grew in Mexico.

3 I was walking along the street when I came a five pound note!

4 Why are you putting that strange voice?

5 Have you worked the answer to number two?

Functions

5 Match the first half of the question with the second half.

1 Do you like	a	rather have lunch now?
2 Would you prefer	b	meet after school?
3 Are you interested	c	at remembering new words?
4 How good are you	d	to take a break now or later?
5 Do you think he'd	e	studying on your own or with friends?
6 Why don't we	f	in learning Spanish?

Now I can ...

- ☐ talk about languages
- ☐ talk about preferences and interests
- ☐ find a language course
- ☐ write a report
- ☐ use verb patterns and passive voice

9

News and media

In this unit you will learn

- **Communication**: reporting your news, watching television
- **Vocabulary**: news, media, types of programmes on TV
- **Reading and Listening**: the life of a journalist, different accounts of an event, media moments in history
- **Writing**: a film review
- **Grammar**: indirect questions, reported speech

Let's get started

1 Work in pairs. Read these two opinions about news and journalism. Discuss.

1 What do you think they mean?

2 Do you agree with their opinions?

'*The real news is bad news.*'
Marshall McLuhan, media expert (1911–1980)

'*Journalism is the entertainment business.*'
Frank Herbert, author (1920–1986)

2 Work in pairs. Which type of news source in the list below do you use to find out more about:

A international news and world events

B national and local news

C news in your school

- television
- radio
- news website
- blog
- local newspaper
- national newspaper
- noticeboard or poster
- newsletter
- magazine

3 Now read these descriptions of news events. Where would you expect to read or hear them?

- the US President is in London for two days of talks
- pupils at your school are raising money for a charity
- a woman's cat was stuck in a tree, so she called the local fire brigade
- a new Hollywood film is coming out
- the government wants to increase taxes
- the national football team has qualified for the World Cup
- a train has crashed on the way to Paris
- there's an outdoor festival near you next month

4 Discuss as a class.

1 How important is news to you? How often do you watch or read the news? Every day? Every week? Never?

2 Do you always believe what you read or hear? How do you decide which news source to trust?

Can I interview you?

Speaking

1 Work in groups. Journalists often interview the types of people in these pictures. What sorts of subjects do they ask them about? Think of two questions a journalist might ask each of these people. Afterwards, tell the class your questions.

2 A journalist interviewed the people (A, B, C and D) above. Match the questions to the person. There may be more than one possible answer.

1 Would you mind telling me whether the government plans to spend less on education? B

2 Do you mind if I ask you about your new film?

3 Could you tell me how much you earn?

4 Do you have any idea how much the operation will cost?

5 I was wondering why your team lost.

6 I'd like to know what you think about the situation.

7 Do you think the public believes you any more?

8 Do you know why she died?

Grammar: indirect ways of asking questions

3 In Exercise 2, the journalist asks the questions in an indirect way. Match the questions in Exercise 2 to these more direct forms of the questions.

1 What do you think about the situation? _6_

2 How much will the operation cost? ___

3 Does the public believe you any more? ___

4 Tell me about your new film. ___

5 Why did she die? ___

6 How much do you earn? ___

7 Does the government plan to spend less on education? ___

8 Why did your team lose? ___

Indirect ways of asking questions

You can ask questions in a less direct (and more polite) way with certain expressions:

Could you / anyone tell me ...?
Do you know / think ...?
Do you have any idea ...?
Do you mind if ...?
Would you mind telling me ...?
I don't know ... / I'd like to know ...
I wonder ... / I was wondering ...

When you ask indirect questions, the word order is the same as for an affirmative sentence:

Do you know <u>why she died</u>?

You don't need an auxiliary verb (*do, does, did*) in the simple tense and the subject comes before the verb:

<u>*Could you tell me why*</u> ~~did~~ *your team lost?*

With questions that need a *yes / no* answer, use *if* or *whether*:

<u>*Would you mind telling me whether*</u> the government plans to spend less on education?
<u>*Do you mind if*</u> I ask you about your new film?

Punctuation rule: Some indirect questions have a question mark (?) and some do not. It depends if the indirect phrase at the beginning is a question or not:

Do you have any idea how much the operation will cost?

I was wondering how much you earn.

See Grammar Reference, page 155

4 Rewrite these questions with the introductory phrases.

1 How do I play this computer game?
Could you show me how to _____?

2 Can I borrow your pen?
I was wondering if _____

3 What time does the film start?
I'd like to know _____

4 What's the name of the actor in the film?
Do you remember _____?

5 Where is the press conference?
Have you any idea _____?

6 Is this new film worth going to see?
Do you think _____?

5 Work in pairs. Take turns to ask and answer questions in these situations. Use indirect questions.

Situation 1: You are at the train station. You want to know the platform number for trains to London. Ask your friend.

Situation 2: There's a film on TV tonight. Your friend has seen it before. Find out about it.

Situation 3: You're in a shop and want to buy a new computer. There isn't a price on it. Ask the shop assistant.

Situation 4: You've bought a new mobile phone but you don't know how to use it. Your friend has a similar one. Ask him/her.

Situation 5: You want your friend's email address. Ask him/her to spell it for you and write it down.

Listening

6 2.14 You are going to listen to an interview with a journalist called Kira Salak. The interviewer has prepared areas he wants to find out about. Listen and write notes about her answers.

> ### Kira Salak
> Reasons for reporting from dangerous places?
>
> _____
>
> Preparation for journeys and extreme conditions?
>
> _____
>
> News story which affected you most?
>
> _____

7 2.14 Listen again and answer questions 1–5. Circle answer A, B, C or D.

1 Which is true about Kira?
 A She usually goes on dangerous journeys.
 B She always travels on her own.
 C She carries a weapon on her journeys.
 D She has been a slave.

2 A journey to a dangerous place is worthwhile if …
 A she gets good photographs.
 B she meets local people.
 C she reports important news from the place.
 D something exciting happens.

3 On her trips she always needs to …
 A defend herself.
 B find a gym.
 C deal with extreme conditions.
 D be physically well-prepared.

4 How does she deal with pain?
 A By ignoring it.
 B By wearing sunscreen.
 C By going inside.
 D By finding a doctor.

5 In the Congo, how did she feel 'OK' to be there?
 A She didn't feel ok to be there.
 B By talking to local people.
 C Because she knew she could escape on a plane at any time.
 D By reporting what she saw.

Speaking

8 Discuss as a class.

1 What do you think attracts journalists like Kira to this kind of reporting?

2 What kind of responsibilities do they have to the people they interview?

9 Write the name of someone famous or someone you admire on a piece of paper. Swap the names with a partner. Prepare five questions for the person on the paper.

10 Now, role-play an interview between a journalist and each of the famous people. Take turns to ask the questions. Try to answer the questions (or make up the information if necessary!).

9B Here is the news

Vocabulary

1 Read these pairs of words connected to newspapers. Match the word to the correct definition.

1 headline ☐ / lead story ☐
   a The most important article on the front page.
   b The words at the top of the article to get the reader's attention.

2 tabloid ☐ / broadsheet ☐
   a Newspapers which report serious news such as politics and international events.
   b Newspapers which report sensational news such as celebrity gossip.

3 editor ☐ / correspondent ☐
   a A person who checks news articles and decides whether to use them.
   b A person who writes news articles (another word for journalist).

4 editorial ☐ / feature ☐
   a A factual article on a particular topic.
   b An article with the opinion of the newspaper on an important news story.

5 front page ☐ / sections ☐
   a Parts of the newspaper covering topics such as sport, food or obituaries.
   b Where you find the most important news of the day.

6 columnist ☐ / reporter ☐
   a A person who regularly writes a particular kind of article in a newspaper.
   b A person who researches and collects information about a news story.

Speaking

2 Read some of the things a news reporter does and discuss why you think they are necessary. Which of these things would you like/dislike to do the most?

Check emails / messages / RSS feeds
Read forum discussions / newsletters
Listen to latest headlines / podcasts
Talk to witnesses / police
Phone contacts / editor / news desk
Update live news blog
Write articles
Send articles
Attend press conferences / meetings

Reading

3 Read the article and say what two areas of journalism are mentioned. How is the writer's new job different from his old one?

A typical day in my life – Martin Coletti: freelance journalist

I should start by saying that there's no such thing as a typical day in journalism. After ten years as a reporter for a newspaper, I got tired of the unsocial hours, the impossible <u>deadlines</u> and spending half my life on the phone. News doesn't only happen on <u>weekdays</u> from nine to five – when there's a <u>breaking</u> story, you have to <u>drop everything</u> and get there as quickly as you can. I also had to knock on a lot of doors and talk to people who didn't want to talk to me!

These days I write articles from home. The deadlines aren't so tight, but I have to work hard if I want to <u>survive financially</u>. The first thing I have to do is decide what I want to write about. It helps to have a newspaper in mind – and to know what kind of articles they usually publish. Then I contact the commissioning editor and send them a proposal (the outline of the story I'm planning to write). I find I get more work if I include <u>alternative angles</u> for the story – giving the editor a choice. That way, they're more likely to see something in my proposal which will fit in with their paper. Then, once we've agreed the details, I can begin researching it. This might mean <u>setting up</u> interviews with people, which is a bit like the old days because I go out and meet people. But today, like most days, I'm sitting at my laptop with a cup of coffee. I've nearly finished the article I'm writing. When I send it, that's normally the last I see of it until it's in print. That doesn't mean that all my work is perfect and doesn't need <u>editing</u>, but in the newspaper world, it's faster for editors to make the changes themselves.

4 Match the underlined words and phrases in the text to items 1–8.

1 stop what you are doing
2 correcting, re-writing or shortening
3 new or developing
4 arranging or organising
5 Monday to Friday
6 different ways of looking at things
7 times or days when work must be finished
8 make enough money to live on

Grammar: reported speech

5 What was Martin talking about when he said these things? Find the answers in the article.

1 I got tired of <u>it</u>.
2 <u>It</u> doesn't only happen on weekdays.
3 I had knocked on thousands of <u>them</u>!
4 <u>They</u> said, "Go away!"
5 I'm sitting <u>here</u> now.
6 I've nearly finished <u>it</u>.

6 Read the rules for reported speech below and report the sentences in Exercise 5.

Martin <u>said that he had got</u> tired of the unsocial hours / the impossible deadlines / spending half his life on the phone / being a reporter for a newspaper.

Reported speech

say and *tell*

Use *say* to report someone's words:
'I love my job.' → He <u>said</u> (that) he loved his job.
Use *tell* to say who someone is talking to:
'I love my job.' → He <u>told me</u> (that) he loved his job.

Move tense backwards

When you report what someone said, you often move the tense 'backwards':
'I'm working from home today.' → He said (that) he <u>was working</u> from home <u>that day</u>.
will often becomes *would* and *can* becomes *could*:
'I'll finish the article tonight.' → He said (that) he <u>would finish</u> the article <u>that night</u>.

No change

With the past perfect, the tense does not change in reported speech:
'I had worked / had been working for the newspaper for ten years when I left.' → He said (that) he had worked / had been working for the newspaper for ten years when he left.

orders and requests

'Start writing.' → He told me <u>to start</u> writing.
'Please phone the office.' → He asked me <u>to phone</u> the office.

See Grammar Reference, pages 156–157

7 Change these sentences in direct speech into reported speech.

1 The critic said, 'The performance is awful!'
2 The police said, 'We are looking for a man with short black hair.'
3 The Prime Minister answered, 'The government isn't going to make any quick decisions about the issue.'
4 She told reporters, 'I've never even met that man in my life!'
5 He explained, 'I planned to change my football club last year.'
6 They said, 'We can't believe the news.'
7 The celebrity couple said, 'We'll announce our news next week.'
8 He told the police, 'I was at work at the time of the robbery.'

Pronunciation: elision of /h/

8 ⊙ 2.15 Listen to these sentences. Notice how the /h/ disappears and the sounds are linked.

1 She asked‿(h)im to call.
2 They told‿(h)er about the dog.
3 She'd kept‿(h)er favourite toy.
4 I said‿(h)e'd be late.

Listen again and repeat.

Speaking

9 Work in groups. Did you watch, hear or read the news recently? What did it say or tell you about …?

- today's weather
- your country's leader
- sport or the arts
- the economy
- any celebrities

Tell the group.

UNIT 9B HERE IS THE NEWS   113

9C Different accounts

Reading

1 What do you know about volcanic eruptions? Have you seen anything about them in the news?

2 Work in pairs. You will each read a different account of the same event. Make notes in the table for your account.

Student A: Read Account 1 on page 115.

Student B: Read Account 2 on page 115.

	Account 1	Account 2
What was the main event?		
Does the article mention any similar events from the past?		
Who was affected by the event? In what ways?		
Is anything said about the way people felt?		
Does the account mention money? What does it say?		
Did anything good come out of the event?		
How would you describe the main 'angle' of the account (e.g. personal / economic / human / historical)?		

Speaking

3 Take turns reporting your account to your partner. As you listen, fill in the column about your partner's account. Then discuss the differing accounts of the event. You can ask and answer questions to get more information. Remember to use reported speech.

The writer of this account mentioned some past eruptions. He said that Krakatoa, for example, had been heard 3,500 kilometres away and had affected the global climate.

Grammar: reported questions

4 Read part of the second account. What questions did the writer ask? What were the answers? Try acting out the dialogue with a partner.

We asked the emergency workers if we were safe and they told us that they couldn't say for sure because nothing was certain. We wanted to know how long the eruptions were going to continue and whether we should leave. They said they didn't know, but that we should stay inside and listen to the radio for more instructions. I had a sore throat and I wanted to know if the air was poisonous. We were just told to wear a mask while we were outside.

5 2.16 Now listen to the conversation and compare it with the text in Exercise 4.

1 Is any of the information different?

2 Do the verb tenses change in the text?

3 What phrases are used to report the questions?

Reporting questions

When you report a question in the past, the tenses follow the same rules as for reported speech. See page 113. The word order of the question is the same as for a statement:

We wanted to know how long the eruptions *were going to* continue.

With yes/no questions, use *if* or *whether*:

I asked the emergency workers *if we were* safe.

We wanted to know whether we should leave.

I wanted to know if the air *was* poisonous..

See Grammar Reference, page 157

6 Read part of an interview below and complete the journalist's report that follows. Use reported questions and reported speech.

Journalist: How long have you been producing this newsletter?

David: I started it when I was at college. About five years ago.

Journalist: And what is your role?

David: I'm the reporter, photographer and editor! I do everything on my own!

Journalist: So, do you produce a weekly newsletter?

David: No, it comes out every two weeks. There wasn't one this week, but there will be one next week.

I began by asking how long David (**1**) _____. He said he (**2**) _____ about five years ago. Then I asked him (**3**) _____ and he told me that he was the reporter, photographer and editor and that he (**4**) _____ on his own. I wanted to know (**5**) _____ a newsletter every week. He said that (**6**) _____ every two weeks. He told me that there (**7**) _____ that week, but that there (**8**) _____ the following week.

7 Work in pairs. Interview your partner about school life. Use these questions:

How long …, Do you …, What …, Are you currently …, Can …

> Watch a video about living with a volcano. Turn to page 140.

Account 1: The cost of the Icelandic eruptions

Public imagination has long been captured by the volcanic eruption of Pompeii, which froze a whole civilisation in time, and Krakatoa, an eruption so strong that it was heard 3,500 km away and affected the global climate. However, the events in Iceland in 2010, although much smaller in scale, brought chaos to the business world.

The eruption of the Eyjafjöll volcano during March and April 2010 had serious and far-reaching effects. Although there was little damage and no reported fatalities, the eruption sent enough ash, steam and smoke into the air to have a serious impact on nearly the whole world. As the ash cloud spread, one country after another banned air-travel. They simply were not prepared to take the risk. European airspace was declared a no-fly zone, resulting in nearly 100,000 flights being cancelled. Millions of people across the world were affected, from holidaymakers who had no way of getting home to businessmen who had to cancel meeting after meeting. The cost to the airline industry was over one and a half billion US dollars. In Iceland, the cost of road repairs alone is said to be around one million dollars.

The travel restrictions affected the sports and entertainment industries, as events had to be cancelled. Transport companies that usually use air travel suffered severe delays as their journeys had to be completed by road. There were fears over food and medicine shortages in Britain. Car manufacturers in Germany and Japan had to suspend production while they waited for parts. A similar fate befell many factories throughout the world. Food items were destroyed because fresh produce could not be delivered. Travel and holiday companies went out of business. And at the very human end of the scale, many people the world over lost money, or their jobs, because of one or more of the above.

But there were some people for whom the travel ban was beneficial. Obviously, anyone involved in road or rail transportation was doing extra business during this period. Local producers in many parts of the world saw their sales figures rise as people were deprived of imported goods. People who live near airports got a sweet, brief reminder of what it was like to live in peace and quiet. And, of course, the media suddenly had a lot more people listening and watching and reading to find out the latest information. Just one more reminder that, in the media, bad news is good news!

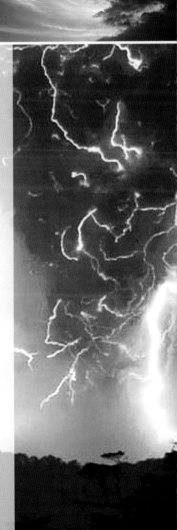

Account 2: Living in the shadow of a volcano

Living in Iceland, we are all well aware of volcanic activity and its effects – they are all around us. A fairly large eruption happens every few years, and they can be dramatic. My grandparents have told me about the eruption of January 1973 in the Westman Islands. Apparently 5,000 people were evacuated safely to the mainland but the eruption lasted for months and the main town was covered in lava and ash. At school, we learned about the massive eruption of Laki in 1783, when around 10,000 people died. But until you live through it, you never really know what to expect.

When the first eruptions happened, on 20th March 2010, my uncle phoned just before midnight to say that there was a red cloud above the mountain – a sign that there was an eruption taking place. Over the next few weeks, the activity continued on and off with explosions increasing in size. It was an amazing sight to see the obvious heat from the volcano and yet there was ice on the ground. The streams of water flowing with mud and ash and ice were quite dramatic. In fact, it was the possibility of flooding that presented the first sense of emergency, rather than the eruption itself. The river was swollen and it looked for a time as though the bridges were going to be washed away. We heard that people from a nearby village had been evacuated and the authorities had started closing roads. I only really panicked when I started to wonder how we would get away with so many roads unusable.

We asked the emergency workers if we were safe and they told us that they couldn't say for sure because nothing was certain. We wanted to know how long the eruptions were going to continue and whether we should leave. They said they didn't know, but that we should stay inside and listen to the radio for more instructions. I had a sore throat and I wanted to know if the air was poisonous. We were just told to wear a mask while we were outside. But, to be honest, even though we were quite close, we didn't suffer too much from the effects because of the way the wind was blowing.

The evacuated farmers were allowed back, and then people were told to leave again. And that was pretty much how it carried on, with roads closing and then opening, people being told to prepare to evacuate and then being told to stay where they were. Flights were cancelled and then the planes were flying again. A year later, in May 2011, the Grímsvötn volcano erupted, causing fear that the same thing was going to happen again. This event lasted just a few days, but it was yet another reminder that we can never fully relax.

9D Reporting your news

Listening: reporting what you've heard

1 Imagine these are some of the news items you and your friends might talk about this week. Which sound interesting? Which sound boring?

1 the current headmaster is leaving the school
2 someone in the government has lost his/her job
3 the football results from yesterday
4 a new TV show started last night
5 results for your last exam
6 an art show opening at a local gallery
7 the wind last night knocked over a tree outside the school

2 2.17 Listen to three conversations. Which news in Exercise 1 are they talking about?

3 2.17 Listen again and write in the missing words.

Conversation 1

A Hey, I've just (1) _____ something really amazing. Apparently, Mr Bruce is going to work at another school.

B Are you (2) _____?

A It's (3) _____! Esta told (4) _____ about it and then I (5) _____ Mrs Reese in maths (6) _____ it was true and she said it was.

B (7) _____! I wonder who'll take his job?

Conversation 2

A Did you see the game last night?

B No, what (8) _____?

A Well, they were losing three nil and they scored four in the last ten minutes.

B That's (9) _____.

Conversation 3

A (10) _____ you heard? You passed!

B What?

A You passed your English exam. You got 98 per cent!

B I don't (11) _____ it!

A It's on the wall outside the classroom. I saw it with my own (12) _____.

B No, you're (13) _____, aren't you?

A Honestly! I'm (14) _____ the truth. Look, here comes your teacher now. Ask him (15) _____.

Pronunciation: sounding surprised

4 2.18 Intonation is important with these expressions for responding to a speaker. Listen and tick which expression (a or b) sounds very surprised.

		a	b
1	No, what happened?	☐	☐
2	Wow!	☐	☐
3	That's incredible!	☐	☐
4	You're joking.	☐	☐
5	Are you sure?	☐	☐
6	I don't believe it.	☐	☐

5 2.19 Listen again to the sentences where the speaker sounds surprised and repeat.

6 Work in pairs.

Student A: Listen to three pieces of surprising news from Student B and respond.

Student B: You have three pieces of surprising news for Student A. Turn to page 143.

7 Swap roles. Student A turn to page 141.

8 Write three pieces of news. Two pieces must be true and one piece must be untrue. Then work in pairs and take turns to tell each other your news. Can you guess which news is untrue?

USEFUL EXPRESSIONS reporting what you've heard

Getting interest
Did you see / hear about …?
Have you heard / seen …?
I've just heard something really … (amazing / crazy / surprising)!

Responding to news
No, what happened?	*You're joking.*
Wow!	*Are you sure?*
That's incredible!	*I don't believe it.*

Convincing
It's true!	*Ask him/her yourself.*
I saw it with my own eyes.	*Honestly! I'm telling the truth.*

Reporting conversations
I heard about if from …	*He/She told me …*
They said that …	*I said to him/her …*
I asked …	*He/She asked me if …*

Writing: a film review

9 Discuss as a class.

1 Where do you normally watch films? At the cinema? On TV? On the Internet?

2 What kinds of films do you like? Which film is everyone talking about at the moment?

10 When you write a film review, it should answer some or all of these questions:

- Which film is it about?
- What sort of film is it?
- What happens? What is the basic plot?
- What famous actors are in it?
- Who directed it?
- Could it be improved in any way?
- What is the aim of the film e.g. to entertain / to inform / to make a statement?
- Does the reviewer like it? Why? Why not?

Read this review from a film blog. Which of the questions does it answer?

The King's Speech, directed by Tom Hooper, is not what you might call a <u>blockbuster</u>. There are no <u>computer-generated</u> <u>special effects</u> to thrill the audience. Instead, despite its relatively slow <u>pace</u>, it is an enjoyable and thought-provoking <u>period drama</u> set in the 1920s and 30s. It is also a true story.

Colin Firth plays the Duke of York, known as Bertie, who has been brought up to believe that his older brother, Edward, would one day be the King of England. However, the <u>plot</u> takes a twist when Edward cannot continue as king, and Bertie is forced to step into the role. But Bertie has a problem – he has a dreadful stammer – and this was at a time when radio was new, so the Royal Family were expected to address the nation through the new sound medium.

In the opening <u>scenes</u>, the young duke stands in front of a microphone talking to a huge crowd and, via radio, broadcasting live to the nation. The embarrassment is obvious as he fails to get the words out and radios across the country fall silent. Bertie's wife (played by Helena Bonham Carter) gets professional help in the form of therapist Lionel Logue (Geoffrey Rush) and the <u>storyline</u> explores the unlikely friendship that develops between the two men as Bertie struggles to overcome his disability.

Perhaps younger viewers might find it lacking in action, but if you're looking for first-class acting with excellent characters, *The King's Speech* is well worth watching.

11 Match the underlined film words in the review to these definitions.

1 the speed something happens   *pace*
2 a very expensive film with lots of action (often made in Hollywood)
3 moments in film which use technology to make something seem real
4 all the parts of the film in different locations
5 film set in the past
6 the story
7 created by computer technology
8 another word for plot

12 When writing a film review, it's important to use interesting adjectives. Use the adjectives in the box to replace the less interesting adjectives in bold to improve sentences 1–5.

> high-speed   fascinating   huge   successful
> spectacular

1 The special effects are **good**. They look so real!
2 The film has a **fast** plot. It never stops!
3 It has an **interesting** storyline.
4 He is a **good** director. He's made lots of famous films.
5 This film will become a **big** blockbuster.

13 Write a review of a film you have seen recently. Write 200–250 words. Remember that your review should answer some or all the questions in Exercise 10 and try to use interesting adjectives.

Reading

1 Look at these pictures of historical events.
How many of them have you read or heard about?

2 Match the pictures A–F to each paragraph on page 119.

3 Match these sentences to the gaps 1–5 in the texts. There is one extra incorrect sentence.

A People were fascinated by the event and were hungry for even the smallest details.

B One reason was that he spoke directly to the viewer.

C Anyone with a television switched it on to watch this event of the century.

D As a result the local government soon closed it down.

E No one had seen the news this way before.

F In 1903, he transmitted a signal across the Atlantic for the first time.

4 Match the words in bold in the text to the definitions.

1 the moment that the facts appeared in the news
2 arranged events when someone speaks to a group of journalists
3 transmitted
4 news media not controlled by the government
5 detailed analysis and information about a news story
6 an attempt to hide information
7 TV stations that only show non-stop news
8 information from people who saw the event
9 twenty-four hours a day

Speaking

5 Discuss as a class.

1 Which newspaper or news channel do you watch or read for in-depth coverage? Does it report around the clock?

2 Do you have independent media in your country? Do you think news media can ever be 100% independent?

6 Work in groups. Imagine you are the editors for a 24-hour news channel. Today your reporters have sent in five news stories. Decide which stories you will …

A break immediately.
B broadcast on the main news in about an hour.
C broadcast if you have time.
D not broadcast at all.

1 The President gave a press conference to journalists about the state of the economy.

2 A famous pop music celebrity has had plastic surgery.

3 Spain's football team drew 1–1 with Germany in a World Cup qualifier.

4 The temperature today was the hottest ever recorded in US history.

5 A lion has escaped from London Zoo.

Compare what you have decided with the rest of the class.

The first American colony landed in Jamestown in 1607, but it wasn't until September 25, 1690 that they had their own newspaper. However, there was only one issue because it was published without the authority of the King of England. (**1**) ___ The colonists tried to produce more newspapers including *The Boston Gazette* which became one of the leading newspapers of the revolutionaries in the War of Independence. It was also possibly one of the first examples of **independent media**.

The Italian inventor Guglielmo Marconi developed his radio telegraph system during the end of the nineteenth and the beginning of the twentieth century. (**2**) ___ Perhaps the most famous moment for Marconi's new media was with the disaster at sea of the Titanic on her voyage to the USA. As the ocean liner sank, two radio operators employed by Marconi broadcast SOS messages and ships rushed to try and rescue survivors, who were taken to New York. At the enquiry afterwards, one person said: 'Those who have been saved, have been saved through one man, Mr Marconi … and his marvellous invention.'

John F. Kennedy is often said to be the first US President who knew how to use the medium of television effectively. (**3**) ___ While running for the presidency he held over 60 TV **press conferences**. He also won the first ever live TV debate against his rival Richard Nixon. Ironically, Kennedy was assassinated in 1963 and the whole event was **broadcast** by TV news cameras. From that moment onwards, TV became *the* medium for breaking news.

(**4**) ___ As Neil Armstrong became the first man to step on the moon audiences were amazed not only to see pictures from the surface of the moon but also to hear the iconic words: 'That's one small step for man, one giant leap for mankind.' Nowadays broadcasts from space seem quite normal but then it was a technical miracle.

In 1974, two reporters from *The Washington Post* newspaper discovered that there was a government **cover-up** of a crime and that the President, Richard Nixon, had lied. When **the news broke**, the scandal, known as 'Watergate', forced the President to resign. The two reporters became famous for their **in-depth coverage** and it took investigative journalism to new levels.

In the run-up to the wedding of Prince William to Kate Middleton in 2011, **24-hour news channels** gave regular updates on the preparations **around the clock**. (**5**) ___ There was frequent talk about such things as who was on the guest list (and who wasn't) and how the bride was going to wear her hair. The wedding itself was, of course, a major TV spectacle. In the USA, over 20 million people watched live coverage and **eye-witness reports** (on breakfast television due to the time difference). Worldwide, it has been estimated that up to two billion people saw the wedding.

Everyday English

On the television

Listening and speaking

1 Work in pairs and discuss the questions.

1 Do you like watching TV with your family? What kinds of programmes do you watch together?

2 Do you think families watch too much TV? What could this family be doing instead?

2 What are your three favourite TV shows? What type of TV show are they? Match them to the types in the box.

> cartoon   documentary
> soap opera   sport   quiz show
> news and current affairs
> reality show   drama series

3 Look at this page from a TV listings magazine.

1 Which different types of TV show can you find?

2 Which programmes would you watch?

4 2.20 Listen to conversation between Katy and Jack. Tick the person for each question.

	Who …	Katy	Jack
1	is watching *The Blue Planet*?		
2	wants to change the channel?		
3	wants to watch the longest programme?		
4	can watch *The Street* on Sunday?		
5	likes a reality TV show?		

5 Work in groups of four. You are a family in the same house with only one television. Read the information on page 141 or 143. Then discuss with the family what everyone is watching tonight on the TV guide in Exercise 3. Try to agree and negotiate if you have to!

Student A: Turn to page 141

Student B: Turn to page 143

Student C: Turn to page 141

Student D: Turn to page 143

	EuroTV	BBC	Channel 3	FX N
6–7	6.00 Blue Planet: Another look at nature under the sea	6.00 Beat the teacher: Four more students compete against their teachers	6.00 National and international news	see
		6.30 The mystery of Sherlock Holmes: The detective solves another crime.	6.30 Wimbledon: Highlights from matches at today's tennis tournament	
7–8	7.00 Who wants to be a millionaire: Another contestant tries to win a million		7.00 Leave me in the jungle: Another celebrity must leave the jungle. Who will it be this week?	7.0 De
		7.30 Local news and weather	7.30 Download Top Ten: Watch music videos of the ten best-selling songs this week	
		7.40 World Cup qualifying match: Spain vs England		
8–9	8.00 The Street: Danny tells Sandra to leave and Wendy has a secret		8.15 Streets of Miami: More action and crime for the Miami police	8.20 Mor
	8.30 The Politics Show: Interview with the Finance Minister about the state of the economy			
9–10	9.00 The Simpsons: More madness from animation family		9.15 Make me beautiful: This week Sally has plastic surgery on her face	9.0 Ma
	9.30 News	9.20 Where are the bees? Scientists try to find out why bees are disappearing from the Earth		

USEFUL EXPRESSIONS watching television

Saying what you want to watch

I want to watch …   *I'd rather watch …*
It's time for …   *We have to watch it.*
It's my turn to watch …   *I always watch … on (Tuesdays).*

Negotiating

But … / We agreed that I could watch … / But they repeat it on …
My show finishes at … / It's only on until …
Then you can watch …
You can watch … if / as long as / on condition that I can watch …

10

Technology changing our world

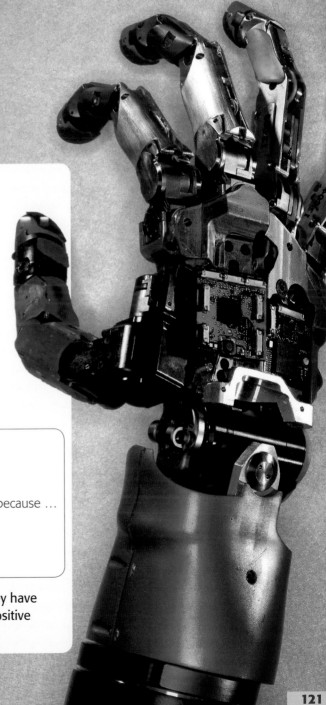

In this unit you will learn

- **Communication**: buying equipment, describing computer problems, calling a helpline
- **Vocabulary**: technology, bionics
- **Reading and Listening**: fame on the Internet, Mary Shelley's *Frankenstein*
- **Writing**: short story
- **Grammar**: verb patterns, conditionals: zero, first, second, third

Let's get started

1 Work in pairs and discuss the following.

1 What technology can you see in the picture?

2 How could it change and improve people's lives?

3 Tell your partner about a time when technology helped you.

2 In the same pairs, make sentences about recent inventions using the words in the table and giving your own reasons.

Example:

Computers have changed work because more people can work from home.

The Internet has improved shopping because you can buy products online.

computers the Internet engines mobile phones TV fast food technology	has have	affected changed destroyed improved speeded up helped	work education shopping the environment transport people's lives	because …

3 Think of two more modern inventions and explain how they have affected the world in some way. Have the changes been positive or negative?

10A Bionics

Vocabulary

1 Study these pairs of technology words. Parts of the words are similar or have similar meaning. Can you guess the difference? Match the words to definition a or b.

1 device / gadget
   a an object or machine for a special purpose
   b a small machine for a special purpose

2 biology / biotechnology
   a the study of living things
   b the use of living things (e.g. DNA) in industry

3 electronics / electrodes
   a the use of electric energy in technology
   b the point where electric energy enters or leaves (e.g. at a battery)

4 network / networking
   a the activity of communicating with lots of different people
   b a large system with many parts which connect people and places (e.g. roads, telephones)

5 wire / cables
   a long thin metal surrounded in plastic to carry electricity
   b a collection of wires covered in plastic to carry electricity, telephone signals, the Internet, etc.

6 motor / engine
   a device that changes electricity into movement
   b a machine that uses fuel to produce movement

7 software / hardware
   a the physical and electronic parts of a computer
   b instructions or program which controls a computer

Speaking

2 Work in groups and discuss these questions.

1 How much technology do you use in your daily life? Is it important to you?

2 Which are the most useful devices or gadgets in your house? Which is your favourite gadget?

3 Which of the devices or gadgets you answered in 2 need
   • wires or cables?   • electronic components?
   • motors?   • software?

Afterwards, summarise and present your answers to the class.

Listening

3 ⊙ 2.21 Listen to a documentary about the woman in the picture and answer the questions.

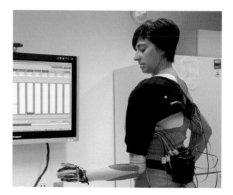

1 What kind of technology does she use?

2 How has it changed her life?

4 ⊙ 2.21 Listen again and answer 1–5. Circle A, B, C or D.

1 Amanda Kitts is …
   A unemployed.   C a doctor.
   B a scientist.   D a teacher.

2 The arm is …
   A silent.   C complex technology.
   B only made of plastic. D noisy.

3 What controls the movement of her arm?
   A her shoulder   C her hand
   B her brain   D electrodes

4 Bionics is also helping people who have difficulties with their …
   A sight.   C movement.
   B hearing.   D answers A, B and C

5 Bionics …
   A always works perfectly.
   B also helps memory loss.
   C is successful with every patient.
   D is helping to improve some people's lives.

Grammar: *allow, let, make*

5 Match the two halves of the sentences from the documentary.

1 The technology allows Amanda ___

2 The electronic device lets Eric ___

3 The message from the brain makes ___

a her elbow bend.

b move his fingers.

c to touch and feel things.

Read the grammar summary and check your answers.

---

allow, let, make

Use *allow* and *let* to say something can happen and nothing can stop it:

- *allow + object + to infinitive: allow it to move*
- *let + object + infinitive: let it move*

(Note: *allow* is slightly more formal than *let*.)

Use *make + object + infinitive* to say something causes or forces something else to happen: *make it move*

See Grammar Reference, page 157

6 Write *allow*, *let* or *make* in this text. Change the form of the word where necessary.

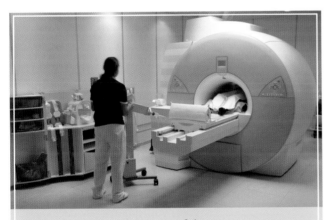

MRI Scanners have been one of the most important inventions in recent years because they
(**1**) _____ doctors see three dimensional images of inside the body. Unlike X-rays, which normally photograph bones or hard tissue, Magnetic Resonance Imaging (**2**) _____ you to study softer tissue such as the brain. If you ever go for an MRI scan, the doctor will (**3**) _____ you remove any metal or electronic objects such as jewellery because the scanner is basically a giant magnet. The patient lies inside the scanner and the doctor sits in another room but there is a speaker system which (**4**) _____ you to communicate with each other. Often, the hospital (**5**) _____ a member of your family stay with you during the process. That can be good – especially if being inside the scanner (**6**) _____ you claustrophobic and nervous!

7 Work in pairs. Look at these pictures of technology and gadgets. Make sentences with *allow*, *let* and *make* to explain what they are for.

Example:

It makes the TV switch on … / It allows you to change channels without moving … etc.

8 Think of three more objects. Prepare sentences using *allow*, *let* or *make* about each one.

When you are ready, work with a partner. Read one sentence. Your partner has to guess what the object is.

Example:

A It allows you to travel very quickly from one place to another.

B Is it a car?

A No. It makes some people feel scared when it takes off!

B A plane!

A Correct.

10B Buying technology

Listening

1 Read this short article and then discuss the questions in pairs.

1 Does the information in the article surprise you?

2 Is the situation similar in your country?

3 Why do you think children feel they need to take these types of gadgets to school?

4 Should the school allow them?

School bags in UK contain more technology than ever!

British school children go to school with bags containing as much as £400 worth of gadgets, research suggests. Almost half of pupils carry mobile phones (average price £50). One in four has a digital music player which can cost £100. One child in 20 takes video games to school. And the really bad news for parents is that children lose these items as easily as their pens and books.

2 2.22 Listen to three conversations. Match the conversation to the technology.

 A  B  C

3 2.22 Listen again and decide if the statements are true or false.

		True	False
Conversation 1			
1	Neither person understands how the device works.		
2	You answer the phone by pressing the green button.		
Conversation 2			
3	The salesperson suggests how the customer might use it.		
4	There is one version of this device.		
Conversation 3			
5	The customer thinks the price is reasonable.		
6	They try to negotiate a better price.		

Grammar: zero, first and second conditionals

4 2.23 Listen again and write in the missing words in these sentences from the conversations.

1 When you _____ it, _____ this button.

2 You _____ when it _____ ringing.

3 If you _____ any more problems with it, _____ me.

4 If I still _____ it in seven days, _____ I change it or get my money back?

5 If you _____ this model, it _____ all of that.

6 This one _____ a larger memory unless you _____ to add some memory to this one?

7 If you _____ it today, we _____ you a discount price of 10 per cent.

8 If it _____ half the normal price, I _____ interested.

9 What if I _____ a DVD player with some new DVDs? _____ you _____ to that?

5 Read the grammar summary on page 125 and write what type of conditional sentences each sentence is in Exercise 4. Write 0, 1 or 2:

0 = zero conditional

1 = first conditional

2 = second conditional

6 Write the correct form of the verb in brackets.

1 When the battery runs out of charge, this light _____ (**go**) out.

2 If the DVD _____ (**not / be**) compatible for this region, the machine doesn't play it.

3 If you decide you don't like the product, we _____ (**give**) you your money back.

4 Old people won't understand modern technology if they _____ (**not / use**) it.

5 Don't pay any extra for the software unless you _____ (**have to**).

6 More people _____ (**use**) robots in the home if they were cheap to buy.

7 If there was a signal, I _____ (**call**) Peter on my mobile.

Conditionals (zero, first and second)

Zero conditional

We use the zero conditional to talk about facts or things that are always true. The verb is in a present tense in both clauses: *If you **turn** left, the supermarket **is** on the right.*

First conditional

We use the first conditional to talk about actions / situations that are likely to happen in the future or as a result of something. The verb in the *if-clause* is the present simple. The verb in the main clause is *will + infinitive*: *If you **buy** this today, we**'ll give** you a 10% discount.*

You can also use an imperative form in the main clause: *Call me if you have a problem with it.*

if or when?

When you talk about things which are generally true, you can use *if* or *when*. There's no difference:

When you press / If you press the green button, it switches on.

However, if you talk about future situations, the meaning can change:

When you have a problem with it, call me. (= The speaker definitely expects it to happen.)

If you have a problem with it, call me. (= The speaker thinks it's possible but not certain to happen.)

unless

unless = if … not

*I'll buy it from you **unless** I see it somewhere cheaper. = I'll buy it from you if I **don't** see it somewhere cheaper.*

Second conditional

We use the second conditional to talk about imaginary situations or unlikely situations now or in the future. The verb in the main clause uses *would + infinitive*. The verb in the *if-clause* is in a past tense: *I**'d buy** it from you if it **was** cheaper.*

Note! Sometimes we use *were* with *he/she/it* with second conditional sentences: *I'd buy it from you if it **were** cheaper.*

Punctuation

When you begin with the *if-clause*, put a comma before the *main clause.*

See Grammar Reference, page 158

7 Match the two halves of the sentences.

1 If you want to get from my house to school, turn
2 My friends and I will go out later unless
3 If I found a large amount of money in the street
4 What would you do if
5 What will you pay me if

a I'd take it to the police station.
b you could visit anywhere in the world?
c I sell you my stamp collection?
d I have to do some jobs at home.
e left down Wood Street and walk for about ten minutes.

8 Work in pairs. Make more sentences with 1–5 in Exercise 7 that are true for you. Then tell your partner.

9 Work in groups of three. In each conversation, two students talk and try to use lots of conditional forms. The third student listens and counts how many conditional forms he/she hears.

Conversation 1 (Student C listens and counts):
Student A: Lend Student B your mobile phone.
Student B: Ask Student A how it works.
Student A: Give instructions.

Conversation 2 (Student A listens and counts):
Student B: You want to go to the cinema tonight with C. Suggest your plan and a film.
Student C: You're really busy tonight and you don't want to see B's suggested film. Suggest another night and a different film.
Student B: Respond to C's suggestion.

Conversation 3 (Student B listens and counts):
Student C: You want to borrow and watch Student A's new DVD. Offer A something.
Student A: Ask for something extra as well.
Student C and A: Make a deal.

After the three conversations, tell each other how many times you used a conditional form.

10C The Internet – a good idea!

Speaking

1 Discuss in groups.

1 How much time do you spend on the Internet?

2 What do you use it for?

3 What are your favourite sites?

Reading

2 Look at this series of stills from YouTube. What is the man, Matthew Harding, doing in the middle of each one?

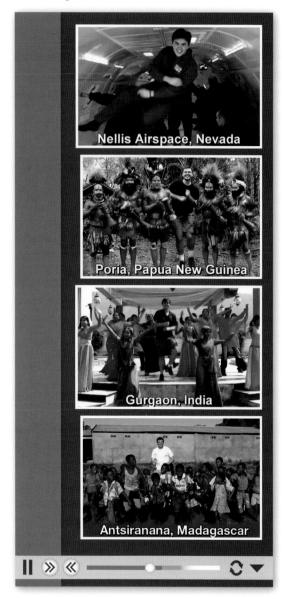

Nellis Airspace, Nevada

Poria, Papua New Guinea

Gurgaon, India

Antsiranana, Madagascar

3 Find out more about Matthew Harding. Read the article and number paragraphs A–G in the correct order from 1–6.

Example:

F = 1

Where is ...
Matthew?

A___

A few months into his trip, Matthew and a friend were taking pictures in Hanoi, and his friend said 'Why don't you stand over there and do that dance. I'll record it.' He was referring to a particular dance Matthew does. It's actually the only dance he does and he does it badly. Anyway, this turned out to be a very good idea because if Matthew hadn't agreed to dance at that moment, then the following story would never have happened.

B___

Things settled down again, and then in 2007 Matthew went back to Stride Gum with another idea. He realised his bad dancing wasn't actually all that interesting, and that other people were much better at being bad at it. He showed them his inbox, which was full of emails from all over the planet. He told them he wanted to travel around the world one more time and invite the people who'd emailed him to come and dance with him.

C___

A couple of years later, someone found the video online and passed it to someone else, who passed it to someone else, and so on. Now Matthew is semi-famous as 'That guy who dances on the Internet.'

D___

In 2006, Matthew took a six-month trip through 39 countries on all seven continents. In that time, he danced a great deal. The second video made him even more famous on the Internet.

E___

The Stride Gum people thought that sounded like yet another very good idea, so they let him do it. And he did. Now, Matthew lives in Seattle, Washington and he hasn't had a real job since Stride Gum called him. He doesn't mind working, but he doesn't much care for having to show up at the same place every day.

F _1_

Matthew is a 33-year-old from Connecticut who used to think that all he ever wanted to do in life was make and play videogames. He achieved this goal pretty early and enjoyed it for a while, but eventually realised there might be other stuff he was missing out on. In February of 2003, he quit his job in Brisbane, Australia and used the money he'd saved to wander around Asia until it ran out. He made this site so he could keep his family and friends updated about where he was.

G___

Because the first video received so much attention, the owners of the product Stride Gum asked Matthew if he'd be interested in taking another trip around the world to make a new video. Matthew asked if they'd be paying for it. They said yes. He thought this sounded like another very good idea.

4 Read the text again and decide if these statements are true or false.

		True	False
1	Matthew's website began as a way to keep in contact with his family and friends.		
2	It was Matthew's idea to make the first film of him dancing.		
3	Lots of people watch Matthew on the Internet because he is such a good dancer.		
4	Stride Gum have paid Matthew twice to travel round the world.		
5	Matthew has never had to work in his life.		

Grammar: third conditional

5 Look at this sentence from the article and answer the two questions about the sentence:

'If Matthew hadn't agreed to dance at that moment, then the following story would never have happened.'

- Did Matthew agree to dance or not?
- Does the sentence describe something that actually happened or an imaginary situation?

Third conditional

We use the third conditional form to talk about unreal and imaginary results in the past. Form it with the *if + past perfect* and *would have + past participle* in the main clause:

If I **had thought** of that, I **would have travelled** round the world.

Matthew **wouldn't have done** it if his friend **hadn't asked**.

Would you **have danced** with Matthew if you**'d known** he was in your country?

Note that we often use the contracted forms of **would** ('d) and **had** ('d) in conversation. They both look the same, so try not to confuse them!

If I**'d** seen Matthew, I**'d** have danced with him.

See Grammar Reference, page 158

6 Write the verbs in the correct form in 1–6.

1 If he _____ (**dance**) well, he _____ (**not become**) famous.

2 If we _____ (**think**) of Matthew's idea, we _____ (**travel**) all over the world.

3 They _____ (**watch**) the video if the website _____ (**work**).

4 If I _____ (**not / click**) on this link, my computer _____ (**not / got**) a virus.

5 If I _____ (**do**) my homework last night, I _____ (**not / be**) in trouble this morning.

6 _____ (**you / come**) to my party last weekend if I _____ (**ask**) you?

Pronunciation: contracted forms in the third conditional

7 ◯ 2.24 Listen and repeat the following sentences. In some sentences the speaker uses contracted forms.

8 Work in pairs. Which of these happened to you recently?

- you came to school on your bicycle this morning
- you scored 100% on your last English test
- you won 10,000 euros on the lottery last week
- you went to the cinema at the weekend
- your family had a holiday in another country

Now make sentences in the third conditional depending on if it happened or didn't happen.

Example:

'I didn't come to school on a bicycle. If I had come to school on my bicycle, it would have taken me about half an hour.'

'I came to school on my bicycle. If I hadn't come to school on my bicycle, my parents would have brought me in the car.'

Speaking

1 Work in pairs. Look at the cartoons and discuss this opinion: 'Computers, the TV and the Internet are destroying families.' Do you agree or disagree? Give your opinion.

2 Look at this list of common problems people have with their computer. Match the underlined words in 1–7 with the definitions a–e.

1 There's nothing on the screen. It's completely <u>blank</u>.

2 The computer has <u>crashed</u> again and the screen has <u>frozen</u>.

3 The Internet is very slow today. I can't download any music or watch videos.

4 My keyboard isn't working properly. When I press the pound key I get a dollar symbol.

5 I think my laptop might have a <u>virus</u>.

6 I tried to <u>log on</u> but I've forgotten my password.

7 My computer has just turned itself off! I didn't press anything.

a sign in using a username and password

b stopped working

c no colour or pictures

d computer software designed to damage another computer

e not moving or changing

3 Tick the problems mentioned in Exercise 2 that you have had with your computer. Compare your list with other students.

4 Work in pairs. Choose from these responses and match them to the problems in Exercise 2. You can choose more than one response.

1 Have you spilled anything on it?

2 Did you write it down anywhere?

3 Have you tried running any anti-virus software?

4 If you restart it, does it work?

5 Try recharging the battery or plugging it in.

6 You should take it back to the shop.

5 Practise a short conversation in pairs.

Student A: Read out different computer problems in Exercise 2.

Student B: Close your book and respond to Student A. Try to suggest a solution to A's computer problems.

Afterwards, change roles and repeat the exercise.

USEFUL EXPRESSIONS describing computer problems

> *There's a problem with …*
> *… isn't working / doesn't work.*
> *My screen is blank / frozen.*
> *The computer has crashed.*
> *The Internet is slow.*
> *If I do X, it does Y.*
> **Suggesting solutions**
>
> *Did you …*   *If you do X, does it*
>   *do Y?*
>
> *Have you …*   *You should …*
> *Try … –ing.*

Writing: a short story

6 Read this short story. Afterwards, discuss the answers to these questions.

1 Who is telling the story? A narrator using the first person (I, me) or a third-person narrator (he, she, it)?

2 Are there a lot of different locations? How many are there?

3 Are there a lot of different characters? How many are there?

4 Is the story over a short or long period of time?

5 Does the writer use dialogue?

6 Is the ending satisfying? Why? Why not?

7 Prepare to write a short story ending with the words: 'If I hadn't complained in the first place, none of it would have happened!'

Before you write, make notes on these questions to help you plan.

- Where is the action?
- Who are the characters?
- What or who do you complain about?
- What happens because of your complaint?
- What do you learn as a result?

8 Now write your story (200–250 words). Use the Tip box on page 143 to help you.

Press one for a new life

I'd been staring at the screen for three hours. Nothing. It was dead. And for what had seemed like another three hours – though was probably more like fifteen minutes – I'd been trying to get through to the computer helpline. 'Press one to hear options. Press two to leave a message. Press three to hear those choices again.' But what was I supposed to press to speak to a human?! Enough was enough. I was going back to the shop where I bought it and tell them exactly what I thought of their Neutron Mega Memory XJ40.

The shop was huge. There were different departments for mobiles, mobiles with extras, mobiles without extras, DVDs, CDs, 3-D DVDs, laptops, laptops that were the size of phones (not laps), laptops that were phones, phones that weren't laptops but could do everything a laptop could. So where did I have to go? There was a human being in a blue shirt standing by the Computer Accessories department.

'Can you help me? I bought this computer but it doesn't work.'

'Are you sure?' he replied, as if I were not a human.

'Yes, I'm sure. The screen is blank.'

'Did you switch it on?'

I was amazed at how rude this person was.

'Customer Service desk,' he said, pointing across to the corner furthest away from us at the back of the shop.

The desk marked Customer Service turned out to be the busiest part of the shop. There were customers holding every type of electronic gadget you can imagine. At the back of the queue, there was a faceless machine which spoke as you arrived: 'Welcome to customer service. To help us with your enquiry, go to desk one for mobiles phones, desk two for audio equipment, desk three for laptops and computers …'

Thankfully, the queue at desk three only had one person in it who was more angry than me and stormed off in furious rage after only two minutes of talking to the woman at customer service. I prepared myself. I had my speech. I was ready to demand a refund. I was ready to be the angriest person she'd ever dealt with. But she looked tired. I was obviously the millionth person she'd met that day. And before I could say anything she began …

'It doesn't work properly, does it?'

'Err, no.' This was not the conversation I'd planned.

'No. They never do. Day after day people come here, buy something, come back with it and they come to the back of the shop to this desk and tell me.'

Suddenly, in that moment, the girl at the back of the shop seemed human. She had brown hair and a sad smile. I suddenly understood what it was like to have a job where the only thing you hear all day is people complaining.

'Why don't you leave?' I suggested.

'I'm saving money to go to college. If I work here another month I'll have enough.'

'But you could work in a shop which sells products that work. Or make people happy. That brings people together. Like a coffee shop.'

'Yes, I see what you mean.'

Our conversation continued like this for some time: with me trying to solve her problems and her mood slowly improving. Later that day, Jane quit her job and is now working at the coffee shop across from my house. I got all the money back for my computer and now I have a laptop that works. I even see Jane every morning as I sit with my cappuccino at the café window and check my emails. She finishes work early today, so I think I'll stay here until then. Maybe she'll want to go to the cinema or something …

10E Frankenstein

Listening

1 Discuss as a class. Have you ever read *Frankenstein* or seen a film adaptation? What do you know about the story?

2 🔊 2.25 **Listen to a short lecture about the book** *Frankenstein*. **What do you think is the best title for this lecture? Choose a, b or c.**

a Why Mary Shelley wrote *Frankenstein*.

b Why *Frankenstein* is still relevant today.

c Famous film adaptations of *Frankenstein*.

3 🔊 2.25 **Listen again and choose an answer for questions 1–5.**

1 Nowadays, *Frankenstein* is _____ when it was written.

    A as popular as

    B more popular than

    C not as popular as

    D less popular than

2 The speaker suggests Mary Shelley's career ended because …

    A her husband was upset.

    B her husband died.

    C she only wrote one book.

    D of the invention of cinema.

3 Very few people have …

    A read *Frankenstein*.

    B seen the film versions.

    C read poetry.

    D read other books by Mary Shelley.

4 The film versions are different from the original book because …

    A they are about bringing the dead to life.

    B Frankenstein is the monster.

    C Frankenstein runs from the monster.

    D they show a monster that is crazy.

5 The speaker believes the book is important nowadays because it deals with issues which are similar to the ethical problems of …

    A society.

    B genes.

    C cloning.

    D monsters.

4 Now read part of the book. Add these missing sentences. There are two extra sentences.

A And so I began the creation of a human being.

B The day of my departure arrived and the journey was long and tiring.

C Then, on a dark evening in November I finally finished.

D I had created a terrible monster.

E It was a question which every great scientist has called a mystery.

F They have discovered how blood circulates and how we breathe.

G The creature suddenly came to life and attacked me.

5 Work in groups. Discuss these questions about the story.

- How would you describe Frankenstein? What kind of a person is he?

- What moments in the story change him the most?

- How does his attitude to his creation suddenly change at the end? Why do you think it changes?

Now summarise your views for the class and compare them with other groups.

130

When I was 17, my parents decided that I should become a student at the University of Ingolstadt. My father decided it would be good for me to study in another country and so learn about the customs of another culture. (1) _____

The next morning I attended my first lecture. Professor Waldman was about 50 years of age, short and his voice was sweet to listen to. He began his lecture, which was a history of chemistry, with a description of modern chemistry: 'Modern scientists have performed miracles. They have looked into the **recesses** of nature and shown how she works in her hiding-places. (2) _____ They have new and almost unlimited powers.' As the professor talked, my mind became filled with one thought. So much has been done but I – Victor Frankenstein – will achieve more, far more. I will find a new way, explore unknown powers and discover the deepest mysteries of creation!

From that day, chemistry became my only occupation. I read with **ardour**, I attended lectures and developed friendships only with men of science at the university. My progress was **rapid**. I astonished other students with my knowledge and my proficiency soon equalled the professor's. Two years passed in this way. Towards the end of this period, I started to ask myself: 'How can we create life?' (3) _____ I read books about the science of anatomy but this was not enough. I concluded that to understand life, you must first understand death. How do we die? To answer this, I must study real human flesh myself.

At night I visited graveyards and studied bodies. I saw how men became wasted. I saw how worms enter into the eyes and brains. I discovered how the muscles and veins worked but – greater than this – I also discovered something that the wisest men since the creation of the world had not. I had the power to **reanimate** dead flesh. No one can imagine the variety of feelings which pushed me forward, like a hurricane. I would break the boundaries between life and death. A new species would call

me its creator and I would bring life where, in the past, death had once seemed the only possibility. (4) _____ It was gigantic, made from different parts of dead bodies.

The summer months passed. It was the most beautiful season but my eyes did not notice it. I worked through autumn towards the winter. I ignored others and behaved as if I was guilty of a crime. (5) _____ I prepared to put life into the lifeless thing. With all the instruments of life around me, I sent **a spark** into the creature. In the fading light I saw the yellow eye of the creature open. It breathed hard, and its limbs moved slightly.

What a catastrophe! What had I done? I had worked hard for two years with the **sole** purpose of **infusing** life into an **inanimate** body. For two years I had **deprived myself** of rest and health. And now I had finished, the beauty of the dream vanished and horror and **disgust** filled my heart. I was unable to look at the being I had created and rushed from the room.

---

ardour great enthusiasm

recesses hidden places

reanimate make something move again

inanimate not moving, not alive

a spark electric charge

infusing putting, adding

rapid fast, quick

sole only

deprive oneself not allow yourself something (e.g. food, rest)

disgust a feeling of dislike for something

Case Study 5 〉 Connecting the world

EARLY DAYS

In the nineteenth century, the telegraph system grew alongside the rail network, with messages being sent down cables which ran alongside the track. Morse code meant that train stations could communicate with each other and pass messages along the track. The following strange story is linked to the use of the telegraph and is believed to be the first use of this system in solving a crime. In 1839, a murder was committed and the killer was seen getting on a train. By sending a message via telegraph to Paddington station, the telegraph operator was able to say where the man was sitting and give his description, which was handed to the police. He was arrested soon after he arrived in London. Of course, the telegraph soon gave way to the telephone and if we hadn't invented the telephone, we would not have developed the Internet.

SCIENCE FICTION

In 1946, Murray Leinster wrote a science fiction short story called *A Logic Named Joe*. The story describes a network of machines that are connected together in order to provide people with information, news and entertainment. In other words, he predicted the Internet. Part of the plot is that people can get answers to all kinds of questions but most of the information given out is about how to make money and how to commit crimes. In the story the main character, who is a technician, manages to 'turn off' the Internet because he thinks the world was better before it. Sometimes I agree with him.

THE FUTURE OF THE INTERNET

It is very difficult to predict what will happen in the future because it depends on so many factors. If, for example, more governments control what people can do online, the power of the Internet will be greatly limited. It will no longer be truly worldwide. The same thing could happen if companies and service providers fail to agree. It will mean that some applications will only work on certain systems. We will be talking about internets (plural), rather than a world wide web. But if things keep going forward, anything will be possible – even pressing a button and having our shopping appear in front of us. The possibilities are only as limited as our imagination!

Morse code was written down as dots and dashes. The letter *s* (three short sounds) was represented by written as three dots (…). The letter *o* (three long sounds) was written using three dashes (---). So the well-known distress signal, SOS, would be three dots, three dashes and three dots (… --- …). Simple!

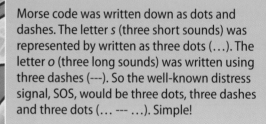

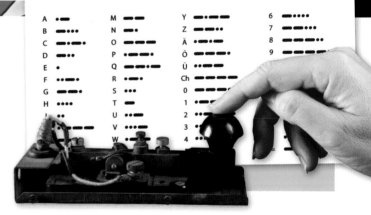

Morse Code

1 Read the three short texts above and find words or phrases which mean the same as the following:

1 next to _____
2 was replaced by _____
3 so that they can _____
4 storyline _____
5 considerations _____
6 specific; particular _____

2 Complete the following sentences using information from the texts and your own opinion.

1 If the telegraph operator had not described the murderer …
2 If the telephone hadn't been invented …
3 If you read the story *A Logic Named Joe* …
4 If the character in the science fiction story hadn't 'turned off' the Internet …
5 If governments interfere with the Internet …
6 If technology progresses …

3 In pairs or small groups, discuss these questions.

• What do you think life was like before the Internet? Was it better or worse?
• What do you think life would be like today if the Internet hadn't been invented?
• Do you think the Internet encourages people to commit crimes?
• What do you think will happen to the Internet in the future? What do these developments depend on?

Review > Unit 9

Grammar

1 Match the two halves of the questions.

1 I don't know what …   a you'd like to come with us.
2 I was wondering if …   b Lillian will come?
3 I'd like to know …   c where he found this.
4 Have you any idea …   d time it starts.
5 Do you think …   e where she is?

2 Rewrite the sentences in Exercise 1 as direct questions.

1 What time does it start?
2 Would _____?
3 Where _____?
4 Where _____?
5 Will _____?

3 Now rewrite the questions in Exercise 2 as reported questions.

1 They asked me what time
   _____.

2 She wanted to know if you
   _____.

3 Your teacher asked me where
   _____.

4 Catherine wanted to know
   _____.

5 He asked if
   _____.

Functions

4 Tick the correct response to the sentence.

1 I don't believe it.
   a But it's true!
   b Wow!

2 Did you see the news?
   a I saw it with my own eyes.
   b No, what happened?

3 I've just heard something really crazy!
   a Are you sure?
   b What?

4 That's incredible! Do you believe him?
   a Honestly! I'm telling the truth
   b Yes, I do but ask him yourself.

5 Sally is off work again.
   a You're joking.
   b It's true!

Vocabulary

5 Complete the crossword by using the clues or writing the missing word.

Across

2 We'll provide in-_____ coverage of all the latest news as it happens.
4 Transmit news by radio or TV.
6 Person who checks articles and decides where to put them in the newspaper.
7 Eye-_____ reports say the crash happened at six in the morning.

Down

1 Round-the-_____ news is on 24 hours a day.
3 Large words at the top of a newspaper article.
5 A newspaper which reports sensational news such as celebrity gossip etc.

Now I can …
☐ report news
☐ talk about media
☐ write a film review
☐ use indirect questions and reported speech

Review 〉 Unit 10

Grammar

1 Complete these sentences with answers A, B or C.

1 Put your money in the machine if you _____ a drink.

   A want   **B** will want   **C** would want

2 If you give them a euro, they _____ you one dollar thirty.

   A gave   **B** 'll give   **C** 'd give

3 If my parents _____ me more pocket money, I'd be able to afford a new camera.

   A pay   **B** paid   **C** will pay

4 If I knew my password, I _____ able to log on.

   A 'll be   **B** was   **C** 'd be

5 I _____ lend her any money if I were you. You'll never get it back!

   A won't   **B** didn't   **C** wouldn't

6 What if I _____ you the case for free? Would you buy the laptop then?

   A gave   **B** will give   **C** would give

7 If you _____ enough money, get some from the cash machine.

   A won't have **B** don't have **C** wouldn't have

2 Complete these sentences about you and your school.

1 The school doesn't allow us _____.

2 One teacher often makes us _____.

3 Sometimes my teacher lets me _____.

Vocabulary

3 Complete each sentence with one word.

1 If you connect this little *machine / gadget* to your computer, you can save all your files onto it.

2 On Mondays we have physics followed by *biology / bionics* at school.

3 This electric fan has a small *motor / engine* inside it which makes it turn.

4 Load the *software / hardware* and press start.

5 The workmen from the telephone company are outside laying *cables / wire* under the road so we can get the Internet.

6 My computer screen is *frozen / blank*. The cursor won't move.

Functions

4 Write the missing words in the responses.

> Did you   You should   Does it
> Have you   Try

1 **A** Why won't this load?

   B _____ tried restarting it?

2 **A** I called the helpline but they couldn't fix it either.

   B _____ ask them to send you a new one?

3 **A** The TV screen keeps going off.

   B _____ hitting it!

4 **A** This cable won't go in this hole.

   B _____ fit anywhere else?

5 **A** I bought this printer this morning but the colours are all blurred.

   B _____ take it back.

5 Put this conversation in the correct order from 1–8.

____ Yes, that's right.

____ Hello, customer service. How can I help you?

____ It's I, E, two, two, zero, A.

____ One moment. I'm just getting a pen and paper. OK. Go ahead.

____ Well, I'm calling because there's no sound on my laptop.

____ I see. What's the model number?

____ OK. I'm just checking now. Yes, there's a problem with this model. You'll need to download a file from our website. The address is …

____ That was I as in India, E as in echo, two, two, zero, A as in apple.

> ## Now I can …
>
> ☐ buy equipment
>
> ☐ describe computer problems
>
> ☐ talk about technological progress
>
> ☐ write a short story
>
> ☐ use verb patterns and the zero, first, second and third conditionals

Irregular verb list

Infinitive	Past simple	Past participle	My Language
be	was / were	been	
beat	beat	beaten	
become	became	become	
begin	began	begun	
bend	bent	bent	
bite	bit	bitten	
blow	blew	blown	
break	broke	broken	
bring	brought	brought	
broadcast	broadcast	broadcast	
build	built	built	
burn	burnt / burned	burnt / burned	
burst	burst	burst	
can	could	been able to	
catch	caught	caught	
choose	chose	chosen	
cost	cost	cost	
cut	cut	cut	
do	did	done	
draw	drew	drawn	
drive	drove	driven	
fall	fell	fallen	
feed	fed	fed	
feel	felt	felt	
fight	fought	fought	
find	found	found	
flee	fled	fled	
fly	flew	flown	
forget	forgot	forgotten	
forgive	forgave	forgiven	
freeze	froze	frozen	
grow	grew	grown	
have	had	had	
hang	hung	hung	
hear /ˈhɪə/	heard /hɜːd/	heard /hɜːd/	
hide	hid	hidden	
hit	hit	hit	
hold	held	held	
hurt	hurt	hurt	
keep	kept	kept	
know	knew	known	
lay	laid	laid	
lead	led	led	
leave	left	left	
lend	lent	lent	

Infinitive	Past simple	Past participle	My Language
let	let	let	
lie	lay	lain	
light	lit	lit	
lose	lost	lost	
mean /miːn/	meant /ment/	meant /ment/	
must	had to	had to	
misunderstand	misunderstood	misunderstood	
pay	paid	paid	
put	put	put	
read /riːd/	read /red/	read /red/	
ride	rode	ridden	
ring	rang	rung	
rise	rose	risen	
run	ran	run	
sell	sold	sold	
send	sent	sent	
set	set	set	
shake	shook	shaken	
shine	shone	shone	
shoot	shot	shot	
show	showed	shown	
shut	shut	shut	
sing	sang	sung	
sink	sank	sunk	
sit	sat	sat	
sleep	slept	slept	
slide	slid	slid	
spell	spelt / spelled	spelt / spelled	
spend	spent	spent	
spill	spilt	spilt	
split	split	split	
stand	stood	stood	
steal	stole	stolen	
stick	stuck	stuck	
swear	swore	sworn	
swim	swam	swum	
take	took	taken	
teach	taught	taught	
tear	tore	torn	
think	thought	thought	
throw	threw	thrown	
understand	understood	understood	
wake	woke	woken	
wear	wore	worn	
win	won	won	

2 One village makes a difference

Before viewing

1 Read this paragraph and then match each underlined word to the definition.

> From its large cities to its small villages, India has a big problem: a <u>shortage</u> of water. Now, people are <u>investing</u> a lot of money to get fresh water to the population. They have spent millions of rupees on building large <u>dams</u> across rivers, creating <u>reservoirs</u> and <u>irrigating</u> dry land. However, some environmentalists have criticised these modern methods. For example, in the Alwar region in the Indian state of Rajasthan, the environmentalist Rajendra Singh is teaching people to use ancient methods to conserve water. His system involves using a series of small dams and <u>wells</u>.

1 places for storing water for later use
2 walls built across a river to stop it flowing
3 deep holes in the ground where water is collected
4 supplying land with water for growing plants
5 not enough
6 giving money to projects or businesses to make money in the future

First viewing

2 In the video the following are mentioned. Number them in the order you learn about them (from 1 to 7).

____ how life has changed for villagers
____ Rajendra Singh's work with people in the Alwar region
_1_ polluted air and water in Delhi
____ the monsoon season
____ big cities should learn from Alwar
____ Rajendra Singh's criticism of the water policy
____ where people get their water in Delhi

Second viewing

3 Match the problems and situations 1–10 to the results a–j on the right. Then watch the video again to check your answers.

1 In New Delhi, there is heavy smog in the sky, so
2 There is industrial waste in the city's river, so sometimes
3 14 million people in and around New Delhi need water, so
4 So many people need water that sometimes
5 In the desert of Rajasthan there is even less water, so
6 Every year the monsoon comes and
7 Many dams have been built but
8 Villagers in the region of Alwar collected stones and rocks so
9 The villagers built smaller dams (instead of larger dams) so
10 The techniques in the village are successful, so

a these may have caused fields, wells and river beds to dry up.
b it doesn't look like a water supply.
c there isn't enough water for everyone.
d villagers must walk miles to get it.
e you can't see the city.
f other villages are also building similar dams.
g they could build smaller dams.
h this provides relief but doesn't replace all the water used.
i the rain water doesn't run off and raises the ground water level.
j communal trucks deliver water every day.

After viewing

4 Work in groups. Plan a TV commercial that will tell people how and why they should conserve water. Then present your commercial to the class. All members of your group should be actors in the commercial. Make notes about how and why below.

How	Why

The lost temples of the Maya 4

Before viewing

1 Work in pairs. Can you answer 1–4?

1 What do you call someone who studies buildings, objects and the culture of ancient civilisations?

2 Name one country in Central America.

3 Name a country with pyramids.

4 What is another name for a tropical forest where the trees and plants grow close together?

2 Check or find answers in this introductory text to the video.

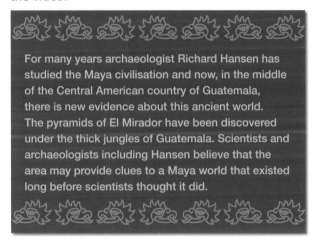

For many years archaeologist Richard Hansen has studied the Maya civilisation and now, in the middle of the Central American country of Guatemala, there is new evidence about this ancient world. The pyramids of El Mirador have been discovered under the thick jungles of Guatemala. Scientists and archaeologists including Hansen believe that the area may provide clues to a Maya world that existed long before scientists thought it did.

First viewing

3 Watch the video. Number these in the order they are mentioned in the video (from 1 to 5).

___ a King called 'Great Fiery Jaguar Paw'

___ comparison of the Maya Kings with the Egyptian Kings

_1_ the great pyramid of Danta

___ nothing on the other side

___ the size of the open space below the pyramid

Second viewing

4 Watch part 1 of the video and underline the correct answer in italics.

1 Hansen travels to the area *on foot / by helicopter / by bus.*

2 The Classic Maya period was between AD250 and AD *19 / 90 / 900*.

3 A Maya civilisation existed in the Preclassic period one *hundred / thousand / million* years before the Classic period.

4 The Danta pyramid at El Mirador is one of the *tallest / oldest / largest* pyramids in the world.

5 Watch part 2 of the video and write the missing words in these sentences from the video.

1 The person that commissioned this building was not a simple chief, living in a grass hut. This was a k_____.

2 Hansen dreams of finding these kings from the beginning of Maya time. He hopes that their t_____ will reveal who they were.

3 Hansen is especially interested in one of the smaller pyramids … one of the s_____ in the pyramid has a large jaguar paw with three claws on it.

4 Hansen believes that this could be a t_____. The tomb of an important king who ruled from 152 BC to 145 BC.

5 It's possible that this king could be b_____ here.

6 The underground imaging system creates a m_____ of what's under the soil.

6 Watch part 3 of the video and answer 1–4.

1 How deep below the ground is the space where there might be a tomb? _____ metres.

2 What are the dimensions of the space? _____ metres long by _____ metres wide

3 Does Hansen find the tomb of the king known as 'Great Fiery Jaguar Paw' and prove he existed?

4 Does Hansen still believe in these early Maya kings after this?

After viewing

7 Imagine you are a journalist with *National Geographic* magazine. Write a descriptive article (200 words) about Hansen and his work. Use and summarise the information in the video to describe his current interest in El Mirador and in particular his search for the tombs of the early Maya kings.

Before viewing

1 Complete the text with the words in the box.

> poisonous antitoxin prepare seafood
> cyanide died enough killed cooked toxins

A lot of foods naturally contain **(1)** _____, which are very dangerous. Although some mushrooms are completely safe, many people have **(2)** _____ from eating Death Cap mushrooms, which are **(3)** _____ – just one bite has **(4)** _____ poison to kill you. You need to find an **(5)** _____ quickly if you are poisoned.

Eating **(6)** _____ is one of the most common causes of food poisoning, but when the food is **(7)** _____, it is usually much safer to eat. Obviously, we have to **(8)** _____ foods like these very carefully, but you might be surprised to learn that people have been **(9)** _____ by eating potatoes, especially if they are green. Almonds, which we use in a lot of breads and sweets, and apple seeds contain **(10)** _____, which used to be the deadliest poison known to man. So be careful what you eat!

2 Read the text below and check you understand the underlined words. Then discuss the questions in pairs or small groups.

The Japanese have been eating different kinds of fish dishes for thousands of years. Fish can contain toxins and it is usually boiled or grilled to destroy poisonous substances. Japanese *sushi* is made of fish, rice and vegetables. Sometimes, *nori* (dried seaweed) is used too. Uncooked fish dishes are called *sashimi* and the flesh of the fish is usually cut very thinly and served with just a little sauce. This can be eaten as a starter or the main course.

1 Have you ever eaten *sushi*?
2 Would you be happy to eat raw fish? Would you eat seaweed?
3 Are there any dishes served in your country that are dangerous or that foreigners find strange?

First viewing

3 Watch the video and complete the missing numbers in these sentences.

1 You can find fugu on more than _____ menus.
2 This famous restaurant is _____ years old.
3 I've been doing this for _____ years.
4 Chef Hayashi took the exam in _____.
5 After World War _____, many people died from eating fugu.
6 Fugu killed _____ people between _____ and _____.
7 About _____ % of the poisonings happen in private homes.
8 A tiger fugu has enough toxin to kill _____ people.
9 The toxin itself is _____ times stronger than cyanide.
10 _____ milligram of the toxin is strong enough to kill a person.
11 A fugu meal is usually _____ different dishes.

Second viewing

4 Watch the video again and answer the questions.

1 Why is Tom Caradonna visiting Tokyo?
2 How does Chef Hayashi reassure Tom that he will be safe?
3 Why did people die from eating fugu after World War Two?
4 What do scientists at the Tokyo University of Fisheries hope to develop?
5 Describe the effect on the body of fugu poisoning using these words: *paralyse nerves lungs breathe*

After viewing

5 Discuss these questions in pairs or small groups.

- Would you try eating fugu, knowing the risks?
- Why do you think the dish is so popular, even though it can kill?
- What other unusual or dangerous foods have you heard about?

The memory man   8

Before viewing

1 Read the text about genes and match the underlined words to the definitions (1–6).

1 individual piece of information or 'code' inside a body

2 biological information inside all living organisms

3 the world around us

4 organ in the head that controls thought, feeling and movement

5 scientists who study the body's nervous system

6 receive something from parents or older relatives

> Throughout history people have always known that we <u>inherit</u> aspects of our parents' appearance. Nowadays <u>neurobiologists</u> also understand that we all carry biological information inside us called <u>DNA</u>. Humans even share DNA with other animals (98% of our DNA is the same as a monkey's). Each piece of this information, or <u>gene</u>, can decide the colour of our eyes or hair. But what these scientists can't say for certain is how much these genes are responsible for what's in our <u>brain</u>. For example, is the intelligence and personality we are born with mainly the result of the world around us or are we born that way? Are we controlled by our genes or our <u>environment</u>? For many scientists, the answer is probably 'yes' to both.

2 Read the text again. Complete sentences 1–3 with *a* (genes), *b* (the environment) or *c* (genes and the environment).

Many scientists think that …

1 appearance is the result of ___.

2 intelligence is the result of ___.

3 personality is the result of ___.

First viewing

3 Watch the video. Look at this list of Gianni Golfera's special abilities. Number them in the order you hear about them (1 to 4).

a has memorised more than 250 books ___

b teaching other people to improve their own memories ___

c repeat a list of random numbers in the correct order ___

d can remember every detail of every day of his life from before the age of one ___

Second viewing

4 Watch the video again and underline the correct word in these comments from the video.

1 'The young Italian man calls it the **skill / art** of memory.'

2 'It's a kind of memory connected to what I **see / hear**.'

3 A person who doesn't have this **gift / present** and who hasn't studied memory tends to just forget things.

4 'Memory is very difficult to understand, and scientists don't really know how it **happens / works**.'

5 'The crucial question is to understand which is the contribution from heredity and which is the contribution which comes from the **environment / atmosphere**.'

6 'Nobody knows why some people lose their **minds / memories** or why so few like Gianni never forget things.'

7 'Since the age of eleven he's been **teaching / training** his brain to remember.'

8 'The question is how much is because of the Golfera family **brains / genes** and how much comes from his maniac type of activity.'

9 'His system involves organisation and hard work. Basically, learning how to **remember / remind** to remember.'

10 'He might just be showing scientists that a great memory can be **made / done** and not just born.'

After viewing

5 Work in groups. Imagine you want to test Gianni Golfera's memory. Plan a way to test his memory. For example, you might test his memory for numbers, words or colours. Afterwards, explain how your test will work to others in the class. You could even try the test on other people in the class.

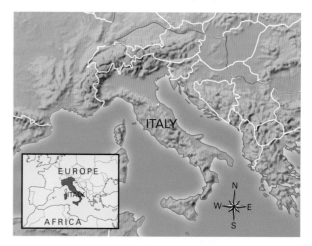

9 Living with a volcano

Before viewing

1 What do you know about volcanoes? Work in pairs and try to complete the facts using the words in the box.

> plates sulphur craters magma active
> surface volcanologists erupts ash

1 Volcanoes are often described as extinct, dormant or _____.

2 Scientists who study volcanoes are called _____.

3 Volcanoes are often formed where tectonic _____ come together, deep under the _____ of the Earth.

4 In a volcanic region, _____ and cones indicate the places where gases and _____ escape by breaking through the Earth's crust.

5 When the pressure builds up, a volcano _____, throwing lava high into the air.

6 The smoke and _____ in the atmosphere make it difficult to see and to breathe. There is usually a strong smell of _____.

First viewing

2 Watch the video and answer these questions.

1 What is Salvatore Caffo's responsibility?

2 What did Salvatore Caffo know at the age of 11?

3 How long ago did Mount Etna begin to form?

4 Name two ways that the people near Etna make a living.

5 How many times has Nicolosi been destroyed?

6 What does Salvatore Moschetto say about the town being destroyed?

Second viewing

3 Watch the video again and complete the sentences.

1 There are over _____ small towns which lie around the bottom of the volcano.

2 In _____, an eruption started that lasted more than _____ days.

3 The lava flow ended just _____ from the town.

4 People visit the _____ to give thanks that the town was _____.

5 Mario Fichera says, 'You _____ to it … you live with it … so it doesn't _____ you.'

6 According to Caffo, volcanoes are an important part of the world's _____ system.

7 Complete the things that Salvatore Caffo does. He:

_____ the black land

_____ the ancient craters

_____ with mountain guides and other scientists

_____ the lava

_____ gases

_____ surface changes

8 Etna has technically been _____ since 1995.

9 Caffo says, 'This is the birth – the _____ of new earth.'

10 If they always knew Etna's next move, their job wouldn't be very _____.

After viewing

4 Work in pairs or small groups. Discuss these questions.

- Do you know any areas in the world where there are active volcanoes?

- What do you know about major volcanic eruptions in history?

- Why do you think people live on and around volcanoes?

- What do you think it would be like to live with the knowledge that your town could be destroyed by a volcano? Would you get used to it?

- Would you visit an active volcano as a tourist? Why? / Why not?

- Do you think you would enjoy doing the job of a volcanologist? Why? / Why not?

Communication Activities

Student A

7D page 90 (Exercise 5)

1 You are the student. You aren't sure about your career but you would like a job where you help other people. You enjoy the subjects of art and music at school. In your free time, you do volunteer work with young children at a nursery. Answer the careers counsellor's questions.

2 Now you are the careers counsellor. Interview Student B and make notes in this form. Try to recommend a possible career.

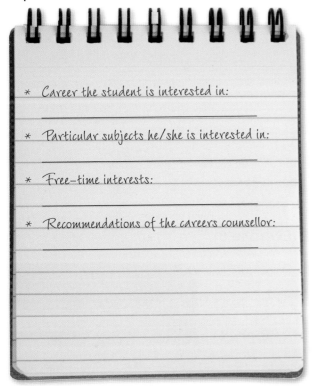

* Career the student is interested in:
  _____

* Particular subjects he/she is interested in:
  _____

* Free-time interests:
  _____

* Recommendations of the careers counsellor:
  _____

9D page 116 (Exercise 6 and 7)

Here are three pieces of news for Student B. Tell him/her the news. Student B will be surprised so you will have to convince him/her and say where you heard / saw it.

News 1: Your favourite actor has made a new film. It's at the cinema this weekend. You saw the poster outside the cinema.

News 2: There's oil at the bottom of your school field. You saw it in the river.

News 3: School is cancelled for the rest of today because there is no electricity. A teacher just told you.

Everyday English page 120 (Exercise 5)

Student A You are the grandmother. You normally watch nature programmes and quiz shows. You also enjoy soap operas sometimes.

Student C You are the daughter. You love soap operas and music and reality TV shows. You always watch *Leave me in the jungle*.

2B page 21 (Exercise 9)

1 You arrive home and the table has lots of cakes on it.
2 You see your friend driving a car for the first time.
3 Lots of people are running out of a restaurant.
4 Someone in class is answering all the teacher's questions about the homework.
5 Your teacher is wearing new clothes.

2E page 26 (Exercise 1)

HOW MUCH DO YOU KNOW ABOUT **WATER?**

1 B **2** C **3** C **4** A **5** B

Communication Activities

3D page 38 (Exercise 6)

English

	―
Useful for doing business Many websites are written in English A common language can help us live in harmony Other? _____	Not everyone needs a job in business Artists/Musicians etc. don't need foreign languages Some people need help with their own language Other? _____

History

	―
Valuable in understanding our own culture Essential if we want to understand the mistakes of the past Helps us realise that other civilisations came before us Other? _____	The past is gone – we need to look to the future Can place too much emphasis on learning dates Simply not interesting for everyone Other? _____

Music

	―
Allows you to be creative Exercises another part of your brain Gives pleasure to many Other? _____	Not likely to lead to a job Some people just can't do it Can be done outside school Other? _____

Geography

+	―
Helps us understand the news We have a duty to know about other countries and their cultures The world is changing and we need to stay up-to-date Other? _____	Not interesting to some Many people will never leave their own country We need to focus on our own culture Other? _____

5E page 66 (Exercise 2)

1 Delhi, India
2 Bangkok, Thailand
3 Prague, the Czech Republic
4 Rio de Janeiro, Brazil
5 Beijing, China

5E page 66 (Exercise 5)

1 A   2 B   3 B   4 C   5 C   6 C

8D page 102 (Exercise 4 and 5)

This year we are going to offer after-school activities, so we'd like to know what kind of activities you'd prefer. Tell us your preferences and interests with this survey.

1 **Here are some of our suggestions. Which would you be interested in?**
   – Chess club ☐
   – Christmas talent show ☐
   – Volleyball ☐
   – Art club ☐
   – Mountain climbing and outdoor adventure society ☐
   – American football ☐

2 **Would you like to suggest some other types of activities? Give your reasons.**

   1 _____
   2 _____
   3 _____

   Reasons and comments:

4A page 45 (Exercise 8)

Communication Activities

Student B

1B page 9 (Exercise 10)

1 There is some information missing in this article about an explorer. Ask Student A questions and write in the missing words.

Example:

Where does Ranulph Fiennes live?

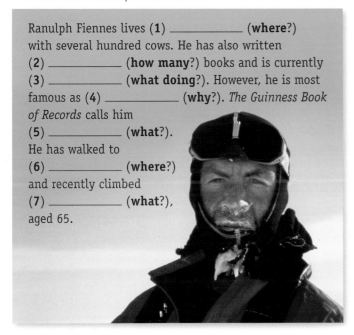

Ranulph Fiennes lives (**1**) _____ (**where?**) with several hundred cows. He has also written (**2**) _____ (**how many?**) books and is currently (**3**) _____ (**what doing?**). However, he is most famous as (**4**) _____ (**why?**). *The Guinness Book of Records* calls him (**5**) _____ (**what?**). He has walked to (**6**) _____ (**where?**) and recently climbed (**7**) _____ (**what?**), aged 65.

2 Read about these explorers and answer Student A's questions.

The explorer Louis Leakey began searching for human fossils in the 1930s. Since then, three generations of his family have explored East Africa. Meave and Louise Leakey work as palaeontologists* in this region. They are currently running a research station at Lake Turkana where there are many ancient remains. Their discoveries have included a 3.5-million-year-old skull.

*palaeontologists = /ˌpæliɒnˈtɒlədʒɪsts/

9D page 116 (Exercise 6 and 7)

Here are three pieces of news for Student A. Tell him/her the news. Student A will be surprised so you will have to convince him/her and say where you heard / saw it.

News 1: Your favourite rock group is coming to play live in your town. You heard it advertised on local radio.

News 2: The President of your country has resigned from the job. You saw it on the TV news.

News 3: Student A passed all his/her exams and got into university. You know because you heard two teachers discussing the results.

Everyday English page 120 (Exercise 5)

Student B You are the father. You usually watch the news and you like detective and police shows unless the football is on! You have to watch that!

Student D You are the son. You don't normally watch much TV but you love *The Simpsons*. Also, a friend of yours from school is on the show *Beat the teacher* tonight so you want to watch it.

10D page 129 (Exercise 8)

Tips for writing short stories
- Set the scene in the introduction (where/when is it? who is involved? what's happening?).
- Write about one main event in a short period of time.
- Only have very few characters (two or three at most).
- Include dialogue because it makes characters interesting and moves the plot forward.
- Use interesting adjectives, adverbs and linking words to make the text more clear and dynamic.
- Endings must be satisfying. Often the main character learns something from what happened.

Grammar reference

UNIT 1

reflexive and reciprocal pronouns

reflexive pronouns

We use **reflexive pronouns** (*myself, yourself,* etc.) with verbs such as *burn, cut, hate, hurt, look at, teach,* etc. when the same person or thing is both the subject <u>and</u> the object of the verb.

I (subject) *told myself* (i.e. me – object) *to stay calm when my boat capsized.*

You (subject) *mustn't blame yourself* (i.e. you – object) *for what happened.*

Karen (subject) *cut herself* (i.e. Karen – object) *while she was chopping vegetables.*

These insects (subject) *disguise themselves* (i.e. these insects – object) *as green leaves, so that birds can't see them.*

Subject pronouns	Reflexive pronouns
I	myself
you	yourself
he	himself (NOT hisself)
she	herself
it	itself
we	ourselves
you	yourselves
they	themselves (NOT theirselves)

We can also use reflexive pronouns for emphasis, to mean 'personally, not (by/with) somebody else'.

I myself think that … (emphasises that this is a personal opinion, and someone else might disagree)

Jerry himself said that we … (emphasises that it was Jerry, not someone else)

We saw the robbery ourselves. (we saw it with our own eyes, not on TV, from someone else, etc.)

The children prepared the food themselves. (emphasises that the children did this alone – they didn't have help from someone else)

reciprocal pronouns

We use the reciprocal pronouns ***each other*** or ***one another*** for mutual actions – that is, when person A does something (for example, *looks at, ignores,* etc.) to person B, and person B does the same thing to person A.

Hannah smiled at Parvati, and Parvati smiled at Hannah.
= Hannah and Parvati smiled at each other.

My pen friend often emails me, and I often email my pen friend.
= My pen friend and I often email one another.

Notice that reciprocal pronouns can also be used in the possessive:

– Miriam checked Jan's work, and Jan checked Miriam's work.
= Miriam and Jan checked each other's work.

the present simple, the present continuous and the present perfect

the present simple

We use the **present simple** to talk about …

- facts, general truths, laws of nature:
  Paris is the capital of France.
  In my country, it snows in winter.
  Water boils at 100° Celsius.
- permanent situations:
  Jorge works as a research scientist.
- regular events, habits, activities often repeated:
  I usually watch TV in the evening.
- feelings and thoughts:
  I love African music.
  I admire people who sail around the world.

the present continuous

We use the **present continuous** to talk about …

- an activity in progress, i.e. which is happening now, at the time when we are talking:
  Please be quiet – I'm trying to study, and you're making so much noise I can't concentrate!
- a temporary situation, around the time when we are talking; the idea of the present here does not refer to this exact moment – it may extend to include 'today', 'this week', or even a period as long as 'this year':
  We're learning about different kinds of explorers in this unit.
- a current trend or development, around the time when we are talking, but extending beyond an exact moment; because a trend or development may be a very long process, the idea of the present may extend to 'this decade' or even 'this century':
  Many of Papua New Guinea's tribal languages are dying out at an alarming rate.

the present simple vs the present continuous

Notice the contrast between the present simple and the present continuous:

Present simple	Present continuous
regular activity permanent situation	activity in progress temporary situation

I often go out with my friends on Saturday (regular activity), *but today I'm studying for my exams* (activity in progress).

Fran usually lives in Rome (permanent situation), *but at the moment she's doing a six-month course in Lisbon* (temporary situation).

stative verbs

Some verbs are called 'stative' or 'state' verbs, because they describe a permanent state, feeling or thought rather than an action. We DON'T normally use continuous tenses with stative verbs. They include:

> *be, believe, hate, have, know, like, love, need, prefer, seem, think, understand, want*
>
> I *know* what to do now. (NOT I ~~am knowing~~)
>
> The new student *seems* friendly.
> (NOT The new student ~~is seeming~~)
>
> I *understand* this exercise. (NOT I ~~am understanding~~)

Some stative verbs have a second, different meaning which is active. For example, *look*, *smell* and *taste* can mean 'have a particular appearance/scent/taste' (stative) or 'use your eyes/nose/taste buds' (active); *think* and *feel* can mean 'have a particular belief/opinion' (stative) or 'use your mind' and 'touch with your fingers' (active). When these verbs are used with their active meaning, they can be used in continuous tenses.

You *look* worried – what's wrong? (stative)

I'm *looking* at some old holiday photographs. (active)

I *think* it's important to help others. (stative)

You're very quiet – what are you *thinking* about? (active)

the present perfect

We use the **present perfect** to talk about something happening in the past, as long as the action or time period has some connection with the present. This includes …

- an action or event that happened during a period of time that started in the past and goes up to the present; exactly <u>when</u> the action happened is <u>not mentioned</u>, because it is not known or not important:

  I've *heard* about this young explorer before. (an hour ago? a week ago? a year ago?)

- a state or situation that began at a specific point in the past, but continues up to the present:

  She *has been* a keen sailor since she was a young child. (She is still a keen sailor now.)

- an action or event that has happened several times in the past, and may be repeated again in the future:

  He *has visited* many parts of the world to study local customs. (He may visit these or other parts of the world in the future.)

- an action or event that happened in the (usually recent) past, but which has a result in the present; notice that, although we understand that the action happened in the past, we do NOT mention exactly when it happened:

  He isn't playing in today's match because he's *injured* his ankle. (Perhaps he injured it a few days ago, but we emphasise the result that this has today.)

UNIT 2
quantifiers

Quantifiers are words which we use to describe the quantity (*how many*) or amount (*how much*) of the thing(s) we are talking about.

We normally use **many** and **much** only in questions and negative sentences (i.e. with the words *How …?* and *not*), or with words such as *too* and *very*; in affirmative sentences, we use **lots of** and **a lot of** instead.

We use **not many**, **a few**, **too many** and **too few** with plural countable nouns; we use **not much**, **a little**, **too much** and **too little** with uncountable nouns. (*A few* means 'not many', and *a little* means 'not much'.)

Number/ Amount	Plural countable	Uncountable
large	lots of / (a lot of)	(lots of) / a lot of
small	not many / a few	not much / a little
not specified	some	some
zero	not any / no	not any / no
correct	enough	enough
incorrect (+)	too many	too much
incorrect (-)	not enough / too few	not enough / too little

the past simple vs the present perfect simple

We have seen that we use the **present perfect simple** to talk about something happening in the past, as long as the action or time period has some connection with the present. In addition to the uses discussed in Unit 1, we can use this tense for …

- an action that was completed a short time ago; this is almost always used with words such as *just, already*, etc:

  Daniel *has just finished* designing a new engine.

- past experiences, i.e. asking or talking about what someone has (or hasn't) done in the whole of their past up to the present; this is often used with words such as *ever, never*, etc:

  I've *never flown* a plane, but I *have driven* a car.

- duration of a continuing state or situation, i.e. asking or talking about when the situation started and/or how long it has continued up to the present; this is used with *for* and *since*:

  I've *lived* in this city for over ten years / since I was a child.

However, we do NOT use the present perfect to talk about a completed action or event at a finished time in the past – we use the **past simple** instead. We use this when …

- we ask, say or understand <u>when</u> the action or event happened:

  Daniel *finished* designing a new engine last week.

- we know that the period of time in which it happened is completely in the past and does NOT continue up to the present.

  Charles Dickens *wrote* lots of famous novels. (He died in 1870.)

the present perfect simple vs the present perfect continuous

We use the **present perfect continuous** to talk about …

- a continuous or repeated activity/event which began in the past, has continued for some time, and is still in progress now; we usually refer to the duration of the activity, i.e. *how long*:

  I've been sending emails all morning.

  It's been raining for hours.

- an activity/event which began in the past, continued for some time, and has recently finished, with a result in the present; we usually refer to this present result:

  I've been jogging, so I'm hot and tired now.

  It's been raining, so the ground is wet and muddy.

- a continuous or repeated activity/event which began very recently, and will soon end, i.e. the activity/event is only temporary:

  I've been walking to school this week, but tomorrow I'm getting my bike back from the repair shop.

However, we use the **present perfect simple** – NOT the present perfect continuous – to talk about …

- a repeated activity/event, beginning in the past and continuing up to the present, which has resulted in a particular total number or amount; we refer to how *many*:

  I've been sending emails all morning. (present perfect continuous for duration)

  I've sent fifteen emails so far this morning. (present perfect simple for total)

  It's been raining for hours.

  It's rained several times in the last few days.

- a state, thought or feeling, beginning in the past and continuing up to the present (see Unit 1: stative verbs):

  I've been reading this book for over an hour, but I haven't understood what it's about. (NOT *haven't been understanding*)

Verbs such as *live, work* and *study* describe activities that naturally extend over several years or even decades. In such cases, there is not a lot of difference between the present perfect continuous and the present perfect simple, and we can use either tense. However, it is more natural to use the present perfect continuous when the activity has begun only recently.

  I've been working here for two months.

  I've worked here for seven years.

Other activities such as reading/writing a book, making a movie, etc. take some time, but lead towards completion in the end. In such cases, present perfect continuous describes an unfinished activity, while present perfect simple means that it has been completed.

  I've been reading a book by Paulo Coelho. (I'm on page 57)

  I've just read a book by Paulo Coelho. (I read all of it)

UNIT 3

the past simple, the past continuous and the past perfect

past simple

We use the **past simple** to talk about …

- an action, event or state which started and finished in the past:

  We won the football match last Saturday.

- a habit in the past, which is now finished:

  I played with my dolls every day when I was a little girl.

- a number of actions in the past which happened one after the other:

  He had a shower, put on his pyjamas and went to bed.

past continuous

We use the **past continuous** to talk about …

- an action or event that was in progress at a certain time in the past; we don't mention when the action started or finished:

  We were playing football at 4 o'clock on Saturday afternoon.

- a past action that was already in progress at the time a second, shorter action happened; we use the past simple for the second action that happened. We use **when + past simple** OR **while + past continuous** to talk about the two actions together:

  They were walking home (past continuous) *when it started to rain* (past simple).

  It started to rain (past simple) *while they were walking home* (past continuous).

Remember that the past continuous is NOT used with stative verbs (see Unit 1: stative verbs).

past perfect

We use the **past perfect** to talk about an action or event that happened at some time before another past action or event, or before a certain time in the past. We do not mention exactly when the earlier action/event happened; this is not important or is perhaps not known.

When I arrived at the station, the train had already left.
(It left at some time – 1 minute? 5 minutes? – before I arrived.)

By six o'clock, the sun had set.
(It set at some time – 5.30? 5.45? 5.59? – before six o'clock.)

We don't have to present the two actions/events in the same order in which they happened, but we must use the past perfect for the one which happened first.

Several countries had already joined the EU before Spain became a member.

By the time Spain became a member of the EU, several countries had already joined.

used to, would and the past simple

used to / didn't use to

We can use **used to / didn't use to** for:

- a repeated past action, a habit in the past or a past state, to show that the situation in the past is no longer true in the present:

  I *used to fight* with my brother a lot when we were younger. (now we've grown up and we don't fight any more)

  This part of Europe *used to belong* to the Soviet Union. (now it doesn't, because the Soviet Union no longer exists)

- something that existed in the past but does not exist now:

  There *used to be* a big, empty field here a few years ago. (now there's a shopping mall)

Used to / didn't use to is followed by the **bare infinitive** of the main verb. Notice that the negative form is NOT *didn't used to*, and the question form is NOT *Did ... used to ...?*

In the past, people from my country *didn't use to travel* to other countries very often. (now they do)

Did you use to live in Argentina? (now you live in Spain)

would / wouldn't

We can also use **would / wouldn't** in the same way as *used to / didn't use to*, to talk about a repeated past action or a habit in the past.

I *would fight* with my brother a lot when we were younger. ✓

In the past, people from my country *wouldn't travel* to other countries very often. ✓

However, we do NOT use **would / wouldn't** with stative verbs.

This part of Europe ~~would belong~~ to the Soviet Union. ✗

There ~~would be~~ a big, empty field here a few years ago. ✗

the past simple

We can always use the past simple instead of *used to / didn't use to* or *would / wouldn't* to talk about repeated actions/habits/states in the past.

I *fought* with my brother a lot when we were younger.

This part of Europe *belonged* to the Soviet Union.

There *was* a big, empty field here a few years ago.

In the past, people from my country *didn't travel* to other countries very often.

Did you live in Argentina?

We use the past simple – NOT *used to* or *would* – to talk about …

- a <u>single</u> past action:

  World War II *ended* in 1945.

- details such as *how long* a past action lasted or how *many times* a past action was repeated:

  Winston Churchill *became* prime minister *twice*. The first time, he *was* prime minister *for five years*.

UNIT 4

modals for speculating (1): the present

Speculating here means guessing what is true or untrue about an event or situation, without knowing all of the facts. We consider a particular explanation, reason, theory, etc. and say if we think it is (for example) probably true, possibly true or probably not true.

Various ways to express how certain we are about the truth include …

- clauses such as *I'm (not) sure/certain … There's no doubt …*, etc.
- adverbs such as *perhaps*, *probably*, *certainly*, etc.
- the modals **must**, **may**, **might**, **could**, **can't** and **couldn't**, with the meanings shown below:

must	may / might / could	can't / couldn't
certain, very likely	possible	very unlikely, impossible

← 100% true   0% true →

Notice that we do not normally use **can** to speculate, and we NEVER use **mustn't**; we normally use **couldn't** only for speculation about the past.

When we speculate about the <u>present</u>, the modals are followed by a **bare infinitive**.

- Situation: I don't know where my keys are:

  They *may / might / could be* in my school bag, I suppose. (It's <u>possible</u> that they're in my bag.)

  They *can't be* in my purse – I've looked there. (I'm certain they aren't in my purse – it's <u>impossible</u>.)

  They *must be* in the pocket of my other jeans – I think that's where I left them. (I'm <u>almost certain</u> that they're in my other jeans.)

modals for speculating (2): the past

When we speculate about the <u>past</u>, we use the modals **must**, **may**, **might**, **could**, **can't** and **couldn't** followed by a bare **perfect infinitive** i.e. **have + past participle** of the main verb.

Notice that "the past" does not mean that we only use modals to speculate about actions, events, etc. in the past simple tense; it means that that we use this construction for any action/event happening <u>before now</u>. As you can see from the examples below, this can include the present perfect and the past perfect.

- Situation: I don't know why my friend didn't call me at 9.00 last night:

  She *may / might / could have fallen asleep*, I suppose. (Perhaps by 9.00 she had already fallen asleep – it's <u>possible</u>.)

  She *can't / couldn't have forgotten* – she always calls me. (I'm sure she didn't forget – it's <u>impossible</u>.)

  She *must have lost her mobile* again. (She has probably lost her mobile again – it's <u>very likely</u>.)

order of adjectives

When we use two or three adjectives together to describe an object, these adjectives usually follow a certain order. Basically, the adjective which is the most objective (i.e. giving factual information rather than an opinion), or which classifies the noun most clearly, goes closest to the noun.

For example, if we wanted to describe a handbag which is brown, made of leather and quite big, the adjectives would follow this order:

It's a leather handbag. (clear, objective fact: leather is leather)

It's a brown leather handbag. (quite objective, but not completely clear: is it almost black? a sort of orange-brown?)

It's a big brown leather handbag. (more opinion than fact, so not clear: big compared to a mouse? big compared to a house?)

The table below shows how this normally works; an adjective in the category nearest to the top of the table goes first (that is, furthest from the noun) and an adjective in the category nearest to the bottom goes nearest to the noun.

opinion	*lovely, beautiful, ugly,* etc.
size/height	*big, small, tall, short,* etc.
weight	*light, heavy,* etc.
price/value	*expensive, cheap, priceless,* etc.
shape*	*round, square, triangular,* etc.
age*	*old, new, antique, brand-new,* etc.
colour	*(dark/light) blue, red, black,* etc.
origin	*African, Chinese, French,* etc.
material	*leather, wooden, plastic, silk,* etc.

* the order of these two categories is often reversed

Notice that we put commas between adjectives in a list when the adjectives are not very objective i.e. adjectives from the first two or three categories in the table above. (This is often used in a story, for example, to show feelings or create a descriptive atmosphere, and is sometimes called 'poetic' description.) However, we don't normally use commas in a list of adjectives from the last few categories in the table above, which give objective facts – that is, 'informative' description.

The sky was full of big, heavy, dark black clouds. ('poetic' description)

Thieves stole several priceless antique Chinese vases. (informative description)

We DON'T use more than two or three adjectives together before the noun. If we want to describe the object further, we should start a new sentence, or start a new clause using *and* or *which*.

It's a big, heavy, square ~~17th-century silver~~ picture frame.

It's a big, heavy, square picture frame. It's from the 17th century and is made of silver.

modals of obligation and ability in the past

The modals *must*, *can't*, *could* and *couldn't* are used for speculation (see page 147) as well as for obligation and ability, and it's important not to confuse the two uses.

- **speculation** – the same modal (e.g. *can't*) can be used for both the present and the past; it's followed by bare infinitive for the present, and by perfect infinitive for the past.
- **obligation and ability** – the modal itself shows if we are talking about the present (e.g. *can't*) or the past (e.g. *couldn't*); it's followed by the bare infinitive for both the present and the past.

obligation

- We use **must** to mainly talk about what the law, a rule, our parents, etc. tell someone to do. The past form of **must** is **had to**:

  You must be quiet in class. (present)

  At school, we had to be quiet in class. (past)

- We use **mustn't** to mainly talk about what the law, a rule, our parents, etc. tell someone NOT to do. **Mustn't** doesn't have a past form; instead, we use *wasn't / weren't allowed to*:

  You mustn't talk in class. (present)

  At school, we weren't allowed to talk in class. (past)

- We use **have to** to talk about what is necessary – either because of a rule, a law, etc., or because of the situation. The past form is **had to**:

  You have to wear a school uniform. (present)

  At school, we had to wear a school uniform. (past)

- We use **don't have to** to talk about something that isn't necessary (but perhaps you can do it if you want to). The past form is **didn't have to**:

  You don't have to go to bed early on Saturdays. (present)

  When I was at school, we didn't have to go to bed early on Saturdays. (past)

Must and **have to** can mean exactly the same thing, and the past form of both is **had to**. But be careful:

- **Mustn't** does NOT mean **don't have to**; it means *not allowed to*:

  You don't have to cycle to school. (you can walk if you like)

  You mustn't cycle on the walkway. (it's against the rules)

ability

- We use **can** to show that someone has enough strength, skill, knowledge, etc. to do something. The negative is **can't**. The past form of **can** is **could**, and the past form of **can't** is **couldn't**:

  I can drive but I can't fly a plane. (present)

  When I was eight, I could ride a bike but I couldn't skate. (past)

UNIT 5

future forms (1): will, be going to, the present continuous

Will is only one of the tenses we use to talk about the future. When we talk about plans, arrangements and predictions for the future, we can use **will**, **going to** or the **present continuous**.

will

- We use **will** to talk about **'on-the-spot' decisions**, i.e. decisions we make at the moment of speaking, usually about the near future. It is just a general decision – we have not yet made any plans or arrangements:
  I'm thirsty – I think I'll make myself a cup of tea.
- We use **will** for **predictions** about the future, based on what we <u>think, believe or hope</u>:
  One day scientists will probably find a cure for cancer.

be going to

- We use **be going to** to talk about **intentions** for the near future, i.e. usually informal plans where we have made no definite arrangements (or without mentioning these); after thinking about it, we know what we want to do and we will arrange the details later if necessary:
  I'm going to start visiting the gym at least twice a week.
- As well as for informal plans about the near future, we use **be going to** for our **ambitions** in the more distant future:
  I'm going to go to university next year. I'm going to study business management.
- We use **going to** for **predictions** about the future, based on what we <u>see or know</u> – that is, based on some evidence in the present:
  Look at those big black clouds! It's going to rain.

the present continuous

- We use the **present continuous** to talk about **definite arrangements** for the near future, i.e. the other people involved know about it and have agreed on the details, bookings have probably already been made, etc. We know (and usually mention) final details such as day/date, time and/or place:
  I'm flying to Rio tomorrow on the ten o'clock flight from Madrid.

Be careful with **be going** (present continuous) and **be going to go**.

I'm going to the mall – come with me!	(present continuous)
I'm going to go to university next year.	(going to)

future forms (2): will (+ adverb) for prediction

We saw in the previous section that *will* is used for predictions based on what we think, believe or hope, rather than on direct evidence. Since we may know little or nothing about the factual background, we are not always absolutely certain about our prediction.

A statement such as 'We will get there by 9 o'clock' (or 'We won't get there by 9 o'clock') doesn't really indicate how certain we feel about this prediction. However, we can show the degree of certainty more clearly by using adverbs, as in the tables below.

100%	*certainly*	
We will	*(almost) definitely*	*get there by 9 o'clock.*
	probably	
50%	*possibly*	

In affirmative sentences, the adverb is placed between *will* and the main verb (*get*). In negative sentences (with *won't*), the adverb is placed before *won't*.

	possibly	
We	*probably*	*won't get there by 9 o'clock.*
	(almost) definitely	
	certainly	

future forms (3): modals for speculating about the future

We saw in the section above that we can use adverbs with **will** to show how certain we are about our prediction; we can also use verbs such as *I'm sure* to show our degree of certainty more clearly.

I'm sure scientists will find a cure for most diseases soon.

I doubt that it will be hot tomorrow.

I suppose that people will possibly live on the Moon in 2200.

We can also use the modals **may**, **might** and **could** to express a medium degree of certainty in a sentence speculating about the future, i.e. to say that this is possible in the future, but not absolutely certain.

may, might, could = perhaps, possibly

They may / might / could win. (It's possible that they'll win)

may not / might not = perhaps not

They may not / might not win. (It's possible that they won't win)

However, notice that **could not** is NOT used in sentences speculating about the future. *They **could not** win* means *They **weren't able to** win* (i.e. ability in the past).

UNIT 6

articles

The articles **a/an** and **the** are placed before nouns (e.g. 'a book', 'the Moon') or noun phrases including adjectives (e.g. 'a good book', 'the Olympic Games'). If there is no article before a noun or a noun phrase, this absence is called the zero article **(-)**.

the indefinite article (a/an)

We use **a/an** before **singular** countable nouns to talk about a person or thing in a general way, i.e. it suggests a meaning such as 'any/no particular/one of several/ thousands etc.'

Basketball is a sport. (There are lots of sports; this is one of them.)

I've never met an Olympic medallist. (There are lots of Olympic medallists, but I've never met one.)

There's a man outside who wants to see you. (There are billions of men; he's one of them, but I don't know anything else about him.)

the definite article (the)

We use **the** before all types of nouns – **singular**, **plural** and **uncountable** – to talk about a specific person, thing, group, etc. The person, thing, etc. is specific because:

- there is only one *(the Moon, the sky, the world, etc.)*:
  The sky is clear today.

- the person, thing, etc. has been mentioned earlier in the same text or conversation:
  I watched a football game on TV. The game was very exciting. (Which game? The game I watched on TV.)

- we explain, describe or define which person, thing, etc. we mean:
  The boy next door is my friend. (Which boy? The boy next door).
  That's my phone – the blue one. (Which one? The blue one.)

- it is clear from the situation which person, thing, etc. we mean:
  This is a good film. The actors are very funny. (Which actors? Obviously, the actors in this film.)
  Come in and close the door. (Which door? Obviously, the door of this room.)

We use **the** before superlative adjectives and ordinal numerals (e.g. *the best player, the third attempt*) because these are automatically defined – that is, they answer the question 'which one(s)?'.

We use **the** before certain adjectives to mean 'all the people in this social/sociological group'; for example, *the rich* means 'all the rich people', *the unemployed* means 'all the unemployed people', and so on. Further examples include *the poor, the young, the elderly* and *the homeless*.

In the same way, we use **the** before adjectives or plural nouns of nationality, to mean 'all the people of this country'; for example, *the French* means 'all French people', *the Germans* means 'all German people', and so on.

the zero article: (-)

We use the zero article **(-)** before **uncountable** nouns and **plural** countable nouns to talk about people or things in a general way.

He's good at (-) most sports. (in general, not one in particular)

I've only seen (-) racehorses on TV. (any, not one in particular)

We use the zero article **(-)** with singular countable nouns in some prepositional phrases:

> **be** at (-) home / at (-) school / at (-) work
> **be** in (-) bed / in (-) hospital / in (-) prison
> **go** by (-) bicycle / by (-) bus / by (-) car / by (-) train
> **go** at (-) home / to (-) school / to (-) work
> **go** to (-) bed / to (-) hospital / to (-) prison

the zero article vs the definite article

In English, the use of the zero article or definite article with names can be very confusing; this use follows certain rules, as shown below, but you should be aware that there are exceptions to these rules.

- people, towns/cities, countries, continents:
  Juan, Seville, Spain, Europe
- countries whose name has a common noun or plural:
  the Czech Republic, the UK, the UAE, the Netherlands
- single mountains, islands, lakes:
  Mount Everest, Cuba, Lake Ontario
- mountain ranges, groups of islands, oceans/seas, rivers, deserts:
  the Andes, the Bahamas, the Pacific, the Amazon, the Sahara
- sports, school subjects, languages:
  football, baseball, mathematics, history, Spanish
- musical instruments, newspapers:
  the piano, the guitar, the Times
- days of the week, months, specific years:
  Monday, January, 1969
- periods of time:
  the weekend, the Sixties/1960s, the Renaissance

the language of comparison

We use **comparative adjectives** to compare one person, thing or group with another. We form the comparative with **adjective + -er + than** or **more/less + adjective + than**.

The Earth is bigger than the Moon.

Bread is less expensive than cheese.

We use **superlative adjectives** to compare one person, thing or group with two or more others. We form the superlative with **the + adjective + -est** or **the most/ least + adjective**. We can use *in the world, of all*, etc. after the noun.

This is the most poisonous snake in the world.

- **adjectives with one syllable**

  With one-syllable adjectives, we form the comparative by adding **-er**, and the superlative by adding **the** ...**-est**:

  long   longer   the longest

  If the adjective ends in **-e**, we just add **-r / the** ...**-st**.

  close   closer   the closest

  If the adjective ends in a **single vowel + consonant**, we double the consonant and add **-er / the** ...**-est**:

  big   bigger   the biggest

- **adjectives with -y**

  With one- or two-syllable adjectives ending in a **consonant + -y**, we change **-y** to **-ier / the** ...**-iest**:

  dry   drier   the driest   pretty   prettier   the prettiest

- **adjectives with two, three or more syllables**

  With most other two-syllable adjectives, and with all three- and four-syllable adjectives, we add **more / the most** (or **less / the least**):

bo·ring	more/less boring	the most/least boring
ex·ci·ting	more/less exciting	the most/least exciting
in·te·res·ting	more/less interesting	the most interesting

- **irregular adjectives**

good	better	the best
bad	worse	the worst
far	further	the furthest
many, much	more	the most
a lot of, lots of	more	the most
little	less	the least

modifiers for comparisons

We use **a little / a bit / slightly + comparative** for comparing small differences.

Skiing is a bit more difficult than snowboarding.

We use **much / a lot / far + comparative** or **easily / by far + superlative** for comparing large differences.

Brazil is a lot bigger than Portugal.

China has got by far the largest number of people.

similarities and differences

We use **(not) as + adjective + as** or **(not) the same + noun + as** to say that two people, things, groups, etc. are (or are not) similar.

James is as tall as Jack. = James is the same height as Jack.

We can use modifiers to show how similar or dissimilar the two people, things, groups, etc. are. We use **exactly the same ... as** to show that there is no difference; we use **almost / about** or **not quite** to show that there is a small difference; and we use **not nearly** to show that there is a large difference

A litre of milk is not quite the same weight as a litre of water.

Finland is not nearly as hot as Egypt.

UNIT 7
relative pronouns

We can sometimes join two shorter sentences together by making the second sentence into a **relative clause**; the relative clause gives further information about a noun or noun phrase in the first part of the sentence.

In order for us to do this, there must be a **pronoun** in the second part that refers back to the noun or noun phrase in the first.

I hate my brother. He likes to win at everything he does. (The pronoun 'he' refers to 'my brother'.)

To form a relative clause, we replace this pronoun with a **relative pronoun**, which we put next to the noun or noun phrase it relates to.

I hate my brother, who ~~he~~ likes to win at everything he does.

(Notice that the relative pronoun REPLACES the original pronoun – we DON'T use both together.)

- For **people**, we use the relative pronoun **who** to replace the pronouns he, she, they, etc.:

  That's Mr White. He teaches us geography.

  That's Mr White, who teaches us geography.

- For **things/animals**, we use the relative pronoun **which** to replace the pronouns it, they, etc.:

  I'm reading an interesting book. It is all about space exploration.

  I'm reading an interesting book which is all about space exploration.

- For **possession**, we use **whose** to replace the pronouns his, her, their, its, etc. (Notice that we can use this for **people** _and_ **things/animals**.):

  My best friend is John. His grandmother used to be a film star.

  My best friend is John, whose grandmother used to be a film star.

  I found a bird. Its wing was broken, so it couldn't fly.

  I found a bird whose wing was broken, so it couldn't fly.

- For **places**, we use **where** to replace **there**:

  A laboratory is a place. Scientists do experiments there.

  A laboratory is a place where scientists do experiments.

  (Notice that 'where' goes next to 'a place', followed by the rest of the relative clause.)

- For **times**, we use **when** to replace **then**:

  'Rush hour' is a time of day. Most people are travelling to work then.

  'Rush hour' is a time of day when most people are travelling to work.

  (Notice that 'when' goes next to 'a time of day', followed by the rest of the relative clause.)

- For **reasons**, we use **why**; this isn't actually a relative pronoun, but it works in a similar way:

  The singer's voice is the reason. I really like the band because of this.

  The singer's voice is the reason why I really like the band.

defining relative clauses

When we join two sentences together using a **relative clause**, the first sentence contains the main information, and the relative clause gives further detail about that information. The meaning of the first sentence is sometimes incomplete without the further information given in the relative clause. In this case, the relative clause underlines defines the noun in the first sentence, and so it is a **defining relative clause**.

My mother is the person. (Which person? The meaning of the sentence is not complete.)

She helps me with my homework. (This defines which person we mean.)

My mother is the person who helps me with my homework.

Notice that the noun which the relative clause refers to is not always at the end of the first sentence. The relative pronoun always goes next to the noun, however, followed by the rest of the relative clause. This means the relative clause may be in the middle of the sentence.

The animals are chimpanzees. (Which animals? The meaning of the sentence is not complete.)

They are closest to humans. (This defines which animals we mean.)

The animals which are closest to humans are chimpanzees.

> In **defining** relative clauses – but NOT in non-defining relative clauses – we can use **that** instead of *who* or *which*.
>
> > *My mother is the person that helps me with my homework.*
>
> Notice that a **defining relative clause** becomes part of the meaning of the main sentence, and so we DON'T use commas to separate the relative clause and the rest of the sentence.
>
> > *The animals which are closest to humans are chimpanzees.*

non-defining relative clauses

If the meaning of the first sentence is complete on its own, the relative clause doesn't define the noun or noun phrase in the first sentence – it simply gives extra information – and so it is a **non-defining relative clause**.

Crows are the world's most intelligent birds. (The meaning of this sentence is complete.)

They can make their own tools. (This gives extra information.)

Crows, which can make their own tools, are the world's most intelligent birds.

> With a **non-defining relative clause**, we DO use commas, before and after the relative clause, to separate the extra information from the main part of the sentence.
>
> > *Crows, which can make their own tools, are the world's most intelligent birds.*

UNIT 8
verb patterns

The main verb in a sentence may often be followed by another verb; the second verb may be an infinitive or an –*ing* form, depending on the pattern used with the main verb. (Remember that the infinitive is the base form of the verb, and has two main forms – the **bare infinitive** and the **to-infinitive**. The **-ing form** is the base form of the verb + -*ing*.)

bare infinitive

We use the **bare infinitive** …

- after **modals** (*can/can't, must/mustn't, should/shouldn't*, etc.):
  I can't understand what she's saying.

- after the verbs **make, let** and **help***:
  The teacher makes us do a lot of homework.

  My parents usually let me stay up late on Saturdays.

  Listening to music helps me (to) relax*.

  * Notice that **help** can be followed by the bare infinitive OR the *to*-infinitive.

to-infinitive

We use the **to-infinitive** …

- after verbs such as **agree, appear, arrange, decide, expect, hope, learn, manage, need, offer, plan, pretend, promise, refuse, seem** and **want**:
  I expect to get good marks in the test.

  You need to buy some new shoes.

  She seems to be upset. What's wrong?

  I agreed to help Carlo with his homework.

- after most verbs which always take an object, such as **advise, allow, ask, encourage, invite, persuade** and **teach**:
  My parents encouraged me to learn French.

- after **it is/was + adjectives describing situations**, such as **difficult/hard, easy, important, necessary** and **nice**:
  It's difficult to remember all these rules.

  It's nice to have lots of friends.

- after **be + adjectives describing feelings**, such as **happy, pleased, sad, sorry** and **surprised**:
  I'm very pleased to meet you.

  We're sorry to hear that you're not feeling well.

-ing form

We use the **-ing form** …

- after verbs such as **avoid**, **consider**, **dislike**, **enjoy**, **finish**, **imagine**, **keep** and **practise**:
  You should always avoid getting into an argument.

- after verb phrases such as **can't help**, **can't stand** and **don't mind**:
  I don't mind listening to reggae music, but I can't stand listening to rap and hip-hop.

- after verbs followed by a preposition, such as **benefit from**, **concentrate on**, **look forward to**, **succeed in** and **take part in**:
  I look forward to hearing from you soon.

to-infinitive OR -ing form

Some verbs can be followed either by the **to-infinitive** or by the **-ing form** without any real change in meaning. Such verbs include **begin**, **continue**, **hate**, **like**, **love**, **prefer** and **start**.

> *I began to play / playing tennis when I was eleven.*
>
> *I love to stretch out / stretching out on my couch after a busy day.*

Some verbs can be followed either by the **to-infinitive** or by the **-ing form**, but there is a change in meaning. Such verbs include:

forget doing – you did it but you can't remember doing it
> *I'll never forget taking my driving test.*

forget to do – you don't remember, so you don't do it
> *I forgot to water the flowers. Can you water them?*

remember doing – you remember now that you did it before
> *I remember seeing him at the gym once or twice.*

remember to do – you remember now that you must do it
> *I always remember to set my alarm when I go to bed.*

stop doing – no longer do something
> *I stopped going to the gym after I hurt my ankle.*

stop to do – stop what you are doing in order to do something else
> *He was jogging, but he stopped to answer his mobile.*

try doing – it's easy; try, but perhaps it won't help you
> *If you've got a headache, try taking an aspirin.*

try to do – it's difficult; try, but perhaps you won't be able to
> *I know you're tired, but please try to concentrate.*

The verbs **hate**, **like**, **love** and **prefer** may be followed by the **to-infinitive** or the **-ing form** …

> A: *Do you like going to the cinema?*
> B: *Sometimes, but I usually prefer going to concerts.*

BUT **would hate**, **would like**, **would love** and **would prefer** are followed only by the **to-infinitive**.

> A: *Would you like to go to the cinema tonight?*
> B: *Yes, I'd love to go!*

the passive form

In active voice, the subject of the sentence is the person or thing that does the action. When we use the **passive**, the subject is the person or thing that the action happens to. In other words, the object of a sentence in active voice becomes the subject of the sentence in the passive. If we want to say who/what does the action (the 'agent') in the passive, we use *by*.

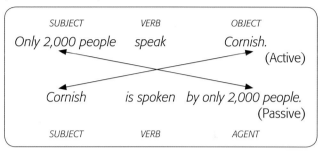

We use the passive when we want to emphasise the subject and/or the action itself. If it is not important or not clear who/what the agent is (e.g. *someone, they, people,* etc.), then we don't include it.

People speak English and Spanish all over the world.
= English and Spanish are spoken all over the world by people.

tenses in the passive

We form the passive with **be + past participle** of the verb which is used in the active sentence; the tense of *be* is the same as the verb tense in the active sentence.

Simple tenses			
present	*is / are*		+ past participle
past	*was / were*		

Continuous tenses			
present	*is / are*	*being*	+ past participle
past	*was / were*		

Perfect tenses			
present	*has / have*	*been*	+ past participle
past	*had*	*been*	

Thousands of tourists visit Cornwall every year. (present simple)
= Cornwall is visited by thousands of tourists every year.

Researchers interviewed the last living speakers. (past simple)
= The last living speakers were interviewed by researchers.

Some children are now using the language. (present continuous)
= The language is now being used by some children.

People have spoken Cornish for 1,500 years. (present perfect)
= Cornish has been spoken for 1,500 years by people.

Nobody had ever recorded the language before. (past perfect)
= The language had never been recorded before by anybody.

the negative form of the passive

We form the negative by adding *n't* to the first modal or auxiliary verb in the sentence, i.e. **isn't/aren't** in the present simple and the present continuous, **wasn't/weren't** in the past simple and the past continuous, **hasn't/haven't** in the present perfect, and **hadn't** in the past perfect.

We can also form a negative meaning by adding **never** after the first modal or auxiliary verb in the sentence, or words such as **nothing** and **nobody** before the first modal or auxiliary verb.

The language is dying out because young children aren't taught to speak it.

Many of these ancient Aboriginal languages were never written down.

A solution to the problem hasn't been found yet.

Until the project began, nothing had been done to prevent the language from becoming extinct.

questions in the passive

We form questions in the passive by putting the first modal or auxiliary verb in the sentence – that is, **Is/Are**, **Was/Were** or **Has/Have/Had** – before the subject.

Were famous places always protected by special laws?

Is the language being taught to the next generation?

Has anything been discovered about the number of speakers who are still alive?

We can also begin questions with **question words** such as **What**, **Why**, **Where**, **How** etc. to ask for extra information rather than a simple 'Yes' or 'No' answer.

How many people is the language spoken by?

Why has the language never been recorded?

When was the language first spoken?

the passive with modals

We have seen that we form the passive with **be + past participle**, and that the tense/form of *be* is the same as the tense/form of the verb in the active sentence.

If a sentence in active voice contains a modal such as **can/can't**, **must/mustn't** or **will/won't**, the modal is followed by the **bare infinitive**. In the same way, if a sentence in the passive contains one of these modals, the modal is followed by the bare infinitive of *be*, and then the past participle of the main verb.

You can't find these languages anywhere else.
= These languages can't be found anywhere else.

We will lose these languages forever.
= These languages will be lost forever.

People must/should do something about the problem.
= Something must/should be done about the problem.

phrasal verbs

A phrasal verb is made up of two (or three) words used together as a single unit of meaning. It combines a **verb stem** with an adverb **particle** (and, in the case of some phrasal verbs, an additional **preposition**).

The meaning of the whole phrasal verb may be very different from the basic meaning of the verb which it contains. For example, *come across* means 'discover by accident', which has nothing to do with the basic meaning of *come*.

Changing the particle changes the whole phrasal verb; although several phrasal verbs may share the same verb stem, this does not show that they all have a similar meaning. For example, *break out* means 'start suddenly' (e.g. a war or an epidemic), *break up* means 'no longer be together' (e.g. a couple or a pop group) and *break down* means 'stop working' (e.g. a car or machinery).

In addition, the same phrasal verb may itself have two or more different meanings. For example, the phrasal verb *go off* means 'explode' (e.g. a bomb) or 'become bad/rotten' (e.g. milk, food).

The verb stem of a phrasal verb is used with the same tenses and forms as a normal verb.

using objects with phrasal verbs

There are three groups of phrasal verbs, depending on whether they can or cannot take an object, and if so, where the object is placed.

Most phrasal verbs are **transitive** i.e. they take a direct object. Some transitive phrasal verbs are **separable** – a short object may be placed between the stem and particle; with phrasal verbs which are **inseparable**, the object must be placed after the particle (and after the preposition, if there is one). The phrasal verbs in the third group are **intransitive** – that is, they don't take a direct object at all.

A: separable phrasal verbs

- A **pronoun object** (*it, us, them*, etc.) MUST go <u>between</u> the verb stem and the particle:

    look it up in a dictionary   ~~look up it~~ *in a dictionary* ✗

- A **short object** (one, two or three words) may go <u>between</u> the verb stem and the particle OR <u>after</u> the particle:

    look the word up in a dictionary

    look up the word in a dictionary

- A **long object** (that is, a phrase or clause) MUST go <u>after</u> the particle:

    look up the meaning of a word you don't know in a dictionary

B: inseparable phrasal verbs

- The object – whether it is a pronoun object, a short object or a long object – MUST go after the particle:

  look after them   ~~*look them after*~~ ✗

  look after the children   ~~*look the children after*~~ ✗

  look after your younger brother and sister

- If there is a preposition (about half of the phrasal verbs in this group have a preposition), the object – whether it is a pronoun object, a short object or a long object – MUST go after the particle AND the preposition:

  look up to them

  look up to your parents

  look up to people who have more experience than you

C: intransitive phrasal verbs

- These phrasal verbs do not take an object, although they may be followed by an adverbial phrase of time, place, etc.:

  Look out!

  I give up!

  The plane takes off at six o'clock.

  You must give way at this intersection.

prepositional verbs

Prepositional verbs are normal verbs which are followed by a preposition; although they look like phrasal verbs, both the verb and the preposition keep their usual meaning.

Some prepositional verbs are intransitive (e.g. *go away*, *sit down*, etc.); almost all of the transitive prepositional verbs follow the same rules as Group A (separable) phrasal verbs.

     put them down   ~~*put down them*~~ ✗

     put your pens down   *put down your pens*

> Some common prepositional verbs include:
>
> *give sth* back (to sb*)*
>
> *go away* (intransitive)
>
> *lift sb/sth up*
>
> *pick sth up* (e.g. off the floor)
>
> *put sth down* (e.g. on a table)
>
> *sit down* (intransitive)
>
> *stand up* (intransitive)
>
> *take sth off* (e.g. clothes)
>
> *throw sth away*

* sth = something; sb = somebody

UNIT 9

indirect ways of asking questions

We ask a **direct question** by using **inversion**, i.e. by putting a modal, auxiliary verb or form of *be* before the subject. If there isn't a modal, auxiliary or form of *be*, we add *do/does/did* before the subject.

Are you looking at me?

Do you live here?

We can also ask a direct question beginning with a **question word** such as ***What***, ***When***, ***How***, etc. Again, we put a modal, auxiliary verb or form of *be* before the subject, and if there isn't a modal, auxiliary verb or form of *be*, we add *do/does/did* before the subject.

Why are you looking at me?

Where do you live?

Sometimes, however, usually in order to be more polite, people ask questions in an indirect way, beginning the sentence with an introductory question or phrase.

<u>*I'd like to know*</u> *why you are looking at me.*

<u>*Would you mind telling me*</u> *where you live?*

There is no inversion in indirect questions. We don't add *do/does/did* before the subject, and the word order is the same as for a statement, i.e. **subject + verb**.

If a question that needs a *yes/no* answer (that is, one without a question word like *who, what*, etc.) is expressed in this way, it is introduced by ***if*** or ***whether***.

Could you do me a favour?

<u>*I was wondering*</u> *if you could do me a favour.*

Are you a university graduate?

<u>*Do you mind if I ask*</u> *whether you are a university graduate?*

Notice that some of the indirect questions above end in a question mark, and some don't. This is because, although the indirect question is no longer a question, some of the indirect expressions at the beginning are themselves questions. *Would you mind telling me ...?* and *Do you mind if I ask ...?* both have a question form, but *I'd like to know ...* and *I was wondering ...* do not.

> Expressions we use to ask questions indirectly include:
>
> **Question form**
>
> *Could you/anyone tell me ...?*
>
> *Do you have any idea ...?*
>
> *Do you know/think ...?*
>
> *Do you mind if I ask ...?*
>
> *Would you happen to know ...?*
>
> *Would you mind telling me ...?*
>
> **Statement form**
>
> *I don't know ...*
>
> *I don't suppose you could tell me ...*
>
> *I'd like to know ...*
>
> *I wonder ... / I was wondering ...*

reported speech
direct vs reported speech

- **direct speech** gives the exact words someone said and uses quotation marks ('…') to show this.

- **reported speech** gives the <u>meaning</u> of what they said, but doesn't use all their exact words and doesn't use quotation marks. We use reported speech when we tell somebody what another person said.

  'I'll meet you here tomorrow,' John said to Susan. (direct speech)

  John told Susan (that) he would meet her there the next day. (reported speech)

backshift

When we report what a person said, the time of speaking is not the same as the time of reporting. For example, what was the present at the time of speaking has usually already become the past at the time of reporting. For this reason, we often use "backshift" in reported speech, i.e. the tense of a verb used in direct speech moves one step back into the past.

Direct Speech	Reported Speech
Present Simple *'I am a writer and a freelance journalist.'*	Past Simple *He said he was a writer and a freelance journalist.*
Present Continuous *'I am working on my second novel.'*	Past Continuous *He said he was working on his second novel.*
Present Perfect *'I have written articles for several magazines.'*	Past Perfect* *He said he had written articles for several magazines.*
Past Simple *'I was a reporter for a national newspaper.'*	Past Perfect* *He said he had been a reporter for a national newspaper.*
Present Perfect Continuous *'I have been writing a lot this year.'*	Past Perfect Continuous* *He said he had been writing a lot that year.*
Past Continuous *'I was earning more money as a reporter.'*	Past Perfect Continuous* *He said he had been earning money as a reporter.'*
will *'Readers will enjoy my new book.'*	would *He said readers would enjoy his new book.*
can *'I can usually write about 2,000 words a day.'*	could *He said he could usually write about 2,000 words a day.*
must / have to *'A writer has to know what their readers want.'*	had to *He said a writer had to know what their readers wanted.*

* Notice that present perfect and past simple both "backshift" to the same tense – past perfect. Present perfect continuous and past continuous both "backshift" to past perfect continuous.

other changes in reported speech

When we report what a person says, the place, listener(s), etc. at the time of speaking are often different to the place, listener(s), etc. at the time of reporting.

For example, imagine that on Monday John speaks to Susan in the park: *'I'll meet you here tomorrow,' John said.*

On Friday, Susan is in the cafeteria, telling a friend about the conversation; what was 'tomorrow' when John spoke is now several days ago, what was 'here' is now far away, and so on. What Susan reports is: *John said he would meet me there the next day.*

Direct Speech	Reported Speech
I; we me; us my; your; our	he/she; they him/her; them his/her; their
here this; these now	there that; those then / at that time
last night/week etc. this morning/afternoon etc. next week/July etc.	the night/week etc. before / the previous night/week etc. that morning/afternoon etc. the next week/July etc. / the following week/July etc.
yesterday today tomorrow	the day before / the previous day that day / the same day the next/following day

reporting verbs

In direct speech, the exact words someone uses can show us if they are speaking (e.g.) politely, angrily, etc.; in reported speech, where we don't use their exact words, we need to use different **reporting verbs** to show this sort of information.

Direct speech	Reported speech
'Sit down – now!' he shouted.	*He ordered me to sit down.*
'Sit down,' he said.	*He told me to sit down.*
'Sit down, please,' he said.	*He asked me to sit down.*
'Would you like to *sit down?' he said.*	*He invited me to sit down.*
'I'd sit down if I was *you,' he said.*	*He advised me to sit down.*

> Reporting verbs we use in this way include:
>
> **advise   ask   invite   order**
> **remind   tell   warn**
>
> The normal pattern is **verb + object (+ not) + to-infinitive**
>
> *The teacher told her students (not) to open their books.*
>
> But: we usually <u>don't</u> *invite* or *remind* someone <u>not</u> to do something
>
>   we usually only *warn* someone <u>not</u> to do something

There are other reporting verbs which don't follow the pattern of **verb + sb* + *to*-infinitive**. *(In the patterns shown below, *sb* means '*somebody*' and *sth* means '*something*'.) These verbs include:

accuse sb* of + -ing

'You stole her bag,' the policeman said to him.

→ *The policeman **accused** <u>him of stealing</u> her bag.*

admit + -ing

'Yes, I stole her bag,' he said.

→ *He **admitted** <u>stealing</u> her bag.*

apologise for + -ing

'I'm sorry I stole your bag,' he said to her.

→ *He **apologised** <u>for stealing</u> her bag.*

deny + -ing

'No, I didn't steal her bag,' he said.

→ *He **denied** <u>stealing</u> her bag.*

describe sth* (to sb*)

'My bag was big and brown,' she said to the policeman.

→ *She **described** <u>her bag</u> (to the policeman).*

offer sb + *to*-infinitive

'I'll carry your bag for you,' he said to her.

→ *He **offered** <u>to carry</u> her bag.*

refuse sb + *to*-infinitive

'No, I won't give your bag back!' he said to her.

→ *He **refused** <u>to give</u> her bag back.*

reporting questions

A **reported question** is very much like an indirect question (see *indirect ways of asking questions*, page 155). It begins with a phrase such as *He asked me ...*, and the rest of the reported question goes back to the same word order as for statements, i.e. **subject + modal/auxiliary** (if there is one) **+ verb**.

However, there are two important differences between indirect questions and reported questions; firstly, we use **backshift** for a reported question, as in reported statements (see *reported speech*, above); secondly, the introductory expression in a reported question is never in question form, as is sometimes the case with indirect questions, so reported questions don't end with a question mark.

'What do you think about the financial crisis?' (Direct question)

<u>I asked him</u> what he thought about the financial crisis. (Reported question)

If the direct question does not begin with a question word, we use **if** or **whether** in the reported question. Again, the word order goes back to the word order of statements.

'Do you feel confident about the future?' (Direct question)

<u>She wanted to know</u> if I felt confident about the future. (Reported question)

UNIT 10

allow, let, make

Taken together as a group, ***allow***, ***let*** and ***make*** have two slightly different sets of meanings.

The first deals with **authority and rules/laws** etc. which affect your actions. If someone *allows* you to do something which you want to do, they give you permission to do it; if someone *makes* you do something which you don't want to do, they give you an order to do it, and you obey.

The second deals with **objects/processes** etc. which affect your actions, or which affect other objects/processes. If something *allows* you to do something, or allows something else to happen, it makes this possible; if something *makes* you do something, or makes something else happen, it causes or forces this result.

Notice that ***allow*** means the same as ***let***, although *allow* is slightly more formal. Notice also that the passive forms ***be allowed*** and ***be made*** are not commonly used with the second set of meanings above.

- **allow**

  The affirmative is ***allow/allows* + object + <u>full infinitive</u>**. We form the negative and questions in the same way as with other verbs. *Allow* CAN be used in the passive (see below):

  The law doesn't allow small children to drive a car.

  Satellites allow us to communicate instantly over great distances.

- **be allowed**

  If someone *allows* you to do something, you ***are allowed*** to do it; in other words, it is the passive of *allow* and is followed by **<u>full infinitive</u>**:

  We aren't allowed to wear jeans at school.

- **let**

  The affirmative is ***let/lets* + object + <u>bare infinitive</u>**. We form the negative and questions in the same way as with other verbs, but *let* CANNOT be used in the passive; we use *be allowed* instead:

  Does your dad let you use his computer?

  Space technology lets us explore beyond our own solar system.

- **make**

  The affirmative is ***make/makes* + object + <u>bare infinitive</u>**. We form the negative and questions in the same way as with other verbs. *Make* CAN be used in the passive (*see below*):

  Our mum always makes us help with the housework.

  Greenhouse gases make global temperatures rise.

- **be made**

  If somebody *makes* you do something, you ***are made*** to do it; in other words, it is the passive of *make*. BUT be careful:

  make is followed by the **<u>bare infinitive</u>**

  be made is followed by the **<u>full infinitive</u>**:

  The boy who broke the window was made to pay for fixing it.

zero, first and second conditionals

zero conditional

We use the **zero conditional** to talk about a relationship between two things that is always true, i.e. a *condition* which always produces the same resulting action or event. The condition is introduced by *if* or *when*, with no change in meaning.

If you heat ice (condition), *it melts* (result).

We use a present tense – usually the **present simple** – in both parts of the sentence.

first conditional

We use the **first conditional** to talk about future actions or predictions which depend on a *condition*, i.e. another (usually future) action, event or situation, where two things are possible.

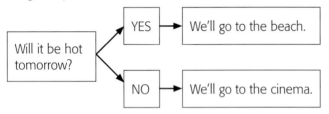

Each of the different possibilities in the condition will cause a different result in the future.

If it is hot tomorrow, we'll go to the beach.

If it isn't hot tomorrow, we'll go to the cinema.

We form the first conditional with **If + present** (usually the present simple) for the condition, followed by a **future** form (usually *will/won't*) for the resulting future action or prediction. We do NOT use a future form for the condition.

If it rains (NOT *If it will rain*) *tomorrow, I'll take an umbrella.*

If they feel (NOT *If they will feel*) *tired, they won't go to the cinema.*

If you don't take (NOT *If you won't take*) *a map, you'll get lost.*

- **if + present … imperative**

  The **imperative** is a command, such as 'Come here!' or 'Sit down!' Its form is the same as the bare infinitive, but it has no subject. In a conditional sentence, it takes the place of the main clause:

  If you need help, call me.

- **if vs when**

  Although we can use *if* or *when* in a zero conditional with no change in meaning, in a first conditional the meaning does change slightly:

  If you need help, call me. (You might need help – it's possible.)

  When you need help, call me. (I'm sure that you will need help.)

- **unless**

  Unless means **if + negative**:

  You'll miss your train if you don't hurry.
  = You'll miss your train unless you hurry.

second conditional

We use the **second conditional** to talk about an imaginary or very unlikely action, event or result which depends on an imaginary or very unlikely condition in the present and/or future.

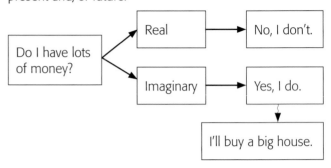

If I had lots of money, I'd buy a big house.

We form the second conditional with **If + past** (usually the past simple) for the condition, followed by **would / wouldn't* + bare infinitive** for the resulting action or event. We do NOT use **would** for the condition.

* We can also use *could/couldn't* or *might/mightn't*, but this is the most common pattern.

We can put the two parts of the sentence in any order – but notice that when the sentence begins with the condition, we must put a comma between the condition and the result.

If I knew the answer (condition), *I'd tell you* (result).

I'd buy a big house (result) *if I had lots of money* (condition).

In formal language, we can use *were* in the second conditional instead of *was* (i.e. following *I, he, she,* and *it*).

If I were you, I would buy this computer.

third conditional

We use the **third conditional** to talk about an imaginary action or event in the past, which is the result of an imaginary past condition.

Notice that the imaginary condition and the resulting action or event are the <u>opposite</u> of what really happened.

> **What really happened:** *He <u>didn't take</u> a map, so he <u>got</u> lost.*
>
> **Imaginary situation:** *He <u>took</u> a map, so he <u>didn't get</u> lost.*
>
> *If he had taken a map, he wouldn't have got lost.*

We form the third conditional with **If + past perfect** for the condition, followed by **would/wouldn't* + have + past participle** for the resulting action or situation.

* We can also use *could/couldn't* or *might/mightn't*.

We can put the two parts of the sentence in any order – but notice that when the sentence begins with the condition, we must put a comma between the condition and the result.

If I'd been careful, the fall wouldn't have happened.

I wouldn't have missed my train if I'd got up early.

Pronunciation guide

Vowels	
/iː/	meet
/i/	study
/ɪ/	middle
/e/	end
/æ/	catch
/ɑː/	hard
/ɒ/	hot
/ɔː/	sport
/ʊ/	put
/uː/	school
/u/	influence
/ʌ/	up
/ɜː/	learn
/ə/	never
/eɪ/	take
/əʊ/	phone
/aɪ/	price
/aʊ/	now
/ɔɪ/	boy
/ɪə/	here
/eə/	where
/ʊə/	pure

Consonants	
/p/	pen
/b/	bag
/t/	table
/d/	dog
/k/	cat
/g/	get
/tʃ/	chair
/dʒ/	jump
/f/	fill
/v/	very
/θ/	thing
/ð/	this
/s/	sit
/z/	zoo
/ʃ/	ship
/ʒ/	treasure
/h/	hat
/m/	man
/n/	no
/ŋ/	sing
/l/	long
/r/	ring
/j/	yellow
/w/	well

CREDITS

Photos

The publishers would like to thank the following sources for permission to reproduce their copyright protected photographs:

Cover: (Shutterstock/sunxuejun)

Inside: pp 5 (Barry Bishop/National Geographic Image Collection), 6 (Daniel Munoz/Reuters/Corbis), 8 (Maria Stenzel/National Geographic Image Collection), 9 (Royal Geographical Society/Alamy), 10tl (FFI), 10tr (Beth Shapiro), 10bl (Zoltan Takacs), 10br (Blue Legacy International/Oscar Durand), 11 (Ian Nichols/National Geographic Image Collection), 12t (hadynyah/iStockphoto), 12tl (Shutterstock), 12tr (subman/iStockphoto), 12bl (anandkrish16/iStockphoto), 12br (Creatista/iStockphoto), 13 (Lev Olkha/Fotolia), 14 (BlackEyedDog/iStockphoto), 15bg (Stanisław Ignacy Witkiewicz, Nowa Era Archive), 15tr (Mary Evans Picture Library/Alamy), 16tl (imagebroker/Alamy), 16tr (Shutterstock), 17a (Susie M. Eising/Stock Food), 18l (Shutterstock), 19b (Peter Menzel), 20tl (Dr Simon Cragg and Graham Malyon, Institute of Marine Sciences, School of Biological Sciences, University of Portsmouth, UK), 20tm (Shutterstock), 20tr (Shutterstock), 22 (Joerg Boethling/Alamy), 23t (chromatika/ iStockphoto), 23tl (Shutterstock), 23tr (Riverlim/iStockphoto), 23ml (Shutterstock), 23mr (Shutterstock), 23bl (ugurhan/iStockphoto), 23br (Shutterstock), 24 (Myhab Ltd), 25 (IakovKalinin/iStockphoto), 26t (Sergey Peterman/iStockphoto), 26tl (Mikko Pitkänen/Fotolia), 26tr (Vasca/iStockphoto), 26bl (GaryAlvis/iStockphoto), 26br (Eli Asenova/iStockphoto), 27 (Lynn Johnson/National Geographic Image Collection), 28th (Shutterstock), 28tr (Shutterstock), 28mr (Shutterstock), 28tl (PBfo/ iStockphoto), 29tr (The Natural History Museum/Alamy), 32tr (Pictorial Press Ltd/Alamy), 32tl (Bettmann/Corbis), 32ml (Wolfgang Eilmes/dpa/Corbis), 32mr (iconeer/ iStockphoto), 32bl (Shutterstock), 38 (Shutterstock), 33 (Bettmann/Corbis), 34 (Shutterstock), 36ml (Shutterstock), 36tr (Aix/Fotolia), 37tl (JTB Photo Communications, Inc./Alamy), 37mr (Thomas Cockrem/Alamy), 37br (Vontica/Alamy), 39 (Shutterstock), 41bg (Lebrecht Music and Arts Photo Library/Alamy), 41tr (Jose Gil/Shutterstock. com), 42 (Ian Geddes/JWG Gallery), 43 (John Stanmeyer/National Geographic Image Collection), 44bg (Shutterstock), 44bl (Tiposy/iStockphoto), 44blm (EMPICS/ EMPICS Sport), 44brm (Bon Appetit/Alamy), 44br (Corbis Premium RF/Alamy), 45tl (Bob Krist), 45tr (Bob Krist), 46tl (The Art Gallery Collection/Alamy), 46tm (The Art Archive/Alamy), 46ml (Interfoto/Alamy), 46mtr (The Print Collector/Alamy), 46tr (James L. Stanfield/National Geographic Image Collection), 46mr (The Art Archive/ Alamy), 47tl (Cliff Walker/iStockphoto), 47tr (Dave Rock/iStockphoto), 47bl (Pgiam/iStockphoto), 47br (kjschoen/iStockphoto), 49 (Shutterstock), 50tr (Pablo Corral V/Corbis), 50mr (Pablo Corral Vega/National Geographic Image Collection), 50br (Cheryl Gerber/epa/Corbis), 51l (Alvaro Leiva/AGE Fotostock), 51r (Danita Delimont/ Alamy), 52 (Interfoto/Alamy/Munch Museum/Munch – Ellingsen Group, BONO, Oslo/DACS, London 2011), 53bg (Arno Burgi/dpa/Corbis), 53mr (Alex Segre/Alamy), 54bg (Sigurgeir Jonasson/Photolibrary), 54mr (Edwin L. Wisherd/National Geographic Image Collection), 55tl (KeystoneUSA-ZUMA/Rex Features), 55tr (ayzek/ iStockphoto), 57 (adel66/iStockphoto), 58t (John McLellan), 58m (Caters Pictures), 58b (Shutterstock), 60 (Shutterstock), 61bl (Do Androids Deam of Electric Sheep? cover: Philip K. Dick/Victor Gollancz, an imprint of The Orion Publishing Group, London), 61bm (Penguin Books/HG Wells, 2005), 61br (Penguin Books/Pierre Boulle, 1966), 62tl (Paul Nicklen/National Geographic Image Collection), 62tm (Pixtal/SuperStock), 62tr (Pete Ryan/National Geographic Image Collection), 62ml (NASA, Johnson Space Center (JSC)), 62mr (Bob Kayganich/illustrationonline), 63 (NASA, ESA. The Hubble Heritage Team (STScI/AURA), J. Bell (Cornell Univ.) and M. Wolff (Space Sci Inst.), 64tl (Shutterstock), 64ml (mbtaichi/BigStockPhoto), 64bl (simongurney/iStockphoto), 65 (Shutterstock), 66bg (David Davis Photoproductions/Alamy), 66l (otvalo/BigStockPhoto), 66br (Shutterstock), 66bm (sculpies/iStockphoto), 66bl (Gary/Fotolia), 66br (Martin Mayer/Alamy), 67bg (Paula Bronstein/Getty Images Ltd), 67tl (Gizmo/iStockphoto), 67tm (Professor25/iStockphoto), 67tr (anzeletti/iStockphoto), 68 (Image Source/Alamy), 69 (Eileen Langsley Olympic Images/Alamy), 70 (George S de Blonsky/Alamy), 71bg (Christopher Morris/Corbis), 71ml (Bonny Makarewicz/epa/Corbis), 73b (gdtaylor/BigStockPhoto), 73tr (compassandcamera/ iStockphoto), 73bl (T_A_P/iStockphoto), 73br (natenn/iStockphoto), 74 (AP Photo/Al Grillo), 75b (Shutterstock), 75bg (dbpetersen/iStockphoto), 76tl (MarkCoffeyPhoto/ iStockphoto), 76tm (Jasper Juinen/Getty Images Sport), 76tr (David Rogers/Getty Images Sport), 79 (Janice Hazeldine/Alamy), 80t (Shutterstock), 80tr (Shutterstock), 80mr (Shutterstock), 80mr (Andy Hooper/Associated Newspapers/Rex Features), 83 (Joel Sartore/National Geographic Image Collection), 84 (Shutterstock), 85 (Mark Thiessen/National Geographic Image Collection), 86 (RubberBall/Alamy), 87 (David Levenson/Alamy), 89 (JohnGollop/iStockphoto), 92 (Mary Evans Picture Library/Alamy), 93 (World History Archive/Alamy), 94t (TatyanaGl/iStockphoto), 95bg (Cary Wolinsky/National Geographic Image Collection), 95br (Raycat/ iStockphoto), 96tl (BigStockPhoto), 96tm (Getty Images), 96tr (goodluz/Fotolia), 96trr (LajosRepasi/iStockphoto), 96mr (Reuters/Ho New), 98bl (Shutterstock), 99tr (Kevin Britland/Alamy), 100tr (Shutterstock), 100h (Lindsay McWilliams/BigStockPhoto), 100l2 (kdrgreen/BigStockPhoto), 100l3 (SasPartout/BigStockPhoto), 100l4 (Marco Desscouleurs/Fotolia), 100r1 (Pushpangadan/Fotolia), 100r2 (Nigel Cole/Fotolia), 100r3 (Wong Siew Tung/Fotolia), 100r4 (Shutterstock), 101bg (Shutterstock), 101tr (Rick Friedman/Corbis), 105 (Shutterstock), 106tr (Shutterstock), 106ml (Shutterstock), 106mr (Shutterstock), 108 (Michael Nichols/National Geographic Image Collection), 109 (seraficus/iStockphoto), 110tl (moodboard/Alamy), 110tr (Comstock/Photolibrary), 110bl (Shutterstock), 110br (Image Source/Alamy), 111bl (Kira Salak), 112tr (Shutterstock), 113br (mddphoto/iStockphoto), 115bg (UPI Photo/Carlos Gutierrez), 115mr (Shutterstock), 117bl (Julian Makey/Rex Features), 117bm (See-Saw Films/ The Kobal Collection), 118tl (Bettmann/Corbis), 118tm (Bettmann/Corbis), 118tr (Owen Franken/Corbis), 118ml (NASA Headquarters – GReatest Images of NASA (NASA-HQ-GRIN)), 118mm (Joseph H. Bailey/National Geographic Image Collection), 118mr (Shutterstock), 119 (NASA Kennedy Space Center (NASA-KSC)), 119tr (MPI/Archive Photos/Getty Images Ltd), 119tr (World History Archive/Alamy), 119mr (MPI/Archive Photos/Getty Images Ltd), 119mr (Ullstein Bild/AP/Press Association Images), 119br (Bettmann/Corbis), 119br (PA Wire/Press Association Images), 120 (Cathy Yeulet/123RF), 121 (Mark Thiessen/National Geographic Image Collection), 122 (Mark Thiessen/ National Geographic Image Collection), 123bl (thelinke/iStockphoto), 123tm (Terraxplorer/iStockphoto), 123tr (Jim Wileman/Alamy), 123mm (paulcraven/iStockphoto), 123ml (TwilightEye/iStockphoto), 123bl (cristimatei/iStockphoto), 124tl (asiseeit/iStockphoto), 124ml (demo/iStockphoto), 124mm (Fatman73/iStockphoto), 124mr (mikered/iStockphoto), 154 (Matt Harding), 127 (Shutterstock), 129 (Shutterstock), 130–131 (Classical Comics and Heinle Cengage Learning), 132t (Vasiliy Yakobchuk/ iStockphoto), 132mr (Shutterstock), 136 (Shutterstock), 138ml (Shutterstock), 138br (Shutterstock), 142ml (Shutterstock), 142mr (Jorge Fernandez/Alamy), 142bl (David Grossman/Alamy), 142br (Steve Allen Travel Photography/Alamy), 143 (Royal Geographical Society/Alamy)

Text

We are grateful to the following for permission to reproduce copyright material:

Team Jessica Watson for an extract in Module 1A from Jessica Watson's blog "Almost Around the Cape and Why I am Sailing Around the World?" 22 February 2010, www. jessicawatson.com.au, reproduced with permission; myhab for details in Module 2D about myhab, www.myhab.com, reproduced with permission; Bob Krist for an extract in Module 4A adapted from 'A Shot in the Dark: Photographing Night Parades' IT Blogon, 3 March 2010, reproduced with kind permission; Sue Leather for extracts in Modules 4A, 6C from the Footprint Reading Library titles 'The Lost Temple of the Maya' and 'A Real Winner', reproduced with permission; MSN Tech & Gadgets for an extract in Module 5B adapted from 'Space: Could It Sustain Life?' by Jane Douglas www.msn.co.uk, reproduced with permission; Canadian Immigrant and Karolina Wisniewska for interview details in Module 6A adapted from 'Peak of victory' by Sabrina Almeida, Canadian Immigrant, 12 March 2010, www.canadianimmigrant.ca, reproduced with kind permission; TNS Research International for the 'Top Ten Most Popular Pets in the UK' 2008, in Module 8C, source: Pet Foods Manufacturers Association, survey by TNS http://www.top-ten-10.com/recreation/pets/uk-pets. htm, copyright © TNS; Dr Kira Salak for interview details in Module 9A, reproduced with kind permission; Cengage Learning for material in Module 10E from Frankenstein: The ELT Graphic Novel by Mary Shelley, adapted for ELT by Brigit Viney, copyright © 2009, Heinle, Cengage Learning, published in association with Classical Comics Ltd; and National Geographic for excerpts adapted from 'Q+A: Josh Ponte, Live from Gabon', National Geographic, 2007; 'Animal Minds' by Virginia Morell, National Geographic, March 2008; 'Winter Celebrations' by Deborah Heiligman and Carolyn Otto, National Geographic, 9 December 2008, http://kids.nationalgeographic.com, (adapted from Celebrate Chinese New Year with Fireworks, Dragons, and Lanterns by Carolyn Otto, 2009; and Celebrate Kwanzaa with Candles, Community, and Fruits of the Harvest by Carolyn, 2008); 'bi-on-ics' by Josh Fischman, National Geographic, January 2010; 'Our Thirsty World' National Geographic, April 2010; 'Hidden Water' by Jane Vessels, National Geographic Supplement, April 2010, www.nationalgeographic.com, copyright © National Geographic, reproduced with permission.; 'Snap judgements decide a face's character, psychologist finds', News Releases, Princeton University, Office of Communications, Chad Boutin; 'Drinking Water: Bottled or from the Tap' http://kids.nationalgeographic.com; http://www.america.gov/st/educ-english/2009/Augu st/20090810110401cMretroPo.8228527.html; 'Award winning teens has more ideas' by George Matlala at Johannesburg News Agency website http://www.joburgnews. co.za/2007/jul/jul11_siya.stm; 'Free-Madrid-Traveller' http://travel.nationalgeographic.com/travel/city-guides/free-madrid-traveler/

In some instances we have been unable to trace the owners of copyright material and we would appreciate any information that would enable us to do so.

Illustrations by Peter Cornwell p 59; Nigel Dobbyn (Beehive Illustration) pp 88, 97, 101, 128; Mark Gerber p 78; Wes Lowe (Beehive Illustration) pp 130, 131; Map Specialists Ltd pp 137, 139; Martin Sanders pp 15, 37, 54, 98, 99, 105; Mark Turner (Beehive Illustration) pp 48, 60; Laszlo Veres (Beehive Illustration) pp 30, 84